EXTINCT HUMANS

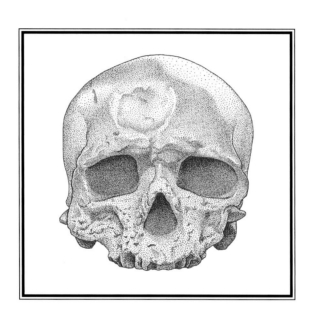

EXTINCT HUMANS

Ian Tattersall and Jeffrey H. Schwartz

Principal Photography by Jeffrey H. Schwartz

A Peter N. Nevraumont Book

WESTVIEW PRESS

A MEMBER OF PERSEUS BOOKS GROUP

Published by Westview Press,
A Member of the Perseus Books Group

FIRST EDITION

A CIP catalogue record for this book is available from the Library of Congress: ISBN 0-8133-3482-2

00 00 01 02 z / RRD lo 9 8 7 6 5 4 3 2 1

Created and Produced by
Nevraumont Publishing Company
New York, New York

President: Ann J. Perrini

Design by Tsang Seymour Design Inc.,
New York, New York

For
Jeanne Kelly
and
Lynn Emanuel

_____

CONTENTS

[Preface]

Pierre Teilhard de Chardin had it right: the human phenomenon is indeed an extraordinary one. But as unusual as humans are in those attributes–braininess, the gift of the gab, artistic expression—that have long attracted philosophers and poets, the evolutionary history of humans and their extinct relatives is not necessarily any more remarkable in itself than are those of squirrels or horses. In the end, as with anything else, it is in the eye of the beholder.

As the beholders, though, we have struggled from the beginning almost uniquely with what it means to be different from other animals, rather than with what it means to be a part of nature. As far back as Aristotle, we humans have sought to isolate those features that distinguish us, and thus remove us, from the rest of the animal world. This has not always been done with a concrete agenda in mind, but the result is often as if there had been. Thus, although Linnaeus, the father of the system of classification that we continue to use, took the bold step of classifying humans together with the other animals as early as the mid-eighteenth century, he did not deal with us as he did with our relatives. For each of those other species, he tried to give a feature or two that would guide his fellow taxonomists in making the same identification. For us, all he gave was the phrase *Nosce te ipsum* (know thyself). And ever since then, that's how humans

have sought to deal with their own past, as if the process of becoming human has in some way been different from the processes of becoming one of the estimated ten million other species inhabiting the world today. Yet even if modern humans are truly a new phenomenon on the evolutionary landscape, they did not necessarily become this way through extraordinary processes. Indeed, even a fairly cursory glance at the human fossil record suggests that the pattern of human evolution has resembled that of most other groups. In other words, although the end result may be extraordinary, the process by which it came about was routine.

Extinct Humans explores this matter of perspective. A linear mindset pervades most work in paleoanthropology, as if the story of human evolution has essentially been one of a single-minded struggle from bestial benightedness to uplifted enlightenment. Not to put too fine a point on it, paleoanthropologists have often been prepared to rewrite the rules of the evolutionary process where their own species is concerned. But if we proceed like paleontologists studying other groups, and let the anatomy of the fossils rather than their ages (i.e., their assumed places in a linear progression) lead us to conclusions about the pattern of human evolution, a very different picture emerges. Certainly up until the origin of our own species, this approach shows us that our pattern has essentially been one of business as usual for the natural world: a story of repeated evolutionary experimentation, diversification, and, ultimately, extinction. And it was clearly in the context of such experimentation, rather than out of constant fine-tuning by natural selection over the eons, that our own amazing species appeared on Earth. Albeit, in the end, with a difference: for unlike even our closest relatives, *Homo sapiens* is not simply an extrapolation or improvement of what went before it. For reasons we will explore, our species is an entirely unprecedented entity in the living world, however mundanely we may have come by our unusual attributes. This central fact of human uniqueness is one with which we urgently need to come to terms, because evolution has done nothing to prepare the biota that not only surrounds but also supports us to cope with this highly destructive new element on the landscape.

Acknowledgments

This book grew out of a long-term (and continuing) project to redescribe and reanalyze the entire human fossil record. This might seem like an excessively far-reaching goal, even an expression of hubris; but in fact the description of the huge variety of human fossils according to a single consistent protocol is greatly overdue. Our colleagues worldwide have been extraordinarily supportive of this venture. Because of this support, we have already been privileged to examine almost all of the fossils, in collections in Europe, Asia, Africa, and the United States, that document the evolutionary history of mankind. We especially wish to acknowledge the hospitality and help of the curators and other staff of the following institutions for access to the fossils and for their assistance in many other ways. In the United States: Harvard Peabody Museum, Cambridge MA; American Museum of Natural History, New York. In England: the Natural History Museum (London). In France: the Musée de l'Homme (Laboratories of Biological Anthropology and Prehistory), Paris; the Muséum National d'Histoire Naturelle, Laboratoire de Paléontologie, Paris; the Institut de Paléontologie Humaine, Paris; the Musée des Antiquités Nationales, St. Germain-en-Laye; the Musée National de Préhistoire, Les Eyzies de Tayac; the Musée du Périgord, Périgueux; the Laboratoire d'Anthropologie, Faculté de Médecine, Marseilles; the Laboratoire d'Anthropologie, Université de Bordeaux 1, Talence. In Monaco: the Musée d'Anthropologie Préhistorique, Monte Carlo. In Belgium: the Institut Royal des Sciences Naturelles,

Brussels; the Université de Liège (Laboratoires d'Archéologie Préhistorique, and of Paléontologie), Liège. In the Netherlands: Nationaal Museum van Naturlijke Historie, Leiden. In Germany: the Rheinisches Landesmuseum, Bonn; the Landesmuseum für Vorgeschichte, Halle/Saale; Senckenberg Museum, Frankfurt; the Museum für Vor- und Frühgeschichte Thuringens, Weimar; the Helms-Museum für Vor- und Frühgeschichte, Hamburg; the Museum für Vor- und Frühgeschichte, Berlin; the Geologisch-Paläontologisch Institut der Universität, Heidelberg; the Staatliches Museum für Naturkunde, Stuttgart; the Osteologische Sammlung der Universität, Tubingen; Forschungsinstitut Bilzingsleben der Universität, Jena. In Austria: the Naturhistorisches Museum, Vienna. In Italy: the Istituto Italiano de Paleontologia Umana, Rome; the Museo Preistorico de Balzi Rossi, Ventimiglia; the Museo Nazionale Preistorico Etnografico "L. Pigorini," Rome; the Universita di Roma "La Sapienza," Dipartimento di Biologia Animale e dell'Uomo, Rome. In Spain: the Department of Paleontology, Universidad Complutense de Madrid; the Museo Provincial de Malaga. In Portugal: the Centro de Estratigrafica e Paleobiologia, Universidade Nova de Lisboa, Monte de Caparica. In Greece: the Department of Geology, Aristotle University of Thessaloniki. In the Czech Republic: the Anthropos Institute, Moravian Museum, Brno; the Institute of Archaeology, Dolni Vestonice; the Narodni Muzeum, Prague. In Croatia: the Hravatski Prirodoslovni Musej, Zagreb; the Institute of Paleontology and Quaternary Geology, Zagreb. In Hungary: the Magyar Nemzeti Muzeum, Budapest; the Magyar Termeszettudomanyi Muzeum, Budapest. In Russia: the Institute and Museum of Anthropology, Moscow State University, Moscow. In Israel: the Rockefeller Museum, Jerusalem; the Department of Anatomy, Sackler School of Medicine of Tel-Aviv University. In Morocco: the Musée Archéologique, Rabat. In Kenya: the National Museums of Kenya, Nairobi. In Tanzania: the

National Museum of Tanzania, Dar-es-Salaam. In South Africa: the Transvaal Museum, Pretoria; the Department of Anatomy and Human Biology of the University of the Witwatersrand Medical School, Johannesburg; the Bernard Price Institute of the University of the Witwatersrand, Johannesburg; the South African Museum, Cape Town; the Nasionale Museum, Bloemfontein. In Indonesia: the Laboratory of Bioanthropology and Paleoanthropology, Gadjah Mada University, Yogyakarta; the Archaeological Service, Yogyakarta; the Geological Survey of Indonesia, Bandung; the Laboratory of Paleontology, Bandung Institute of Technology, Bandung; and the Museum Negeri Propinsi Jawa Timur "Mpu Tantular," Surabaya. To all those who have helped us at these institutions, our heartfelt thanks.

We also want to express our appreciation to the many colleagues worldwide whose insights and ideas have influenced our own. Equally, we owe deepest thanks to Karl Yambert, our editor at Westview Press, for his commitment to this project, and to Peter N. Nevraumont, Ann J. Perrini, Simone Nevraumont, and Ruth Servi Zimmerman of Nevraumont Publishing Company for initiating the project and seeing it through to fruition with their usual flair. Ron Clarke went beyond the bounds of duty to provide illustrations and advice. Patrick Seymour and Kevin Smith of Tsang Seymour Design gave this book its elegant design, for which we thank them. The book could not have appeared without the dedication of the indispensable Kenneth Mowbray, who kindly prepared the index and whose efforts were particularly valuable in organizing the figures appearing in this book.

CHAPTER 1

The Path to Human Evolution

The Path to Human Evolution

Almost every week or two, so it seems, there's a piece in the news about a new discovery of a fossil human relative, such as the species *Australopithecus garhi* from Ethiopia that is currently being touted as *the* ultimate ancestor of the modern human lineage. Or a new piece of information on an already known human fossil, such as our discovery of previously undescribed features within the nasal cavity of Neanderthals, or the extracting and analyzing of DNA from the fossil bones of the first described Neanderthal skeleton. Perhaps the oddest recent pronouncement was the attribution of the distinctive cranial and skeletal anatomies of Neanderthals to maladies of the thyroid gland producing cretinism. Who knows what stories tomorrow's popular media will bring?

Although we take being bombarded with this kind of information for granted—almost as if we expect it along with our morning coffee—the path followed by human evolutionary scholarship over the past century and more has not been a smooth one. Indeed, it has been fraught with problems from the very beginning—problems that persist as the field doggedly pursues the fleshing-out of our evolutionary past. The influence of the dead hand of tradition can perhaps be seen most dramatically in that many contemporary specialists in human evolution continue—whether they realize it or not—to be

influenced by the work of earlier scholars who were not themselves evolutionists. To understand where we are today involves knowing where we were yesterday, so let's begin by looking at the development of ideas about humanity's place in nature.

In the Beginning

We find the first recorded musings about how the natural world works and how humans might fit into it in the writings of Greek and early Roman scholars. Common to many of these intellectuals was an interest in how the environment might affect how people look and behave. In this pursuit Herodotus (484–425 BC), who is best remembered as the first historian, made comparisons between the skulls of Persian and Egyptian soldiers killed in battle. He was impressed by how easily, so it seemed, the head of a Persian could be cracked in contrast to an Egyptian's. Perhaps, he speculated, this was because Persians were in the habit of wearing felt hats, which made the bone of their skulls thin and brittle. In contrast, Egyptian males had shaved heads throughout their lives. Could it be that their thicker cranial bones derived somehow from the constant exposure of their heads to the sun?

Hippocrates (b. *c.* 460BC), the acknowledged father of medicine, and Aristotle, that all-around naturalist and philosopher, also subscribed to an environmental explanation for the existence of differences among individuals living in different places and climates. Hippocrates thought that it was a damp and cold climate that made the Scythians of Asia Minor the "ruddy race" he portrayed in his writings. Aristotle (b. 384BC) picked up on this environmental theme and threw in another feature of the Scythians (and, while he was at it, of the neighboring Thracians, as well)—their straight hair—as being caused by the inhospitable climate in which they lived. In contrast to these groups, Aristotle's "Aethiopians" (from the Greek *Ethiop*, meaning "burned face") had woolly hair and dark, sun-burnt skin.

But Aristotle went further than merely speculating on why humans from different parts of the known world looked or acted differently from one another. As the first comparative anatomist on record, he was interested in trying to find out how the world and life on it fit together. In pursuit of answers to this conundrum, Aristotle came up with a scheme of grouping organisms that not only triumphed in his day but that dominated biological thought for almost two millennia.

As Aristotle saw it, life emerged from the inanimate. From this beginning, he conceived of a hierarchy of life (which has become better known in the Latin of medieval scholars as the *Scala Naturae*) that was planted at one end in an inorganic source, such as the sludge on the floor of a swamp, from which it ascended to its other end. Humans sat on the upper rungs of this *Scala Naturae*. Plants and non-human animal life forms were distributed among the other rungs of this ladder in a hierarchy of increasing complexity that linked the lowly inorganic with humans, the most perfected forms of life on Earth. Aristotle thought that some organisms just popped out of thin air (by spontaneous generation, as this notion would later be called), whereas others emerged from mud or fecal matter. Humans and those animals we call mammals and birds, however, either started out in life as larvae, or developed from eggs.

Although science would have to wait nearly two thousand years until the Swedish botanist Linnaeus (Carl von Linné) (1707–1778) would create the taxonomic group that we refer to as Mammalia (he called them Quadrupedia), Aristotle had succeeded in sorting out many of the fundamental features of this aggregate of animals. Starting at the broadest level, Aristotle identified those animals we call mammals as four-legged animals that both had true blood coursing through their veins and gave birth to live young. Now, he could have included birds in this group, because, as he rightfully acknowledged, birds are technically quadrupedal or four-footed animals. As he would have put it, just like mammals, birds locomote via four "points." And, again like mammals, birds are true blooded. But birds do not give birth to live young. To Aristotle, that meant that birds belong to one group, and mammals to another, within the larger group to which birds and mammals both belong.

In Aristotle's eyes, humans are like mammals and birds in having true blood coursing through their veins. Additionally, humans are similar to mammals because they give birth to live young. Superficially, humans are also like birds in walking only on two legs. In contrast to birds, however, in which the forelimbs are in the form of wings and are the individual's primary means of getting about, the arms and hands of a human are freed of this locomotory obligation. Aristotle thought that humans also differ from birds, and from all mammals for that matter, in the direction in which their knee joint flexes. He mistakenly believed that this joint bends backward in birds and mammals and forward in humans. On the basis of this seemingly profound difference, Aristotle singled out humans from other animals and proclaimed that their bipedalism reflected divinity both in their nature and in their essence. Aristotle's anatomical misconception stayed on the books until the fifteenth century, when Leonardo da Vinci finally pointed out that the joint that Aristotle had mistaken for the knee in birds and non-human mammals was really their ankle joint. That is why the joint Aristotle took to be the knee of a bird bends backward. The real knee of a bird, which, like a humans, bends forward, is hidden under the feathers up against the body. To make his point, Leonardo pictured a human standing on tiptoe. In this pose, the ankle is up and points back, just like Aristotle's birds' "knees."

Thanks to Aristotle—the orientation of the knee joint notwithstanding—bipedalism early on took center stage among the most diagnostic criteria used by comparative anatomists, and later by paleoanthropologists, to distinguish humans from other living animals. To this character Aristotle added the ability to think and reason. As attributes of the large human brain, these features put this organ also at or near the top of the list of features separating humans from the rest of the animal world. Furthermore, these two attributes—bipedalism and braininess—were assumed to be correlated. According to Aristotle, no animal could be bipedal if its body was top-heavy; with a large and heavy trunk and forelimbs, an animal just could not stand. And, he believed, weight just plain interferes with intellect and common sense. Centuries later, philosophers such as Rousseau and Lord Monboddo would wrestle with the question of whether any other animals, particularly among the apes, had the human capacities of intellect and reason. And centuries later again, with the discovery of human fossils, the debate over which feature evolved first—bipedalism or the enlarged, thinking brain—would witness vicious intellectual battles.

Indeed, the early twentieth-century Piltdown forgery, which put together a modern human skull with an apelike jaw, was evidently concocted as a direct counter to the *Homo erectus* fossils found in Java at the end of the nineteenth century that consisted of a modern human-looking femur and a "pithecoid" skull cap. The Javanese specimens seemed to suggest that bipedalism evolved first, whereas the fraud—despite the absence of the rest of the skeleton—was taken as demonstrating the possession of a large brain prior to the conversion of the rest of the body from ape to human. We'll never really know the reasons for the Piltdown forgery, as we'll never really know who fabricated it. But a reasonable speculation is that it would have ensured England's place as yielding the world's oldest fossil human. And, because its skull looked more human than "Java Man," and because it had housed a large brain, "Piltdown Man" could more readily be embraced as a possible human ancestor. Add to this the prevailing bias that the West was civilized and the rest of the world was not, and it is not difficult to understand how the large-brained Piltdown Man could be an easy sell.

As you might well expect, scholarly interest in the emergence of "civilized" humans has had a long and also checkered history. For instance, the Greeks and early Romans wrestled with questions about the origin of their particular state of civilization. One scenario held that the history of civilization paralleled the life cycle of an individual. The best and healthiest days are in one's youth, after which one declines into old age and then death. Likewise, the heyday of healthy and vigorous human civilization had occurred in the good old days of yesteryear. Since then, everything had gone to pot, with civilization degenerating and falling into moral decay and decrepitude. Pompeii, where streets were lined with brothels, and Rome, with couples fornicating on the steps of the Senate, come to mind as examples. The alternative view of the history of human civilization was much more optimistic. It held that in the beginning, everyday life had been more primitive and simpler than today's. Over a long period of time,

humans developed technology. As technology improved, so, too, did the human condition, which eventually resulted in the high level of civilization enjoyed by the Greeks and Romans. True or not, the image of Rome's place at the top of the world's greatest cities did much to inspire the Caesars' legions as they conquered most of the Mediterranean world and lands beyond the Mediterranean. The overall theme of this view of civilization was that there was a continuum of progress from primitive to advanced humans.

Of these two themes, the general idea of degeneration would be co-opted and reconfigured into their depiction of the origin of human races by eighteenth-century naturalists such as the Comte de Buffon and by the father of physical anthropology (and also, we suggest, paleoanthropology), Johann Friedrich Blumenbach. These scholars claimed that the longest continuous record of "high" civilization was to be found in Asia, and concluded that Asia was where humans must have originated. From there, humans migrated west, to the Caucasus Mountains. The Caucasians (that is, those immigrants who stayed in the region of the Caucasus) and those others who migrated into Africa became the "white" and "black" races, respectively, through a process of degeneration from the original stock. It is interesting that, in their speculations on the demise of the Neanderthals, archeologists and physical anthropologists of the twentieth century have kept alive the notion of an invasion from the East of an overpowering, more sophisticated "race" of humans.

But it would be the theme of progress that would later pervade evolutionary thought. On a grand level, the acceptance of the reality of evolution at first had little impact on perceptions of how life was arranged. The comparative anatomists and taxonomists of the Dark Ages had kept alive Aristotle's *Scala Naturae* by infusing it with a Christian creation motif. This produced a taxonomic hierarchy of life's forms with humans being the closest to the image of a divine creator. This arrangement of life from the supposedly lowest to highest became known as the Great Chain of Being. When evolutionary ideas were eventually infused into paleontology, the Great Chain of Being was itself transformed into an evolutionary succession of life, from the simplest to the most complex. Among vertebrates, for example, the evolutionary succession was supposed to be from fish to amphibians, to reptiles, and thence to mammals.

On a more individual level, it is noteworthy that Charles Darwin devoted the first volume of *The Descent of Man* entirely to a discussion of how progression had played out in human evolution. Incorporating countless comments on how primitive humans differed physically and intellectually from those more civilized, Darwin spent chapter after chapter in this work detailing how one could follow the transformation of humans from something apelike in body and mind, through the "savages" and "barbaric" humans, to the most sophisticated of the "races," the Europeans. It is not surprising that this vision of evolutionary progress was not derived from study of the fossil record. For, by 1871, when *The Descent* was published, little

more than the original Neanderthal skull from the Feldhofer Grotto in Germany had been presented to the scientific world in publication. Thus Darwin essentially followed the precedent of the Great Chain of Being in perceiving the ascendancy of humans through a sequence of living forms that went from monkeys to apes, to the most primitive and uncivilized humans, and on up to the most advanced and civilized humans. Having established to his satisfaction that one could trace such a transformation series through living apes and humans, Darwin could turn this horizontal comparison ninety degrees and imbue it with the element of evolutionary and geological time. But there were few fossils known that could support his contention. The only potential candidates for such a human-ape ancestor were from deposits in France and were no more than a few broken jaws—which didn't help at all. Nevertheless, Darwin speculated with supreme assuredness that, were the fossils known, a similar evolutionary transformation—from monkey through ape to primitive and then civilized human— would certainly be played out.

The idea that the human condition arose from the primitive, savage, and wild—portrayed by whichever "race" or fossil qualified as representing the lowest human condition—was not novel with Darwin. There is a long history of such formations, which are epitomized in the writings of the Roman philosopher Titus Lucretius Carus (*c.* 99–55BC), more widely known just by his middle name. Compared with the puny Romans of his day, Lucretius' first humans were larger and had harder and stronger bodies. Unlike Romans, who depended on the comforts of civilization, these first humans—although lacking both fire and clothing—could endure any kind of environmental circumstance. Like other animals, they traveled in bands and, depending on the weather, either slept on the ground, in thickets, or in caves. They could eat anything without consequence and rarely fell ill. How much more similar to nineteenth- and early twentieth-century reconstructions of the life of early humans—not to mention modern cartoon strips such as Alley Oop—could Lucretius' account have been?

In and Out of the Dark Ages

Although the ideas of degeneration and progress in Greek and early Roman natural philosophy might seem naive to us today, they arose from within a tradition that honored scientific investigation, questioning, and individuality of thought. This was the world of Aristotle, Hippocrates, and Herodotus, among others. In this world there was also an appreciation of humans being as much a part of nature as other animals, and, like them, being subject to the whims of their surroundings, environmental or, in the case of humans, also cultural. But both the idea that nature somehow played a role in the development of each organism's attributes and a generally healthy scientific attitude toward gathering data from the real world just for the sake of learning about it were squelched by the rise of Christianity in the first and second centuries A.D. Inquiry within the confines of a monolithic church could only proceed through the acts of prayer and revelation. Personal experience and direct observation no longer counted in the assessment of what should have been a scientific problem. In fact, inquirers were often burned at the stake or drawn and quartered as a heretics and infidels. With the resulting demise of unfettered inquiry, the biblical story of creation came to be supported by the oddest of supposed forms of proof. For instance, around the turn of the seventh century, Isadore, Bishop of Seville, noted that the Latin word for man, "homo," could be derived from the Latin word "humus." Because "humus" refers to the organic part of soil, Isadore argued, there must be truth to the story of the creation of Adam from dust as presented in the Old Testament in the Book of Genesis.

Although the naturalists of the Dark Ages were intellectually stymied, their search for evidence of the work of a divine creator did fuel the desire to clarify the details of the Great Chain of Being. To be sure, the Chain was nothing more than a translation of Aristotle's *Scala Naturae* in which organisms were lined up from the simple to the complex. But its demonstration became the task of the comparative anatomists of the emergent Renaissance—such as the German Konrad von Gesner, the Englishman Edward Wotton, and the Italian Caesalpinus of Arezzo, all of the mid-sixteenth century—who expressed the results of their labors in taxonomies or classifications. The common desire of these naturalists was to elucidate the supposed natural order of creation for which, of course, there could be only one scheme. And they did so through the search for organisms that would close in the gaps of, and provide the missing links in, the Great Chain. For if, according to doctrine, all life forms that could have been created had been created, then discovering them was ultimately achievable. Despite this common goal, the classifications that these scholars generated as demonstration of the divine arrangement of life were often as different from one another as the taxonomists themselves. Not only was there no coordinated or agreed-upon system of classification, there was no clear sense of what the basic unit of nature was. The idea of the species, which would ultimately be seen as the basic unit of nature, was to be long in its gestation.

There was a profound consequence of trying to pigeonhole the organic world into a taxonomy demonstrating a continuum from the most primitive to the most advanced in perfection: how did one deal with the human end of the classification? In the context of a Great Chain of Being, there had to be some humans that were closer to the "brutes" than were others. And because it was necessary for a taxonomist to provide in his classification the transition or link between the apes and the rest of humanity, various human groups were put forward as being the most primitive, or brutish, of living humans. Favorites among some early taxonomists were the Hottentots or "Bushmen" (the Kalahari San), then known in Europe by little more than rumor. Even in the nineteenth century, such rationalists as Thomas Henry Huxley and Charles Darwin had their favorite "savage." For Huxley, it was the Australian

Aborigine, and for Darwin, the Tierra del Fuegian. [Figure 1] From such supposedly transitional forms—the most brutish of humans—the taxonomists proceeded to line up the races as they perceived them, leading, of course, to the pinnacle of perfection, white Europeans, with males, of course,—at the top. Some taxonomists even segregated males and females hierarchically within each perceived non-European race.

Although documenting the Great Chain of Being may have been the motivating force behind the works of these early taxonomists, the implications of such a Chain were not also uniformly shared. For some taxonomists the simple, straightforward biblical creation story encompassed all life. For humans this meant that, no matter how many different races a taxonomist carved out, they all shared the same history. They were all, according to this "monogenetic" interpretation, descendants of Adam. So far, perhaps, so good. But there was a dangerous and less attractive side. The flip side of monogenesis was polygenesis; and from the polygenists' point of view, the differences between races were simply too great for all to be traceable to the same Adam. Different races, therefore, had to have arisen from different Adams.

As late as the early nineteenth century, and still in the pursuit of the Great Chain, one taxonomist, Jean Baptiste Bory St. Vincent, went so far as to recognize fifteen species of human, which he sorted into two subgenera within the genus *Homo*. Clearly, this is pushing the envelope of such a presumed hierarchy in nature.

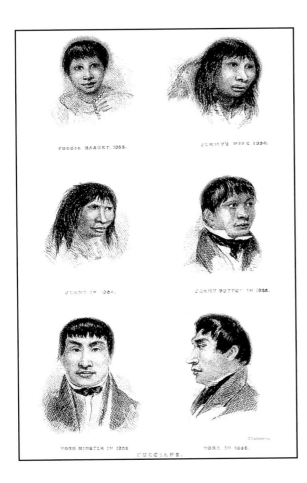

post-World War II paleoanthropologists to keep the number of extinct hominid species to a minimum. For, by grouping ourselves and such wildly different hominids as Neanderthals and a host of other fossil humans in the same species, the differences between groups of living humans become even further diminished by comparison.

To explain further how some early taxonomists dealt with humans, one easy way in which the differences between "us" and "them" (the rest of the organic world) could be highlighted was by not classifying humans at all—despite the agreement of virtually all taxonomists that humans were anatomically similar to the other animals that Linnaeus would eventually classify in Primates. This is precisely what the sixteenth-century Swiss comparative anatomist and taxonomist, Konrad von Gesner, did. He specifically excluded humans from his comparisons and classification. Fortunately, at least for the history of taxonomy as a discipline, Gesner did attempt to bring some order to the art of classification. He proposed the rank of genus, which he used as the base level of a classification denoting the links of the Great Chain of Being. A century and a half later, the Swedish botanist and taxonomist Linnaeus would take Gesner's genus and put it together with the species that the seventeenth-century English zoologist and comparative anatomist, John Ray, had proposed as an even more basic unit of classification. And in what would be his most radical move in the same work, his *Systema Naturae*, Linnaeus would place humans not only in their own genus and species, *Homo sapiens*, he would

Even Darwin, who used the device of a transition from identifiably primitive to civilized "man" in *The Descent of Man*, was committed to the membership of all humans in the same species. One cannot but wonder if a latent resurgence of belief in polygenesis has not been unconsciously behind the tendency among place them in an order together with other animals.

But it was not easy getting to the point where Linnaeus could steel himself against the calumny of his colleagues and the church by classifying humans with other animals. First there had to be a scientific recognition that humans were even like other animals. In 1632, Joannes Jonstonus took the taxonomic bull by the horns and discussed humans simply in comparison with other animals. But even this was pushing the limit of what was considered acceptable. So Jonstonus stopped there, refraining from classifying humans with other animals. He kept them by themselves, as would be expected of a view of creation in which humans were ultimately regarded as being inextricably different from other forms of life. When all else was considered, humans would seemingly always have to be set apart from the rest of the animal world because of their ability to reason and in their possession of language. Alas, revelation, not personal observation, still governed the pursuit of organismic science. Still, by this point humans were at least more visibly part of the general concern of taxonomists.

Although John Ray is acknowledged today as father of the science of systematic zoology, even he could not break free of the stranglehold of the Great Chain of Being. The place of humans as closest to their creator continued to dominate Ray's conceptions no matter how clear it was becoming that, anatomically at least, humans were like other animals—especially the apes and monkeys. By virtue of their ability to reason and their possession of language,

humans would, for Ray, always be apart from their near look-alikes, monkeys and apes. It is thus something of an odd irony that Ray was the first taxonomist to recognize formally in his classification the great similarities between humans and that subset of other animals we now refer to as primates. He did so by introducing the term Anthropomorpha, which means "man shaped." But, no matter how anthropomorphic apes and monkeys obviously were, they were fated to be classified apart from humans.

Perhaps it was because of his weddedness to the doctrine of the Great Chain of Being that Ray took that one step that no other taxonomist had done previously. He went below Gesner's genus to the level of the species, a term he coined to designate the most fundamental units of life. Until Ray, even Gesner's genus was at best only a vague referent to a collection of specimens that might not even constitute a real group in nature. But Ray's species, derived as it was from the Latin word referring to a particular "kind" of something, was meant to identify true groups of individuals. Here, then, was a way to reflect the most fundamental acts of creation, to identify the kinds of animals that a divine creator had placed on the face of the earth. Species, not odd collections of organisms or single individuals displaying pathological conditions, were the real and fundamental units of nature. Although he eventually broke intellectual ranks with the taxonomists who were enslaved by the Great Chain of Being, Linnaeus would draw both on Ray's species and Gesner's genus to create the basic elements of the classification system we still use today.

A botanist by training, Linnaeus, like all good taxonomists, embraced and feverishly studied all specimens that came his way—from the inorganic to the organic, animal as well as plant. In 1735, at the ripe old age of twenty-five, this Swede became the first taxonomist formally to put humans and other animals in the same group. In the first edition of his major work, *Systema Naturae*, he placed humans in a group whose name he borrowed from Ray—Anthropomorpha. It was not until the tenth edition of the *Systema*, which was published in 1758, that Linnaeus replaced Anthropomorpha with the name Primates, the "chiefs of creation."

The broad impact of Linnaeus' work on taxonomy in general came, however, from his recruitment of Gesner's genus and Ray's species into formal usage. Under Linnaeus' scheme, every individual organism had to be assigned to a species, and every species had to be assigned in turn to a genus. The attractiveness of this formulation, and probably a major reason for its rapid and wide adoption, lay in Linnaeus' demand that each species and each genus be defined on the basis of at least one tangible feature or trait. Until Ray introduced the concept of the species and Linnaeus formalized its usage, taxonomists were not bound by any common rules. But, under Linnaeus's scheme, the description of each species conveyed the details that made that particular organism distinct from all others.

If there were some number of species that appeared to hve some features in common that suggested that they, in turn, constituted a natural group, then they were placed together in the genus, which was defined on the features that these species shared that were not specific to each as a species. The genus was then defined on the basis of a next higher order of information. Linnaeus did this with what he thought consitituted different species of humanlike animals, including the orangutan, which he lumped with our own species in the genus *Homo*. And if it appeared that several genera (the plural of genus) shared certain features, then they would be grouped into a higher taxonomic rank, which would be defined on the basis of this still higher order of information. What were you supposed to do if a species appeared to stand alone? According to Linnaeus, it still had to have a genus name, but, in this case, the genus and species shared the same definition. But if a genus came to subsume more than one species, its definition was based on those unique features common to all of its species.

By following Linnaeus' rules of classification, taxonomists could know the criterion or criteria that another taxonomist had used in creating, for example, a new genus or new species. They would also then be able to decide if an unclassified specimen should be allocated to a known genus or species or if it deserved to be distinguished in its own, new species or a new genus and species. In the *Systema* of 1758, Linnaeus' Order Primates came to embrace the genera *Homo*, *Simia*, and *Lemur*. The genus *Lemur* subsumed the "lower" primates and *Simia* included monkeys but not apes because the two apes that were then known to science, the orangutan of southeast Asia and the chimpanzee of central Africa, were classified as species of *Homo*. Although Linnaeus labored to define each genus and its species by at least one anatomical feature that seemed to be distinctive of it, he did not do so for *Homo*. *Homo* was simply defined by the phrase *Nosce te ipsum*, know thyself. Apparently, if Linnaeus had been totally free of the religious and political shackles of his day, he probably would not have created a separate genus for humans. As he admitted in a letter to a colleague, he did not believe that any feature of note separated *Homo* from *Simia*. He did so only to minimize the amount of opprobrium he would attract with his brazen act of classifying humans in a group with other animals. Although the phrase *Nosce te ipsum* may have been useful advice in a philosophical sense, it was to be of no help whatsoever when it came to dealing with the fossil record.

Putting Humans into Evolution and Fossils into Human Evolution

Although evidence has always existed of the presence of different kinds of past humans, its significance was long in being recognized and was misinterpreted well into the Renaissance. For instance, large megalithic structures, such as Stonehenge, were thought to have been the work of giants of superhuman strength who had once roamed the face of Earth. Stone artifacts, which were exposed along river banks or

uncovered when fields were plowed or foundations for roads or houses were dug, were interpreted in one of two ways: either they came from the heavens (the smaller projectile points and arrowheads often being referred to as "elf arrows" and the larger implements as "thunderstones") or they were formed in the bowels of Earth, just like any rock or stone. Konrad von Gesner coined the term ceraunia for such objects. Not only would ceraunia come to embrace a cornucopia of geological objects, it would subsume all excavated hard objects. Thus, ceraunia come to include stone artifacts that had been modified by humans, as well as fossils, which are bones and teeth that become rocklike through the process of mineralization. For centuries fossils, stone tools, and everything else geological were often illustrated in the same plates by one scientist or another who lumped them all together as "things that had been dug up."

The odd thing is that, by the sixteenth century, Europeans were aware of the existence of humans elsewhere in the world who actually used stone instead of metal tools. However, only the sixteenth-century Italian Renaissance scholar Michele Mercati made the proper connection. Before the end of that century, he had suggested that people in the past had also made stone tools, and that such implements were represented among the ceraunia that were being discovered. Unfortunately, Mercati's treatise, although possibly read by some of his contemporaries while in manuscript, was not published until the eighteenth century. Thus the class of ceraunia began to unravel only in the second half of the seven-

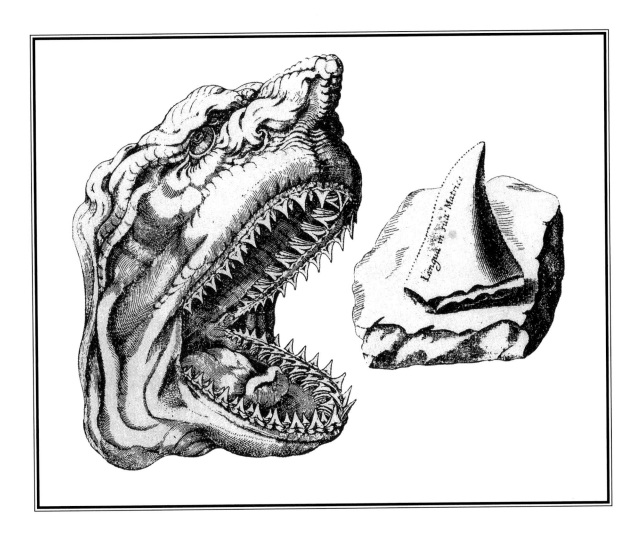

teenth century, with the demonstration by the Danish geologist and anatomist Nicholaus Steno that the structure of rocks that were identical with clams and mussels or shark's teeth were not rocks at all. Instead, Steno explained, these objects had the detailed features of the shells of living clams and mussels or sharks teeth precisely because they were the remains of living organisms that were simply contained in rocks as they formed. [Figure 2]

[Figure 2]
Until the geologist and anatomist, Nicholaus Steno, demonstrated that fossil clams, mussels, and shark's teeth were the mineralized remains of once-living organisms, scholars believed that they were just odd-looking stones.

With the realization that there had actually been ancient organisms whose remains had been incorporated into the rock record, you might think that the stage had been set for the acceptance of human antiquity. And indeed, in 1686, the English natural historian Robert Plot became the first to publish a work on the manufacture of stone tools by earlier humans. He even illustrated stone tools in the same plates as seventeenth-century implements, toys, sculpture, and monuments. There was now no turning back. Stone tools from the past had become an accepted reality.

But there was a downside to this recognition. Another English natural historian, John Woodward, had emphatically stated in 1728 that if you made stone tools, you were not only technologically unsophisticated, you were nothing more than a barbarian and savage. Stone tools that were dug up in the fields had to have been made by earlier humans, who, of course, had been barbaric and savage compared with eighteenth-century Englishmen. But the course of human history had been away from the barbaric to the civilized, away from stone tools to the advanced technology of metallurgy. Truly civilized humans of the eighteenth century had followed this path of progress. The consequence of adhering to this simple-minded chain of thought, however, was that if you were to find any living humans who still made stone tools, they had to be savages. And, unfortunately, western European explorers had discovered many groups of people who still used stone and other non-metal tools. If you belonged to a western society, this simple dichotomy—metal-tool use equals civilized, non-metal tool use equals savage—gave justification to conquest and subjugation. If you were the "other," you were out of luck. As we saw,

even Charles Darwin was not exempt from these temptations.

Despite scientists' acknowledgment of the reality of fossils and stone tools, and of the implications from stone tools uncovered in the fields that there had been earlier primitive humans, only non-human animals were allowed by Scripture to be older than the general time of the Great Flood. This was because, if you followed the sequence of creation, non-human animals preceded humans. Because animals still inhabited Earth, obviously fossils of now extinct animals not only represented the historical sequence of creation, they also reflected the reality of the biblical flood that had killed off those unfortunate enough not to be saved by Noah. Humans, however, had been created last and in the image of God. Since the period of the Great Flood began with Adam and Eve, humans—primitive or not—would not have existed earlier in time. Thus, in 1857, when Schaaffhausen and Fuhlrott became the first to publish on a fossil human, the evident antiquity of this important specimen—the famous Feldhofer Grotto Neanderthal—was far from universally accepted. [Figure 3]

The miners who discovered the Feldhofer Neanderthal gave the specimen to Johann Karl Fuhlrott, a school teacher. Fuhlrott was convinced that the skull cap had come from a layer that also contained the bones of animals that all scholars agreed were now extinct, such as mammoths and cave bears. Unfortunately, his collaborator Hermann Schaaffhausen, the much revered Professor of Anatomy at the University of Bonn, saw things differently. Schaaffhausen

[Figure 3]
Although the German school teacher, Carl Fuhlrott, thought
that the Feldhofer Grotto Neanderthal skull cap represented an extinct human relative, the eminent Professor
Hermann Schaaffhausen won his case for this specimen as
nothing more than a remnant of an individual from a
savage and barbaric race of diluvian human. Photograph
courtesy of Rheinisches Landesmuseum, Bonn.

did everything he could during their public presentation on the Feldhofer Grotto skull cap to dismiss Fulhrott's claims, and to argue that there was no reasonable conclusion other than that the bearer of this oddly shaped cranium and skeleton had been a recent human of barbaric aspect. Perhaps, Schaaffhausen mused, this individual had belonged to the one of the wild tribes mentioned by Roman historians. But, whatever the true identity of this individual, it had been from a savage and barbaric race, but not necessarily more so than the most savage and barbaric of known living races, such as the aboriginal Australians.

Thus the indisputable contemporaneity of ancient humans and their stone tools with the bones of extinct mammals had to await 1886, with the discovery by Julien Fraipont and Max Lohest of two partial Neanderthal skeletons at the Belgian site of Spy. Prior to that event, the evolutionary significance–or, more precisely, its lack—of the Feldhofer Grotto skull cap and skeleton had come under the scrutiny of none other than Thomas Henry Huxley. Although Huxley's essay on the anatomical bases for distinguishing humans and the apes as a group (with the apes constituting their own subgroup) is perhaps the best known of the three essays he published together in 1863 under the title of *Man's Place in Nature*, it is to the one in which he discussed the evidence for human antiquity that we now turn. At the time Huxley wrote this essay on human evolution, we must admit, the fossil evidence was pretty scrappy. Indeed, there was not much more than a partial skull from the site of Engis, near Liège, Belgium, and the

remains from Feldhofer Grotto. As for the Engis specimen, there was no doubt that its features matched those of living humans, although it was possible, according to the eminent English geologist Charles Lyell, that it could have been contemporaneous with extinct mammals.

The Feldhofer Grotto Neanderthal was a less clear-cut case. Huxley reconfirmed Schaaffhausen's descriptions of the ways in which this Neanderthal differed from living humans. For example, the bones of the Neanderthal's skull and skeleton were thicker. The skull was longer, wider, and lower and bore thickened and continuous brow ridges. The ribs were more circular in cross-section. And the collar bone was significantly longer. Not too humanlike, it would seem. But this was no deterrent to Huxley. Using an illustration in which the outline of the Neanderthal skull cap was drawn over that of the skull of an Australian Aborigine (which he chose as representative of the most primitive members of the presumed graded hierarchy of living humans that led up to Europeans), Huxley blithely went on with his argument for including the fossil in the species *H. sapiens*. [Figure 4] In short, Huxley proclaimed, "the Neanderthal cranium is by no means so isolated as it appears to be at first, but forms, in reality, the extreme term of a series leading gradually from it to the highest and best developed of human crania." Indeed, Huxley told his audience, "[a] small additional amount of flattening and lengthening, with a corresponding increase of the supraciliary [brow] ridge, would convert the Australian

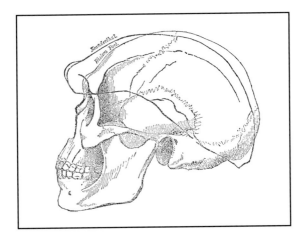

[Figure 4]

The idea that human fossils represented merely a projection of modern human variation into the past was first presented by Thomas Huxley, who suggested that it would not take much to transform the thick-browed and low-profiled Feldhofer Grotto Neanderthal's skull cap into an Australian Aborigine's. As far as Huxley was concerned, the Australian Aborigine was perhaps the most primitive of living humans. Reproduced from Thomas Huxley's *Man Place in Nature* (1863); courtesy of American Museum of Natural History.

brain case into a form identical with that of the aberrant fossil."

Voilà. In one fell swoop, Huxley had projected the perception of a continuum of human variability into the past, swallowing up the odd-looking fossil specimen in its wake. He also, inadvertently, provided an example of how scientists can abuse the notion of evolution. For if he, the leading comparative vertebrate anatomist of his generation, could imagine how easy it would be to transform an Australian Aborigine's skull into a Neanderthal's, the sky was the limit in terms of which other not-so-human-looking specimens could also be sucked into the species

H. sapiens on the grounds that they were nothing more than variations on a general theme.

Huxley's apparent legacy to paleoanthropology—of seeing a continuum of human variation extending from the present into the past—is somewhat difficult to reconcile with his general view of how evolution works. In contrast to Darwin, who argued for an evolutionary continuum through the gradual accumulation of minute variations, Huxley counted himself among those comparative anatomists who embraced saltationism. Whereas Darwin devoted *On the Origin of Species* to arguing that nature does not make leaps from one kind of organism to another, Huxley believed that this was the case. Although Huxley defended Darwin's right to his intellectual position, he admonished him in a letter for rejecting the notion *natura non facit saltum* (nature does not make leaps). As a saltationist, Huxley could not envision how an organ or novel feature that had any kind of functional significance could be put together gradually. What, the saltationists argued, would the series of ancestral organisms do, or how would they even survive, until the new trait was completed and up and running?

We shall probably never know what Huxley really had in mind when he was writing about the Feldhofer Grotto Neanderthal. Perhaps he was hedging his bets. The human species may have originated in saltatory fashion, but once in existence, the transformation from primitive to civilized human took place gradually. Huxley may have even found himself forced into this intellectual corner as a result of embracing the notion that some living humans, such as the

Australian Aborigines, were more primitive than others, such as western Europeans. If we are correct, then Huxley certainly set the stage for Darwin's lengthy discourse in *The Descent of Man* on a similar theme. Further, because Huxley believed that Australian Aborigines and western Europeans were members of the same species, he had to view their anatomical differences as a matter of variation. As such, it would not be a great stretch of the imagination to extend the range of variation to include the Neanderthal specimen. Had a third kind of distinctive fossil human been known at the time, it is difficult to say how Huxley would have dealt with it. Regardless, he introduced, at the very beginning of paleoanthropological studies, the basis for thinking of human evolution as a continuum of shifting variation.

The weight of Huxley's reputation notwithstanding, there was at least one lone voice that could not accept the notion that the Neanderthal was merely a variant of living *H. sapiens*. That individual was William King. In 1864, the year after Huxley published his three essays in *Man's Place in Nature*, King, a professor of geology at Queen's College in Galway, Ireland, gave a paper at the meeting of the British Association for the Advancement for Science in which he argued for recognizing the Neanderthal as a species apart from *H. sapiens*. With the publication of King's paper the same year, *Homo neanderthalensis* entered the literature as the first species name to be given to an extinct human.

In his presentation, King rejected the various suggestions that had been offered by Schaaffhausen and others to explain why this particular human looked so different from living humans. Following Huxley's descriptions in great detail, he went on to list the features of the skull and skeleton in which this individual differed so markedly from living humans. These features, he asserted, made it clear that any claims of resemblance between the Neanderthal and any living human were based on assumption rather than reality. After dispensing with Huxley, King turned to Darwin. Darwin had argued that living humans differed so much from the Neanderthal, most notably in their smaller and thinner-boned brain cases, because they have not had a "natural" natural history. Instead, Darwin argued, because of their particular circumstances of being able to manipulate the environment and thus themselves, the diverse lot of humans should be treated as domesticated animals. And, as everyone knows, domesticated animals, being subjects of artificial rather than natural selection, can come in a much greater variety of sizes and shapes than wild animals. King also rejected this conceit of Darwin's. Humans were not like domesticated animals at all. Clearly, King argued, domesticated animals, being "so remarkably differentiated by cranial peculiarities, are *artificial*, whereas the varieties of mankind are *natural.*"

King was certainly brave to buck the leading authorities. He had based his taxonomic assessment on the morphological differences between *H. sapiens* and Neanderthals instead of being swayed by a particular model of how they should be interpreted, as Huxley and Darwin had. Even so, he was undoubtedly constrained by the political and intellectual atmosphere of his time. For example, he admitted, he could have gone beyond suggesting that Neanderthal was a species apart from *H. sapiens*. In truth, he believed that, because the Neanderthal was more similar to the chimpanzee—especially in the brow ridges and low cranial profile—than to living humans, the extinct human should really be put in its own genus. But King's thoughts of placing Neanderthals in a separate genus may also have been tempered by his belief that, like the ape, the Neanderthal had lacked the human qualities of language and moral attitudes.

King's speculations about the "mind" of Neanderthal aside, one might have predicted that future discoveries of fossil human relatives would have solidified his argument that distinct anatomical differences between this fossil and living humans were taxonomically relevant. But little happened, despite the fact that the fossil remains that we now regard as representing *H. erectus* were first relegated to different genera. These fossils, discovered in Java in the 1890s, were first called *Anthropopithecus erectus* and then *Pithecanthropus erectus;* those discovered a few decades later in China were classified as *Sinanthropus pekinensis*. Shortly after the turn of the century, a jaw found in Germany was given its own species, *Homo heidelbergensis*. As the twentieth century progressed, less recognizably human fossils were discovered in South and then East Africa. And as the fossils were discovered, they were variably assigned to different genera and species. By the late 1940s, the picture of human evolution looked for all the world like that of other animals: different genera and species, some going extinct, and, in the case of humans, only one surviving.

The Evolutionary Synthesis: Exempting Humans from Natural Selection

The potential for recognizing diversity in human evolution was cut short with the invasion of the halls of paleoanthropology by the leaders of the "evolutionary synthesis," the ornithologist Ernst Mayr and the fruit fly geneticist Theodosius Dobzhansky. They brought with them the biases of Huxley and Darwin. From Darwin came the argument that humans are exempt from natural selection as we know it to work in the wild, and, because of that, their evolutionary history has also been different from other organisms. From Huxley and Darwin came the basis for the idea that, rather than resembling a bush with many branches, human evolution proceeded upward in a straight line. In this context, differences between specimens were seen as mere extensions into the past of versions of modern human variability, rather than as clues to an evolutionary past that was characterized by many species.

Dobzhansky and Mayr had both published monographs on general aspects of evolution that contributed to the formulation in the 1930s and 1940s of the grand evolutionary synthesis, through which Darwinism and Mendelism were formally melded in the form of the neo-

Darwinism we know today. In the 1950s, no doubt buoyed by their apparent success in promoting neo-Darwinism above all potential alternative evolutionary theories, Dobzhansky and Mayr branched out to include humans in their bailiwick.

Dobzhansky's pet notion was that humans had to be thought of as a special case because they had culture. Because culture removed humans from the effects of the natural environment, humans as organisms were also removed from the evolutionary vicissitudes of natural selection. Culture became the human environment and, with it, came our species' manipulation of its own evolution. If, as Dobzhansky firmly believed, toolmaking, and perhaps even tool use, constituted a reflection of human control over their environment, so, too, he argued, must human evolution have long ago veered off on its own unnatural course. Because culture allowed its bearers to adapt to a diversity of situations, the differences that existed among extinct and living humans were no more than different adaptations of members of a single, continuously evolving lineage. By the same token, culture also precluded the existence of more than one hominid species at any given point in time. It just couldn't happen that two species could bear culture.

Mayr approached human evolution from a slightly different angle—that species evolve from subspecies and that speciation can only occur when there is a vacant econiche that a subspecies can invade. Having done so, the species can then set off on its own course of evolution. Because, Mayr argued, living humans are so widespread geographically and so diversely adapted, there are now no vacant econiches into which any subset of the species could move. Therefore, we cannot expect that humans will ever speciate. From this speculation Mayr then declared that this must have been the way it was for most, if not all, of the time humans had existed. As such, except perhaps at the very beginning, there never was, as with other organisms, any speciation, or any diversification of human species. Allowing at most two species of australopith (early biped) to have existed—only because they would supposedly have occupied different econiches—Mayr proclaimed that forever thereafter there was only one species of human at a time: an australopith had evolved directly into *H. erectus* which, in turn, had become transformed into *H. sapiens*. When *Homo habilis* was announced, Mayr incorporated it as a stage in the continuum from an early biped to *H. erectus*.

In one fell swoop, Mayr and Dobzhansky determined the course of human evolution and the format into which most paleoanthropologists would thereafter allocate fossilized hominid specimens. If the specimen was old, it was supposed to be one of two types of australopith. If it was a bit younger, then it was eventually *H. habilis*. Younger still and it was *H. erectus*. And, finally, there was modern *H. sapiens*. Gone forever was the diversity that the different taxa assigned to previously discovered fossils indicated was there. Even if some of those genera, such as Pithecanthropus and Sinanthropus, should (in retrospect) have been kept to the level of the species, diversity would still have characterized human evolution.

But how could anyone, much less a bunch of paleoanthropologists who were not equipped with the supposedly more biologically informed backgrounds of Mayr and Dobzhansky, disagree with them? No one could. Or, at least, no one would who didn't want to be accused of being anti-evolutionary—or, much worse, anti-Darwinian. And with humans now removed from the realm of biological evolution as it affected every other organism that ever walked the face of Earth, the door was wide open for non-biological elements, such as culture and time, to dominate the discussion of human history. Because human evolution was now conceived of as a straight line of continuous transformation of one species into the next, there was no need for concern about the method and theory of determining evolutionary relationships. Species identification of human fossil became basically a matter of time and place. Because of this, it was now much less important to the determination of species what any particular fossil hominid looked like. Consequently, a wildly diverse assortment of hominid fossils were lumped together as mere variations on a theme because they came from roughly the same period. And once this was done, one could look back on this presumed assemblage and marvel at how incredibly variable humans had been in the past.

With the sequential stages or phases of human evolution defined essentially by time, study of the comparative anatomy of fossils from a taxonomic standpoint was put on the back burner. Elevated in importance were the scenarios that had to be devised to explain the

mechanisms behind the supposed continuum of human evolutionary change and how, at any point in time, there could have been such wildly variable populations of the same species of human ancestor. From the 1950s until the very present, these concerns have characterized the major efforts of most paleoanthropologists.

But the monopoly of this dogma is beginning to crack. More and more paleoanthropologists are finding it increasingly difficult to sustain this artifice of interpretation. Humans, as special as they may think they are, and indeed may be, have enjoyed the same kind of evolutionary history—involving both speciation and extinction—as the rest of life. Just as with other organisms, our evolutionary past resembles a many-branched bush of diversity, with many species coming into existence and almost as many dying out. At first glance, it might appear that it would be a simple matter to tease out the species from the continuum to which Mayr and Dobzhansky exiled them. But, as we have learned the hard way, it is not. As practicing paleoanthropologists, the problem that we face right now in discussing human evolution is that, since our fossil record (unlike those of other organisms) has so rarely been approached from the perspective of diversity, we have often found ourselves obliged to sort out specimens from scratch, so that we can begin to ask what we hope are the right questions. In some instances, particularly with Neanderthals, we have been able to contribute new data and new interpretations. In others, such as with the australopiths, we are just beginning to find our way. And in yet others, such as *H. erectus*, which we initially thought was a relatively clear-cut case, our initial studies have led us to suspect that, even there, the picture may have been much more complicated than we had assumed.

A large part of the problem is because human fossils were regarded as merely representatives of a continuum of variability through time leading to present-day humans, with an emphasis on comparative anatomy for purposes of delineating species relegated to secondary citizenship. Once this happened, efforts to define on anatomical grounds the handful of species and the two genera that were permitted to exist, *Australopithecus* and *Homo*, disappeared. This is a shame because, had the field of paleoanthropology followed the course of comparative study that had been initiated over two centuries ago by Johann Friedrich Blumenbach (1752–1840), things might have been completely different.

Defining *Homo*

In 1775, forty years after the first edition of Linnaeus' *Systema Naturae*, Johann Blumenbach of Göttingen published his dissertation, *On the Natural Varieties of Mankind*. Although he would pursue the study of other organisms, Blumenbach's work on humans would have the greatest impact because of its focus. Although he could not be considered an evolutionist, and there were no human fossils for him to incorporate into his studies, we consider this scholar to be the "father" of paleoanthropology. For, whether or not they know it, virtually all paleoanthropologists follow his lead when they

attempt to define the characteristics that identify the genus *Homo*. This is particularly interesting when you consider that a major preoccupation of paleoanthropology is the sorting out of fossils into a minimum of species within the genus *Homo*. In Blumenbach's day, the concern was who among the living "races" could be considered a member of the species *H. sapiens*. And it was in his pursuit of the answer to that question that Blumenbach emerges as a major player in the history of our discipline.

Although Blumenbach was an admitted fan of Linnaeus, he thought that his intellectual idol had failed by not offering any anatomical features—not even one—to back up his taxonomy of humans. And even if he had, Blumenbach was not convinced that it would have been very helpful. Despite his secure place in history as the father of modern classification, Linnaeus was very limited in how he defined not only species and genera but also the higher taxonomic ranks of a classification. When discussing mammals he often focused strictly on dental differences. Blumenbach, in contrast, thought that Linnaeus' approach could be usefully broadened to include a more diverse base of anatomical information.

In *On the Natural Varieties of Mankind*, Blumenbach argued against the polygenists, maintaining that all living humans, regardless of perceived differences, belonged to the same species, *H. sapiens*. How else could one explain the fact that all humans, regardless of where they lived and what they looked like superficially, stood erect and had the same detailed features of skull, jaw, and body? This was a critical beginning for his later life's work, in which he strove to go well beyond Linnaeus' dictum "know thyself" and delineate anatomical features by which to distinguish humans from other animals. But before he could discuss humans as a group in comparison with other groups of animals, he first had to establish that, variation aside, all humans were united as a species. So, in his dissertation, Blumenbach painstakingly went through the features of hard- and soft-tissue anatomy that all humans shared regardless of the differences that were emphasized only in regional populations. This having been done to his satisfaction, Blumenbach then proceeded to his next major work, *Of the Difference of Man from Other Animals*, which was finally published in 1795, twenty years after his dissertation. There he elaborated upon the distinguishing features of humans that, as we will see in later chapters, essentially became the "list" that guided many paleoanthropologists in their interpretations of particular fossil specimens as well as, more generally, the picture of human evolutionary history.

Blumenbach began his presentation in the second work with a discussion of Linnaeus' ideas, particularly the Swedish botanist's conviction that he, at least, could not find a single character by which to distinguish humans from apes. Not only had Linnaeus failed to define the genus *Homo* by anything more useful than a fanciful phrase, he had not defined the species *sapiens*, either. The only seemingly concrete taxonomy Linnaeus had done with regard to *H. sapiens* was to present a list of races and to describe each by an idiosyncratic conglomeration of physical, cultural, and behavioral characteristics. Nonetheless, Blumenbach greatly admired Linnaeus as a systematist, and was determined to complete his work.

Blumenbach delineated four areas of anatomical distinction by which he thought humans—*H. sapiens*—could easily be defined: the development of erect posture, a broad and flat pelvis, two-handedness, and closely set, as well as morphologically and sequentially related, teeth. First, harking back to Aristotle's list of characters, was the distinctive erect posture, which, Blumenbach argued, was both natural for and specific to *H. sapiens*. He defended the "natural" aspect of this claim by reference to stories of abandoned or lost infants who had been raised in the wild by animals, and who had grown up, without any external input, to walk bipedally. Obviously, these individuals had naturally and spontaneously learned to stand upright and locomote on two legs.

To prove that bipedalism was specific to *H. sapiens*, Blumenbach invoked a whole series of anatomical differences between humans and other animals. For example, human infants differ from quadrupeds because they crawl on their hands and knees, not on all four feet. Further, the bones of the human ankle develop earlier than those of the wrist, rather than simultaneously or the other way around as in quadrupeds. Humans have long, strong legs and a short trunk, together with short, relatively weak arms. Among quadrupeds the legs are either short and the arms very long and strong as in apes and various other primates, or, as in many primates and indeed mammals in general, the hindlimbs are only slightly longer than the forelimbs. The human chest is wide from side to side and compressed from front to back; in quadrupeds the reverse occurs. Also, a human's shoulder joints are widely separated and the shoulder blades ride along the back. In quadrupeds the shoulder joints are closer together and the shoulder blades lie along the sides of the body. And finally, humans have a short breast bone and rib cage, which together leave the viscera less well encased than in quadrupeds, which have a long breast bone and a more extensive rib cage.

After looking at bipedalism, Blumenbach went on to discuss the human pelvic region, which, he declared, is the only true pelvis among animals. By "true pelvis" Blumenbach meant that the details of the different bones—the bones in which the hip joints reside and the intervening sacrum, which is composed of a series of five vertebrae that fuse together—create a broad basin that cups a human's viscera; in quadrupeds, which have a narrow pelvic girdle, the internal organs are confined by the rib cage and the stomach muscles. As for distinctive features of the soft tissues of the human pelvic region, Blumenbach followed Aristotle and the Comte de Buffon in recognizing the presence of swollen buttocks. These exist because the gluteal muscles (which are swathed in a thick layer of fat) that attach to the enlarged posterior portions of the human pelvis are huge compared with those of quadrupeds.

One of the human gluteal muscles—the gluteus maximus, so named because it is the largest of the set of three—connects to the back of the femur. There it creates an attachment scar that runs partway down the leg bone's midline. When this muscle contracts, it pulls the leg back, propelling the individual forward in the characteristic gait of human bipedalism. This scar on the human femur was identified by early anatomists as the linea aspera (meaning "line of hope"). This name derived from the notion that quadrupeds, which lack the human arrangement of the gluteal muscles, are desirous (but, regrettably, incapable) of achieving that attribute of human perfection, bipedal locomotion.

Because walking on two rather than four legs changes the orientation in which an individual holds its torso, it is reasonable to expect significant differences between humans and quadrupeds in the pelvic region, and that these differences would impact on the processes of carrying and giving birth to infants. In humans, Blumenbach pointed out, the sacrum and the vestiges of the tail bones at its end (which form the short coccyx) are curved inward toward the center of the pelvic opening. Although this adds slightly from below to the supportive bowl shape of the human pelvic region, it also (according to Blumenbach) causes the woman's vagina to point forward instead of back, as it does in quadrupeds with their narrower, longer, and straighter sacra. The curved human sacrum and coccyx may aid in cupping the viscera and the developing fetus, but, in turn, the forwardly angled birth passage presents an extra obstetric obstacle that quadrupeds do not encounter. In discussing this topic, Blumenbach referred to a comment Lucretius (of the strong, silent savage scenario) had made to the effect that humans' preference for a frontal position during copulation was for the best position possible, as well as to Leonardo da Vinci's anatomical drawings, and notes about how natural this position was for humans because of the orientations of their sex organs.

After examining the pelvic region, Blumenbach went straight to the human hand, which, he recalled, Aristotle had declared as being the "organ of organs." As far as Blumenbach was concerned, the human hand is perfected by its long, opposable thumb. From the hand he then went on to the foot and especially its big toe. In humans, the big toe, although long like the thumb, is in line with the other toes and is thus not adept at grasping, like the big toe of apes and other primates. Indeed, it is because most non-human primates have hands and feet that are capable of grasping that Blumenbach, Buffon, and others classified them in the category "Quadrumana." Humans, having only one pair of grasping extremities, were classified as "Bimana."

Blumenbach did not stop with features of the foot. Although he had criticized Linnaeus for relying too much on dental characteristics in his diagnoses of species, he did not reject teeth as an important part of the comparative base. As for how humans differ from apes in their jaws and teeth, he began with the observation that, in humans, the lower front, or incisor, teeth are vertically implanted, not tilted forward, or procumbent, as in apes. In both the upper and lower jaw, but especially in the upper, the

human canine tooth is not much taller than the incisors, with which it is closely aligned. In apes, the canines are large (the upper being the larger) and much taller than the incisors. Further, in the upper jaw of an ape, the canine is separated from the incisor nearest it by a distinct gap, into which the lower canine fits when the jaws are closed.

Staying with the chewing apparatus, Blumenbach pointed out that the molars of *H. sapiens* are somewhat rounded in outline and bear relatively flat cusps. In the African apes, at least, the lower molars in particular are longer and more rectangular and the cusps more pointed and distinct. However, as we have been reminded time and time again, especially from our study of fossils from Vietnam and Indonesia, teeth that had traditionally been identified as *H. erectus* have often turned out to be those of orangutans or of extinct species closely related to these apes. Had Blumenbach compared human and orangutan teeth, he might have been quite surprised to see the general similarities.

From teeth, Blumenbach went on to features of the jaws themselves. With regard to the lower jaw, he noted that the midline of the human mandible is usually adorned with a noticeable swelling, or "chin." The result is that, among living primates, we are the only species whose lower jaw is not smooth and vertical or backwardly sloping in front, as it is in all the apes. It was the emphasis various comparative anatomists placed on the possession by "advanced" humans of a large protrusion at the front of the lower jaw that inspired them to pro-

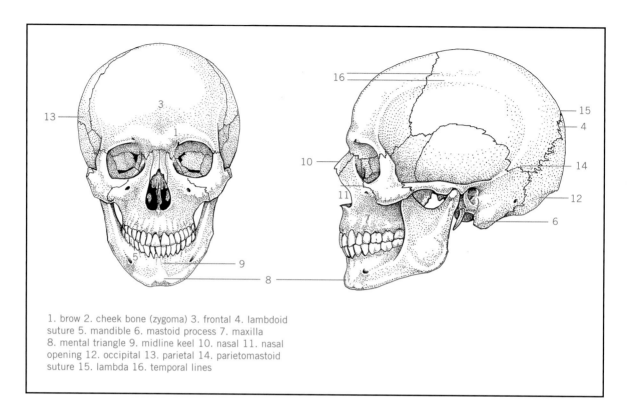

1. brow 2. cheek bone (zygoma) 3. frontal 4. lambdoid suture 5. mandible 6. mastoid process 7. maxilla 8. mental triangle 9. midline keel 10. nasal 11. nasal opening 12. occipital 13. parietal 14. parietomastoid suture 15. lambda 16. temporal lines

claim that "primitive" humans were actually intermediate between apes and the most "civilized" of humans. [Figures 5a, b, and c]

Thus, the eighteenth-century Dutch human anatomist and "physiognomist" Pieter Camper thought that Africans viewed in profile looked more like "lower" animals, with their forwardly angled snouts, than did Europeans, with their flatter faces. His perception of the facial angle also incorporated whether the front teeth were inclined forward or vertical and whether the front of the lower jaw sloped backward or bore a chin and thus protruded forward. Dogs and monkeys, for instance, had acutely protruding facial angles. "Civilized" Europeans had no real facial angle. Apes were somewhere in between

[Figures 5a, b, and c]

Front, side, and basal views of a skull of *Homo sapiens* illustrating and identifying various regions and features discussed in the text. J. Anderton, with permission

these groups. And Africans were supposed to be in between the apes and so-called civilized Europeans. Clearly, as far as Blumenbach was concerned, this was a ridiculous proposition and one that took no heed of the reality of the situation: all humans have a chin, regardless of its absolute degree of prominence.

As for the human upper jaw, Blumenbach tackled a long-standing debate: do humans have one or two pairs of bones comprising this structure? In most mammals, especially in juveniles

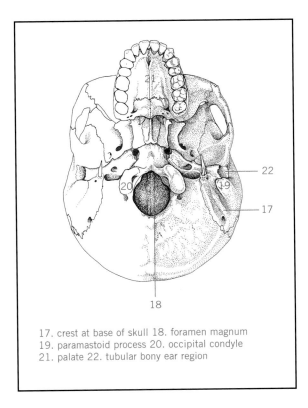

17. crest at base of skull 18. foramen magnum
19. paramastoid process 20. occipital condyle
21. palate 22. tubular bony ear region

whose bones have not yet begun to fuse together along their lines of contact, one can see two sets of bones. There's a pair of small bones—the premaxillary bones, or premaxillae—at the front of the jaw. They meet at the midline, they contribute to the floor of the nasal opening above, and they house the roots of the incisor teeth. Next to the premaxillae, the bulk of each side of the upper jaw consists of a large maxillary bone, or maxilla. Since Blumenbach's time, the contact, or suture, between these bones has come to be known as the premaxillary-maxillary suture. This suture is visible in juveniles and even on into adulthood in every living mammal with the glaring exception of humans. The apparent absence of this suture in humans was taken by

various taxonomists, as well as by anatomists such as Pieter Camper and Andreas Vesalius, as indicating that our species has no premaxillae, only the pair of maxillary bones. And this, in turn, was taken as unassailable evidence that we are something special, to be set apart from all other animals. For Camper and others, the lack of a premaxillary bone was proof that humans were special and not like any other animal.

Some anatomists could not accept this interpretation. One of them was Blumenbach. But Blumenbach's argument in this regard was actually quite odd. In his quest to demonstrate that humans were similar to other primates–and also like other animals—he failed to identify a premaxillary bone during his dissections both of orangutans and of a species of the Old World monkey *Cercopithecus*. Thus, Blumenbach declared, humans and other primates all resemble each other in *lacking* a premaxillary bone! Ironically, at about the same time, Johann Wolfgang von Goethe, brilliant anatomist as well as literary and philosophical figure, was also dead set on proving that humans were similar to other animals. However, Goethe did so by demonstrating— accurately—that humans actually *do* possess a premaxillary bone.

The discrepancy in identifying a premaxillary bone aside, Goethe and Blumenbach were both in agreement on one attribute that they thought truly set humans apart from the rest of the animal world: the ability to reason. It was reason, as Blumenbach saw it, that made it possible for humans to dominate other animals. After reason, Blumenbach singled out the capacity for invention as a major distinguishing feature of being human. In parallel with Benjamin Franklin, he saw that the uniqueness of human inventiveness applied to both language and toolmaking. The feature of human language that he thought distinguished it from animal communication was its infinite arbitrariness and variety. In being arbitrary, human language and reason were, Blumenbach proffered, quite similar to one another.

Blumenbach's Legacy

Because Blumenbach had absolutely no idea about evolution, much less the possibility that humans had arisen through such a mechanism, he would probably be dumbstruck at the prospect that his arguments for distinguishing *H. sapiens* from other animals would have had the impact they did on the field of paleoanthropology. We need only list the anatomical features he delineated: bipedal posture and locomotion; a chin; feet unlike the hands; and small upper and lower canines without gaps between them and neighboring teeth. There were also the shapes and chewing surfaces of the cheek teeth, in addition to attributes of the brain, such as reason and the arbitrariness of language and invention.

Have we progressed much beyond Blumenbach's initial work during this century? In some ways, yes. Technology has made the study of morphology a pursuit of finer detail. Evolution has become part of the formulation. And there are more fossils than anyone could

ever have predicted would be discovered. But in other ways, the answer is no. The basic arguments still persist, although now they have to do with where to draw the lines of the taxonomic fence: the genus *Homo* versus the earlier genus *Australopithecus* versus not being a hominid at all. The major differences between questions raised now and those addressed by Blumenbach are simply of degree. Just how much like us in pelvis and foot was a particular hominid species and how proficient was the form of bipedalism? Is there a real chin or an incipient chin? Are the canines really small or on the way to getting there? Just how high or low are those molar chewing surfaces, and, is the enamel covering them really like ours structurally? And, if we can identify correctly the grooves and raised areas of the surfaces of brain casts taken from the inside of fossil skulls, are they in the same places that are supposed to reflect intelligent thought and language in ourselves?

The fossils have been unwitting victims of these interpretations because, for the most part, they have been pawns in an evolutionary scenario that portrays human history as a smoothly transforming continuum of change. But this intellectual stranglehold on our evolutionary notions is beginning to loosen. The past few years have witnessed the discovery of such an unexpected array of early human species, with combinations of brain, jaw, tooth, and limb that clearly cannot be accommodated by the traditional notion of a single evolving lineage, that it is impossible (although the attempt is still made) to avoid reality. There were a lot of species, and they weren't all necessarily in our direct line of descent. It remains commonplace to refer collectively to the earliest of these early human relatives as australopiths because the first-named of them was called *Australopithecus africanus.* But more genera will likely have to be introduced to reflect these fossils' disparate relationships. And although the picture of diversity in human evolution has been even harder to picture when discussing fossils attributed to the genus *Homo,* it is becoming easier with every passing day. There simply is too much anatomy that speaks to the distinctiveness of, say, Neanderthals as a group apart from ourselves, or of many other fossils that received wisdom has forced into just two species: *H. erectus* and *H. habilis.*

Although we must recognize Blumenbach's importance in setting the stage for paleoanthropological pursuits by presenting the first anatomically based definition of the genus *Homo,* we must also realize that fossils were not part of his consciousness. Blumenbach's vision of the genus *Homo* was the same as his vision of *H. sapiens.* From his perspective, the goal was to argue that all humans—which, for him, meant only living humans—belonged to the same species. And in this context, Blumenbach's effort was a huge success. However, many problems in paleoanthropology today derive from of trying to pigeonhole fossils into the categories he established, as if they define exclusively what a hominid is. Blumenbach's work served a long and useful purpose, and its historical significance must be acknowledged. But the world is intellectually a different place now, and if we are ever fully to understand "man's place in nature," we must shed the legacies of the constraints—not only Blumenbach's, but Mayr's and Dobzhansky's—that continue to make us think about humans in a very particular and actually very idiosyncratic way.

We have been doing our part in trying to deal with human fossils on their own terms, as their anatomy, not as tradition, dictates. We cannot claim that we have all, or even most, of the answers. But we can present our understanding of how the picture of human evolution is shaping up—in part from our firsthand experience with specimens, and in part from a scrutiny of casts of specimens and their presentation in the literature.

This, then, is a work in progress, one which we hope will provoke a much needed rethinking of human evolution, not just by ourselves or our colleagues, but by every one of us. For, after all, there would seem to be greater grandeur in the view that we humans have and always will be a part of nature, than there is in thinking that we are and have been so special that we are removed from it.

CHAPTER 2

Evolution Today

[Evolution Today]

To understand evolutionary histories—of humans or any other group of organisms—it is necessary to understand the evolutionary process itself. Misunderstand the process and you'll misunderstand the history. And although you'd hardly guess it from looking at the paleoanthropological literature, the views of more general evolutionary biologists on how evolution actually works have radically altered over the past quarter-century. To grasp the present situation, we have to introduce a little more history.

The story goes all the way back to Charles Darwin—who, it must be remembered, had what was essentially a political problem. His message was that all living organisms are related by descent from an increasingly remote series of common ancestors; the mechanism by which he proposed this had occurred was natural selection. The argument was simple: in every generation, many more individuals are produced than ever survive to maturity and to reproduce themselves. Those that succeed—the "fittest"—carry heritable features that not only promote their own survival but are also passed along preferentially to their offspring. In this view, natural selection is no more than the sum of all those factors that act to promote the reproductive success of some individuals (and its lack in others). Add the dimension of time, and over

the generations natural selection will act to change the complexion of each evolving lineage, as advantageous variations become common in the population at the expense of those less advantageous. And this is where the political problem came in: Darwin lived in a world still dominated by Christian notions of special creation and of species fixity. Thus, to establish his basic view of the common descent of all living forms, it was clear that he was somehow going to have to demonstrate that these biblical dictates were wrong. Darwin's solution to this dilemma was a simple one. He couldn't deny that species had reality in space—clearly, anyone looking around at the world could see that nature was organized into discrete "packages"—but what he *could* do was to deny them reality in time. Given enough time, Darwin claimed, one species would evolve into another under the benign direction of natural selection. This formula did not in fact broach the problem of how new species actually *originate*; but the assumption was that, repeated many times, it was this process that had ultimately given rise to the millions of species known today.

Contrary to received wisdom, and to stories of fainting bishops' wives, Darwin's central tenet—that all living organisms (including humans) are related by common descent—was quite rapidly accepted by scientists and public alike. What was not accepted so readily was the notion of natural selection. Even after the basic principles of genetics had been rediscovered in 1900 (they had actually been first enunciated in 1866, but in a very obscure publication), the mechanisms whereby new species arose and new hereditary variations were incorporated into populations (two very different things) remained the subject of acrimonious debate. Some early geneticists and other evolutionists were saltationists, believing that new species arise suddenly, by wholesale reorganization of the genome (the total genetic makeup of the organism). Others felt that the evolutionary process was driven by "mutation pressure": the rate at which smaller genetic novelties were introduced into the population. Yet others cleaved to various notions of "orthogenesis," whereby an inherent drive existed within lineages toward change in a particular direction. Few, however, favored natural selection as the principal agent of evolutionary change.

In fact, natural selection did not return to its central place in evolutionary theory until the 1930s and 1940s, a time when geneticists, naturalists, and paleontologists came together to embrace what became grandly known as the great Evolutionary Synthesis. By this time, the mathematical geneticists J. B. S. Haldane, Ronald Fisher, and Sewall Wright had laid the statistical basis for understanding how genes could be shuffled in populations over time, given various assumptions of natural selection. Then in a series of highly influential books, the geneticist Theodosius Dobzhansky, the ornithologist Ernst Mayr, and the paleontologist

George Simpson brought their various fields into the fold by demonstrating to their satisfaction that virtually all evolutionary phenomena could be boiled down to long-term changes in the genetic make-up of populations, under the guiding hand of natural selection.

This, of course, was fine for the geneticists, who thereby held the key to the mysteries of the evolutionary process. It also worked for the ornithologists and other naturalists, who could still think of species as discrete entities in space as they went about their task of cataloguing the basic units of nature, and assessing their evolutionary relationships. The ones who were really shorted by the Synthesis were the paleontologists, those scientists whose efforts were directed at understanding evolutionary histories and processes by analysis of the fossil record. For, under the Synthesis, time, the unique dimension of their study, robbed species (the basic paleontological unit) of their identity. Species became ephemera that simply evolved themselves out of existence. Thus the Synthesis effectively left paleontology without a theoretical framework because paleontologists were relegated to the essentially clerical task of sorting out the mundane historical details of what had evolved into what.

During the period preceding the outbreak of World War II, paleoanthropologists had been little more than onlookers upon the development of the Synthesis. Indeed, it is hard to discern in the paleoanthropological literature of the time anything more than the most superficial interest in the modes and processes of evolution itself. After the war ended, then, there was in paleoanthropology a plethora of names applied to extinct hominids; plus a yawning theoretical gap just waiting to be filled. Dobzhansky and Mayr were more than pleased to fill that gap, and to supply paleoanthropology not only with the theoretical framework it so clearly lacked, but also with ready-made interpretations of the human fossil record. We have already briefly noted the details of the Dobzhansky and Mayr proposals in the last chapter, and will return to them in the next. Enough to repeat that, unsurprisingly, they were linear in nature. For, if it was a general rule that species slowly evolved themselves out of existence by gradual change under natural selection, then the history of human evolution, too, must have boiled down to a long, gradual slog from primitiveness to perfection: a process of fine-tuning over the eons. [Figure 6] Even leaving aside the magisterial and unassailable authority of Dobzhansky and Mayr, this view of human evolution was highly congenial to a science already steeped in notions of the Great Chain of Being, and it came rapidly to dominate the paleoanthropological mindset. Indeed, it still dominates that mindset today, despite the fact that for decades evolutionary biologists have been pointing out that the Synthesis presents at best an incomplete picture of the very complex evolutionary story.

Unsurprisingly, it was from paleontology that the first grumblings of this kind were heard. [Figure 7] If the "neodarwinian" dictates of the Synthesis were correct, then the fossil record should be replete with intermediate forms. Yet it was not, as had long been recognized. A hundred years earlier Darwin himself had been acutely aware of the "gaps" in the fossil record and had concluded that they resulted from that record's incompleteness. A century later, the discovery and study of many millions more fossils had failed to change the essential picture: the record is marked by a *lack* of intermediates. It was time for someone to ask whether the gaps in the record, far from being deficiencies, might actually be telling us something. The question was articulated in 1972 by two invertebrate paleontologists, Niles Eldredge and Stephen Jay Gould. [Figure 8] They contrasted the traditional expectations of "phyletic gradualism" with an alternative notion of "punctuated equilibria," whereby the history of most species is one of "stasis," or non-change. Most true evolutionary innovation, they contended, takes place in relatively short episodes, probably linked to the process of speciation in which new species are born of old ones. No less than Ernst Mayr himself had been a leading advocate of the notion of "allopatric" speciation, whereby small peripheral isolates of a "parental" population could bypass the "genetic inertia" of large interbreeding populations, and thereby incorporate true genetic novelties on their way to becoming new species. And with this mechanism, ironically, he had paved the way to an explanation not simply of the gaps that exist in the fossil record, but of why we should expect them to be there.

Recent work by one of us (JHS), presented in some detail in the recent book *Sudden Origins*,

[Figure 6]
The process of speciation as envisaged by Ernst Mayr in his 1942 book *Systematics and the Origins of Species.*

Stage 1. A uniform species
with a large range

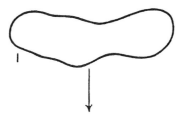

Followed by:
Process 1. Differentiation
into subspecies

Resulting in:
Stage 2. A geographically
variable species with a more
or less continuous array of
similar subspecies (2a all
subspecies are slight, 2b
some are pronounced)

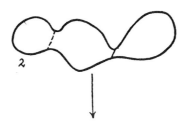

Followed by:
Process 2. a) Isolating actio
of geographic barriers between some of the popula-
tions;
also b) development of isolating mechanisms in the
isolated and differentiating
subspecies

Resulting in:
Stage 3. A geographically
variable species with many
subspecies completely isolated, particularly near the
borders of the range, and
some of them morphologi-
cally as different as good
species

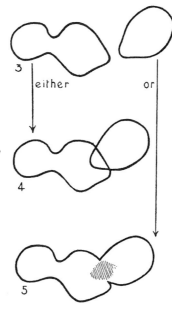

Followed by:
Process 3. Expansion of
range of such isolated populations into the territory of
the representative forms

Resulting in either
Stage 4. Noncrossing, that is,
new species with restricted
range
or

Stage 5. Interbreeding, that
is, the establishment of a
hybrid zone (zone of secondary intergradation)

FIG. 16. Stages of speciation.

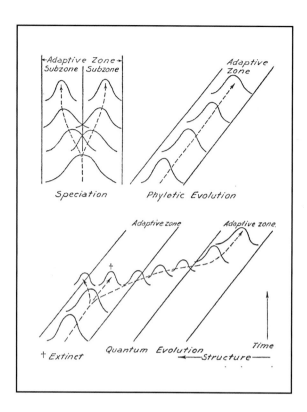

the individuals and populations bearing them. It has for long been known that any important structure must reach a certain minimal threshold of development or its possessor will be aborted. Thus in extinct three-toed species of horse, the lateral digits always consist of three phalangeal elements, even if they are small relative to the size of the central digit. With the appearance of the first single-toed horses, the lateral digits are entirely absent. There is no intermediate condition between three toes and one.

At the level of the regulatory genes, and thus of the developmental advent of structures, we also see a picture of the abrupt appearance or disappearance of features. Each individual possesses two copies of each gene; you are known as a homozygote if both copies are the same, and as heterozygote if the two are different. In heterozygotes one copy will be "dominant" to the other, "recessive," copy, and will mask its effects. In the case of the vertebrate eye, for example, studies on the mouse *Rx* gene showed that individual mice that were either homozygous or heterozygous for the active gene had both an eyeball and a bony socket. In contrast, homozygotes for the experimentally mutated inactive, or recessive, *Rx* gene lacked both structures. Again, there was no in-between state.

It has long been known that non-lethal mutations typically arise as recessives. Genes controlling new physical features therefore likely emerge in a population through a slow process leading to the production of homozygotes for the mutation. But when these features appear, it will be as if "out of nowhere." They will also appear in their full-blown state in a

suggests a genetic basis for how we so often find innovations appearing suddenly in the fossil record, rather than being slowly fine-tuned over the ages by (presumed) natural selection. There is a class of genes whose function it is to regulate major developmental patterns in each individual, and seemingly minor changes in such regulatory genes can have major consequences for

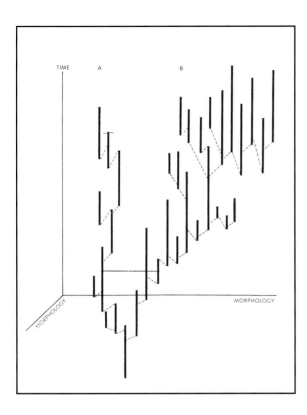

[Figure 8]

Three-dimensional sketch published by Niles Eldredge and Stephen Jay Gould in 1972 to contrast two patterns that might be observed in the fossil record. The vertical bars are species as they exist through time, and the dashed lines are speciations, as one species gives rise to another in a short-term event. On the left we see a pattern of relative morphological stability over time, while on the right is shown a "trend," where speciation is also associated with morphological shift. In both cases, the evolutionary pattern might be interpreted retrospectively as a straight line, but in fact the actual patterns are of stasis within species, with intermittent speciation and extinction. The "trend" is explained by the differential success of species which do not themselves undergo continuous modification during their histories. Courtesy of Niles Eldredge.

number of individuals, because as recessives they will have remained "silent" until a critical mass of them had accumulated in the population, permitting them to be expressed in the homozygous state. Finally, at some point, and by a mechanism that remains unknown, the mutant recessive is converted to the dominant state. Here, then, we have a potential explanation at the genetic level for why, for instance, the acquisition of modern human body form in the paleoanthropological record appears to have been virtually instantaneous, rather than the result of perfecting transformation over the ages. [Figure 9]

None of this is to suggest that natural selection is not an active ingredient of the evolutionary process. Indeed, it seems to be central to the process of local diversification that all successful species undergo. Every widespread species develops regional variants, doubtless for reasons of adaptation to local conditions; and it is such variants that provide the basis for future new species. It is significant, however, that natural selection is not related to the process of speciation itself, which is caused by genetic events that are random with respect to adaptation. And the upshot is that species play two distinct roles in evolution. One is as discrete, bounded entities, with births (at speciation), lifespans, and deaths (at extinction). The other is as dynamic units that usually consist of multiple local populations, each in itself an individual engine of evolutionary innovation. Such populations usually do not enjoy independent historical existences, however, until they have been "validated" by the process of speciation, which makes them into historically and genetically independent entities. Once thus validated, species can as a whole assume their unique roles in the "ecological theatre and the evolu-

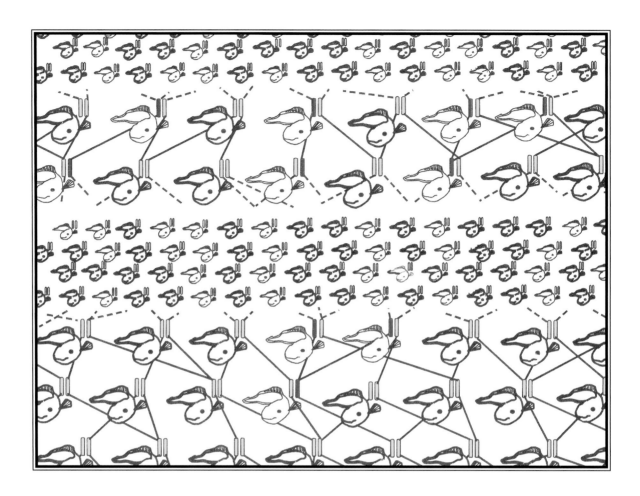

tionary play," as the great ecologist G. Evelyn Hutchinson once put it. Genetically isolated from the rest of the world, species can enter into competition with other species that will ultimately winnow them in a fashion analogous to the winnowing of individuals by natural selection. Indeed, it seems that any long-term "trends" we see in the fossil record (increasing human brain size, for example) may well be much more frequently caused by the differential survival of species in this ongoing drama than by the within-population workings of natural selection. After all, environments tend to change, often very abruptly, on a time-scale that is much shorter than that with which traditional natural selection could be expected to cope. Thus the evolutionary process takes place on multiple levels, with populations and species playing roles just as important as the role of traditional natural selection among individuals.

What does all this mean for our interpretation of the human fossil record? Most importantly, it means that we have to abandon the linear dictates of the Evolutionary Synthesis in favor of a recognition that the evolutionary process is much more complex and many-layered than these dictates suppose. We should not expect evolution to represent a ladder we have climbed (with ourselves at the top). Instead, the evolutionary histories of most groups will be stories of evolutionary experimentation, with new species constantly being spun off and fending for themselves in the ecological arena. Such close relatives will compete with each other and with ecologically similar, if more distantly related species, and will succeed and fail within the context of unpredictably changing habitats. Above all, it is because of this complexity, both systematic and ecological, that we should not expect that uncovering human evolutionary history will simply be a matter of discovery—find enough fossils, and all will somehow be revealed. Instead, the fossil record consists of multiple species, whose relationships need to be analyzed on the basis of their morphology (which is really all that carries the imprint of their evolutionary histories) rather than on that of their age (which implies an assumed position in a long linear sequence). As a consequence, we have to abandon the expectation that only a single species of hominid—or as few of them as possible—existed on Earth at any one time. Scientists are often scoffed at for proposing or resuscitating unfamiliar names for fossil hominids—thank Dobzhansky and Mayr for this attitude. But names are not just inconveniences to be minimized before paleoanthropologists can get to the really interesting stuff. For better or for worse, names are our way of expressing the evident complexity of nature. Human evolution is a history of experimentation, of constant exploration of the very many ways there are to be hominid. And if we insist on cramming these complexities into the smallest number of species possible, as advocated by Dobzhansky and Mayr, we will inevitably wind up oversimplifying and thus distorting the story of human evolution. We may somehow feel, because *Homo sapiens* is the lone hominid on Earth today, that this is a natural state of affairs. Not so, as we will explore in the succeeding chapters of this book.

But if we cannot simply discover evolutionary histories, as if we were fitting links into a chain, what should we do? One very positive development in paleoanthropology during the 1970s and 1980s was the introduction of "cladistic" methods (from the Greek word for "branch"). Before the mid-1970s, paleoanthropology, like systematic biology in general, had admittedly come a long way just on the basis of a subliminal realization that some characteristics are more useful than others in reconstructing the evolutionary relationships that exist among species. However, if we are to produce truly scientific—testable—statements about such relationships, we need an articulated theoretical basis for what we are doing. And such an explicit basis was finally supplied by the German entomologist Willi Hennig, the father of cladistics, whose work, *Phylogenetic Systematics,* was translated into English in the 1960s. Hennig pointed out that morphological characters (or more properly, *states* of characters) fall operationally into two categories: primitive (plesiomorphic) and derived (apomorphic). Primitive states are those that were present in the common ancestor of a subsequently diversified group of organisms (a clade); derived states are any departure from the primitive condition. It's important to realize that being primitive or derived are not in themselves inherent qualities of particular anatomical conformations. A particular state (say, feathers among birds) may be derived for a particular larger clade (birds, or any other group of species all derived from the same exclusive common ancestor); however, the same state will obviously be primitive for subclades within the major clade (perching birds, for instance, or ducks).

Thus if the ultimate goal of evolutionary reconstruction is to reveal patterns of common ancestry in the living world, the quest for relationships becomes the explicit search for shared derived character states. A derived character that is unique to a particular species is not of much

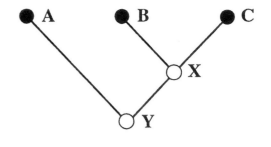

[Figure 10]

A very simple cladogram, stating no more than that species B is more closely related to species C than either is to A. This is known by the common possession of at least one derived character state by B and C that is absent in A. The common ancestors Y and X are hypothetical, and as such will rarely be demonstrable in the actual fossil record – for, in principle, any ancestor must be primitive in all characters relative to its descendants. From Tattersall (1995).

use in this context, because it provides no links with other species. And neither are shared primitive characters helpful, because they do no more than indicate that two species shared a common ancestor at some degree of remoteness. Shared derived character states, on the other hand, carry a strong signal of relatedness, although there is still the problem of "homoplasy," the development of similar anatomical conditions separately in different lineages. How homoplasies may most efficiently be recognized is one of the major outstanding problems in systematics, the study of diversity in the organic world.

The distributions of character states within clades of related organisms are expressed in simple branching diagrams known as cladograms. [Figure 10] Essentially, a cladogram will state that species A is more closely related to species B than either is to species C, because A and B share derived character states not present in C. Cladograms imply nothing more than this, and they are in fact the only kinds of statement in systematics that are actually testable. If we add to the information in a cladogram by specifying what kind of relationship is involved between two species (ancestor and its descendant, for example, or descent from a common ancestor), we get what is known as a phylogenetic tree. And because it is impossible to demonstrate one kind of relationship as opposed to the other, trees are not susceptible to scientific testability. However, they are certainly more interesting than cladograms, and in the case of fossil species will also incorporate information about geological age. The most complex statement of all is the scenario, which throws in everything else you know or believe about the species involved: ecology, adaptation, and so forth. Such narratives depend as much on the skills of the storyteller as on the facts; but if scenarios are explicitly based on trees that are, in turn, derived from specified cladograms, how they were arrived at is at least evident.

Evolutionary relationships, then, are reflected in systems of resemblance that cannot simply be discovered, like fossils themselves, but that have to emerge from a process of morphological (anatomical) comparison and analysis. That is why you will encounter a fair amount of anatomical description in this book, as we follow out the human fossil record; for it is what fossils look like (rather than how old they are, or where they come from) that provides the essential key to their roles in the evolutionary drama.

CHAPTER 3

Early Bipeds:
African Origins

Early Bipeds: African Origins

In 1893, the same year in which the Dutch physician Eugène Dubois set sail for southeast Asia in the search for human ancestors that led to his discovery of the first specimens of Java Man (*Homo erectus*), the scholar who would name *Australopithecus* was born in Australia, near the city of Brisbane. Christened Raymond Arthur Dart, his upbringing was imbued with Methodist and Baptist teachings as well as with the fundamentalism of the Plymouth Brethren. In 1911, at the age of 18, Dart was introduced to evolutionary studies through courses in biology at the University of Queensland. Bitten by the scientific bug, he entered the University of Sydney as a medical student in 1914. The same year, he attended a series of four lectures given by Professor (later Sir) Grafton Elliot Smith, Chief of Anatomy at the University of Manchester in England. Smith was an internationally eminent ethnologist and physical anthropologist, as well. Only a few years earlier, he had put another academic feather in his cap through his demonstration of the near-human-like qualities of the Piltdown brain, estimating its large size from the "fossil" skull and its surface features from impressions left on the inside of the vault.

During World War I, Dart was allowed to teach anatomy while fulfilling the more tradi-tional duties of military service. He became increasingly intrigued by the nervous system, particularly the brain, and set his sights on studying with Elliot Smith. Fortunately, in 1919, Elliot Smith became professor and head of the anatomy department at University College, London. The two met, and Elliot Smith hired Dart as Senior Demonstrator in anatomy. Dart continued his studies on the nervous system and soon came to reject one of the long-standing "givens" of developmental neurology: that nerve cells in the body arise from the spinal cord during its early phases of development. According to Dart, these nerve cells had an independent origin. He was, of course, incorrect. But his adamant defense of his position gave him the reputation of being a troublemak-er, which, deserved or not, would plague him throughout his career.

After a two-year stint on a fellowship in the Department of Anatomy at Washington University in St. Louis, Dart returned to London. At Elliot Smith's insistence, he applied for and received the position of Chair of the Department of Anatomy at the newly estab-lished University of the Witwatersrand ("Wits") in Johannesburg, South Africa. He and his wife moved to Johannesburg in January, 1923—and the rest, to use a cliché, would be history. For just over one year later, Dart was presented with a fossilized skull that would turn the paleoanthropological world on its head, and, unfortunately, also against him for his interpretations of it.

The specimen in question was one of an untold number of fossils that had been unearthed during the mining of lime deposits at various sites in South Africa. Lime is an important component in the process of refining precious metals. And where this mineral had dripped in dissolved form into subterranean fissures and abysses, so, too, had fallen the bones of animals and debris from the outside world. As the lime precipitated, everything became cemented together. Thus, when chunks of lime were blasted out, they brought with them the fossilized remains of animals that had existed at the time of their formation. Sometimes, animal skulls—frequently baboons—would be saved by one of the miners, either as a keepsake (a paperweight, perhaps) or as an object for sale to local collectors. But, as recorded in the notes of one of the quarry directors, most fossilized skulls and skeletal bones ended up with the limestone in the refining kilns, where they would make a noticeable "puff" as they disintegrated in the heat. Subterranean caves make great catchment basins for bones, but they are next to impossible to date directly, and figuring out how old the South African fossils are has and continues to depend on comparing them with more easily datable fossils from elsewhere.

Through a complicated and improbable series of events, late in 1924 Dart received a box of rocks and fossils from the Buxton limeworks at Taung, an obscure village far away on the fringes of the Kalahari Desert. As a comparative neuroanatomist, Dart recognized immediately that two of these specimens were not fossilized bone, but were, natural casts of the inside of the brain cases of fossil baboons. These "endocasts" were not exact replicas of the original brains but rather were general representations of the topography and proportions of the brains as reflected through the tissues and intervening fluids that had surrounded them. There was another specimen—part of a skull that was still largely encased in the hard "breccia" of rock pieces cemented together by lime. And this fit with a third endocast that was definitely larger than and different from the monkey endocasts.

Dart set to work on removing the breccia from this specimen and, two days before Christmas 1924, managed to expose its left side. The exposed left side which revealed much of a fairly vertical forehead; part of a smooth brow region, and the tall ovoid eye sockets below it; part of a slender cheek bone; a small lower face and nasal region; a curved, not very protrusive upper jaw; and part of the lower jaw. In the next few days, Dart exposed the better-preserved right side, which told the same story: a very thin-boned, lightly built, young individual. [Figure 11] Dart was impressed by how humanlike this specimen was in the small size of the opening of its nasal region, in the profile of its teeth, particularly the very low, non-projecting upper and lower canines, and in the proportions of its lower face and mandible (small)

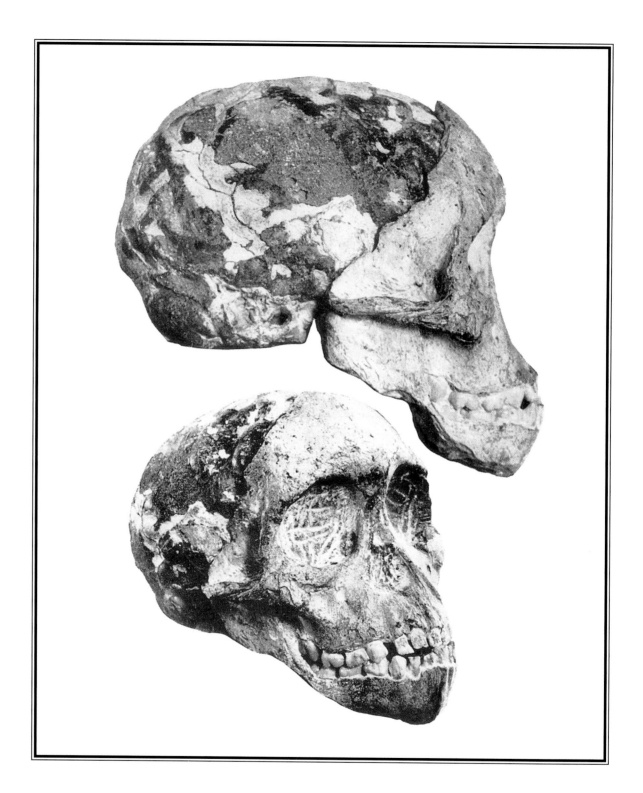

Extinct Humans

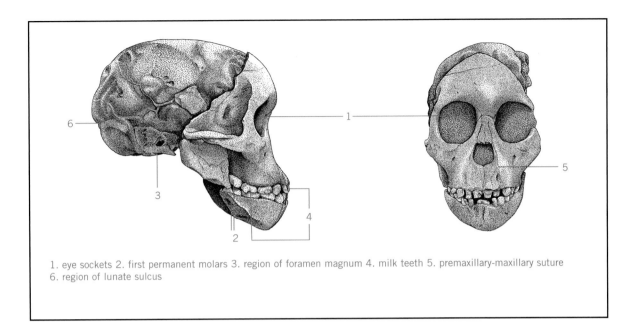

1. eye sockets 2. first permanent molars 3. region of foramen magnum 4. milk teeth 5. premaxillary-maxillary suture 6. region of lunate sulcus

[Figure 11]

In 1925, the young anatomist Raymond Dart, shook up the scientific world with his publication on the fossilized partial skull and brain cast (facing page) of a child from the limeworks at Taung, South Africa. He made this specimen the basis of a new genus and species— *Australopithecus africanus*—which he argued had been intermediate between humans and apes. From Robert Bloom's *The South African Fossil Ape-Men* (1946).

[Figures 12a and b]

Among the human-like attributes of the Taung child specimen, Dart was particularly impressed by the large (above) brain with its posteriorly placed lunate sulcus, forwardly positioned foramen magnum, short snout, small canines, large and rounded eye sockets, domed forehead, and smooth and unprotruding brow region. Drawings by Don McGranaghan.

compared with the skull overall (large). But Dart was even more astonished by how huge the endocast, which fit perfectly into the partial skull, was in comparison with the size of the face. Dart also noticed a few pieces of fossilized bone adhering to the base of the endocast. These pieces represented the perimeter of the hole through which the spinal cord exits the brain. To his further amazement, this hole— the foramen magnum, or "great hole"—had been situated quite far forward under the skull,

as in bipedally erect humans. [Figures 12a and b] By the end of the first week of the new year, Dart had completed a manuscript on this specimen and sent it off the British journal *Nature*, where it was published on February 7.

With characteristic boldness, Dart began his article on the Taung specimen with the emphatic declaration that it represented "an extinct race of apes *intermediate between living anthropoids and man.*" The lack of the stout features of brow, jaw, and canine tooth characteristic of the African apes made this individual, in Dart's eyes, of "delicate and humanoid character." He had not removed the limey matrix that held together the upper and lower jaws, so he could not see the details of the chewing surfaces of the teeth. But he could tell that all the milk teeth were in place and that the first permanent molars were in various final stages of eruption. Because the first permanent molar erupts at about the age of six years in humans, but much earlier in apes, Dart concluded that his Taung individual must have been the same age as a human at the same stage of development would be. (On the basis of microscopic analyses of tooth enamel and bone formation rates, we now believe that the Taung child, and other juvenile australopiths, for that matter, grew at the pace of apes, not humans—which means that these extinct humans would have reached various stages of development at earlier ages than a living human would. Consequently, the Taung child was probably closer to two or three years of age at death, not six.)

After discussing the features of skull and tooth that supposedly demonstrated the Taung child's intermediacy between humans and apes, Dart, the neuroanatomist, devoted a lot of space to discussing its brain. He pointed to the forward position of the brain stem indicated by the foramen magnum. The apparent forward position of the foramen magnum could only mean that the brain stem had traveled straight down after leaving the skull. In turn, this could only mean that the head had been balanced atop a vertical vertebral column—a suggestion was supported by the fact that the two raised areas

that articulate with the first vertebrae lie on each side of the foramen magnum. And if the Taung child's vertebral column was held vertically, this could only mean that it had been bipedal, because humans also have a vertical vertebral column on top of which their heads are balanced and are the only truly bipedal primates. In contrast, the more quadrupedal an animal is, the more backwardly facing is the foramen magnum and the more horizontal is the vertebral column.

From this speculation about bipedalism arose a cascade of other questions. The most central of these for Dart was that the hands of the Taung "humanoid" must have been freed from involvement in locomotion, as they are in bipedal living humans. In contrast, chimpanzees and gorillas walk not only using the soles of their feet, but also the knuckle-surfaces of their hands. Freed from the requirements of locomotion, the Taung child's hands could now assume "a higher evolutionary role not only as delicate tactual, examining organs that were adding copiously to the animal's knowledge of its physical environment, but also as instruments of the growing intelligence in carrying out more elaborate, purposeful, and skilled movements, and as organs of offence and defence." And because its hands were not tied up in getting about, the Taung child could use them to make tools. Having implements available to hunt, prepare, and process meats and other foods meant that the jaws did not have to be thick and sturdy; nor did the teeth, especially the canine teeth, need to be massive. Tools could also be used in defense, so there was yet another reason why the canines did not have to be tall, pointed, and ferocious looking. Following Darwin, Dart put the whole thing together to suggest that the more one relied on implements, the smaller one's canines and jaws could become—because, to play on the old Darwinian adaptive saw, there was no need for teeth and jaws to perform roles either as tools or as weapons.

Although most people might think first of stone as being the material from which early tools were made, Dart thought that early humans could have used anything at their disposal that was readily available and durable. When, in the decades after the Taung discovery, other australopith sites were excavated and the bones and jaws of antelope and other extinct animals were exhumed along with those of the hominids, Dart would develop his theory of an "osteodontokeratic tool culture." In this scenario, he imagined his humanoids relying on tools and weapons made from the bones (the osteo part), teeth (donto), and antlers and horn (keratic) of contemporaneous animals. For example, the toothed jaws of a grazing animal, such as an antelope, could, he argued, have been used as a saw, because the edges of the teeth are sharp and platelike, and their pointed tips are regularly spaced. He also noted that the upper end of a femur from a larger quadruped would have made a perfectly good hammer to be used in peaceful activities as well as during confrontations.

The image of a brutish cave man standing guard at the mouth of his domicile holding intruders at bay as he swings the femur of a mammoth may not be as outlandish as one might think. A great story about one of our colleagues, Daris Swindler, is that, during the university riots of the 1960s, he defended his skeletal lab from an angry mob with a femur that he grabbed out of instinct when he heard noises coming up the stairs. But a large part of Dart's vision of his early human ancestors was that they had an innate tendency toward aggressiveness and conflict. As he saw it, a killer-ape ancestor would explain a lot in terms of the atrocities of war that the world had known from the beginning of written history and through which he himself had lived during World War I. From speculating about the role of bipedalism in the evolution of the Taung humanoid, Dart proceeded to the features of the endocast. As far as size went, the Taung child's brain had been larger than an adult chimpanzee's, and indeed was almost as large as an adult gorilla's. Had the child survived, its brain would, of course, have continued to enlarge, perhaps, as in living humans, tapering off in the twenties. In being high and rounded the Taung child's brain was shaped more like a human's than an ape's. To Dart this meant that the Taung child had been capable of associative memory and intelligence, with both faculties being well developed and in harmony with one another. But Dart was even more impressed by two other observations. It appeared that the side of the Taung child's brain had been expanded. Dart thought this was certainly a humanlike characteristic. But, perhaps more astonishingly, Dart identified the location of a particular groove—the lunate sulcus—which represents the posterior-most border of the brain's thinking gray matter, as being much farther back and down on the endocast than one would find in an ape's brain. In humans, the lunate sulcus lies well down, almost under, the hugely expanded gray matter.

Certainly, if true this was an important discovery. For there is nothing more seductive than having a reason to speculate about the evolution of the human brain and its intangible attributes. But was Dart correct? Identifying structures on the surface of a cast of the inside of a skull as being actual features of the brain itself is not an easy task. The living brain is encased in three layers of membrane, all of which are separated by layers of fluid. And all of this keeps the surface of the brain at a distance from the inside wall of the skull. As history would have it, identifying the lunate sulcus in the Taung child's endocast has not in fact been so easy, although the professional stakes have been high. The paleoneuroanatomists Ralph Holloway and Dean Falk have been fighting a heated battle for more than twenty years over the exact location of the lunate sulcus on the Taung child's endocast. Each thinks the other's lunate sulcus is merely an artifact. As seems to be the case in general in science, the less certain the parameters of the anatomy being described, the more hotly debated are its interpretations.

Dart's final foray into the cerebral depths of the Taung humanoid, as he called it, came from the now-vacant bony eye sockets. Because these cavities were large, forwardly oriented, and positioned close together, Dart concluded that the eyes had demanded a considerable amount of gray matter (the cerebral cortex) both for

vision and for processing the visual information received about the surroundings. Putting this together with his belief that the Taung individual had been a very tactile animal with its hand, Dart was certain that this humanoid's cerebral cortex had resounded with sensory information. He believed that not only had the Taung humanoid been capable of appreciating input from sight, sound, and touch much more thoroughly than that of any ape, but that it had crossed the threshold that would be critical for acquiring language. Truly, by any standards, this was quite a sequence of extrapolations!

Convinced of his specimen's centrality in understanding human origins, Dart rejected all other candidates that had been proposed as direct human ancestors. This included England's famous Piltdown Man (which would not be discovered for the forgery it was for decades to come), which Dart thought was much too apelike in its lower jaw. As for Eugène Dubois' Java Man, Dart dismissed it out of hand as "a caricature of precocious human failure." No, it was obvious that the Taung humanoid represented "a creature well advanced beyond modern anthropoids in just those characters, facial and cerebral, which are to be anticipated in an extinct link between man and his simian ancestor."

Having dispensed with the competition, Dart now had to name his new humanoid. Dubois had described his Java Man as an "ape-man," giving it the genus name *Pithecanthropus*—which the German anatomist and embryologist Ernst Haeckel had earlier coined in anticipation of the discovery of a missing link between humans and apes. Dart, however, saw his fossil as a "man-like ape" that had taken that crucial step to becoming human: acquiring language. In recognition of the presumed evolutionary status of the Taung humanoid, Dart proposed not only a new genus and species for it, *Australopithecus africanus*, but also a new family, Homo-simiadae. In a grand finale, Dart closed his article on the Taung child with a generous nod to Charles Darwin. Darwin had been the first to buck tradition by arguing that human ancestry lay not in Asia, as Buffon among others had forcefully argued, but in Africa. But Darwin had no proof of this. Only his speculation that the harsher conditions and predators of southern African would have provided the grist for natural selection to mold a fragile but thinking biped from an ape.

Dart's intellectual association with the revered British naturalist did not deter his detractors for a minute. Within weeks of the issue of *Nature* that carried Dart's announcement of *A. africanus*, many of the most powerful anatomists and paleoanthropologists of Great Britain and the United States—including Grafton Elliot Smith—published letters to the editor denouncing this discovery and its discoverer. These tirades covered all bases, from rejecting Dart's authority as a taxonomist because he had violated convention by combining Greek (*Australo-*, meaning southern) and Latin (*-pithecus*, meaning ape) in the same genus name, to disqualifying him as a competent anatomist because—as anyone who knew anything could plainly see—this was merely a fossil ape, perhaps a chimpanzee.

Among the most vocal of Dart's detractors was Sir Arthur Keith, whose fame had been assured by his validation of the Piltdown remains. As a brain expert himself, Keith could take on Dart—which he did in a chapter devoted entirely to this pursuit in his book *New Discoveries Relating to the Antiquity of Man*. Step by step Keith set about dismantling Dart's claims about the Taung child. For instance, he and colleagues had found gorilla brains with the same shape as the fossil, and, anyway, some Neanderthals (particular the specimen from Gibraltar) had possessed ape-shaped brains. The grooves and fissures in the endocast's surface were not human, but apelike—period. [Figure 13]

As for general and specific cranial features, comparison with a juvenile chimpanzee, Keith argued, was sufficient to show that the Taung individual was merely an ape. One of his points of attack lay in the presence of a premaxillary-maxillary suture in the Taung child. If it were humanlike, the Taung child should not have shown this suture. Keith even dismissed the position of the Taung child's foramen magnum as irrelevant. In human children, Keith remarked, this hole at the base of the skull lies farther forward than in the adult, which means that its position shifts backward with growth. In the Taung child, the foramen magnum was farther back than in a human child. Ergo, it would have shifted even farther back with growth. So much for Dart's claims of bipedalism in the Taung child. As far as Keith was concerned, all of the important anatomical comparisons lay with the African apes. Despite the eventual

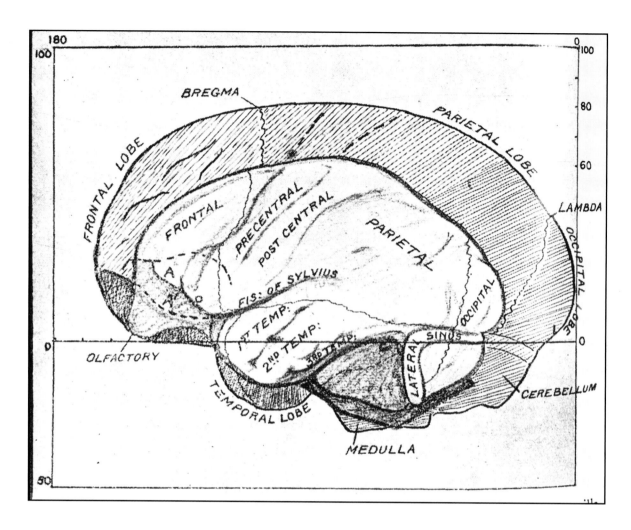

acceptance by all paleoanthropologists of the reality of early hominids, and of the genus and species *A. africanus*, Dart would never fully recover from public assaults such as Keith's.

Forever Australopithecus

Robert Broom, South African physician and world-renowned vertebrate paleontologist, read with keen interest Dart's *Nature* article on the

Taung child. Perhaps because he was not a pale-oanthropologist, Broom was not influenced by the attacks on the young neuroanatomist and arranged to see the specimen for himself. His experience working with fossil mammals predisposed him to finding clues to evolutionary relationships in the details of tooth morphology. Upon scrutiny of Dart's specimen, Broom was truly convinced that first in its teeth, and then in its skull, the Taung child was indeed more humanlike than apelike. He wrote up his descriptions, which he sent, accompanied by good illustrations, to the Oxford University Professor William J. Sollas. Sollas had become famous for his theory that modern humans arriving from the east had driven European Neanderthals to extinction. He not only embraced Dart's interpretation of the Taung child, but also managed to convince Elliot Smith of its correctness. Sollas sent a quick note of support to *Nature* and then, in 1926, published a longer article on the humanlike contours of the Taung skull's cross section.

Although an obvious supporter of Dart's, Broom was not able to pursue any fieldwork that might add to the human fossil record until the mid-1930s. His medical practice was far off in the township of Maquassi, but it was in the Transvaal region near Johannesburg that lime was being quarried. Through the efforts of friends and colleagues, in 1934 Broom landed a position at the Transvaal Museum in Pretoria. In 1936 he turned from fossil reptiles to human paleontology and ventured to the limeworks at Sterkfontein, 40 miles from Pretoria and 30 from Johannesburg.

During his first two visits to Sterkfontein, Broom found fossilized bones of various mammals, including baboons, which were common. But on his third visit he was presented by the quarry manager, G. W. Barlow, with most of an endocast of something that seemed to be either apelike or humanlike. [Figures 14a and b] In searching the breccia deposits for more material, Broom found the depression at the top of the skull that had housed the endocast. Spurred on by this discovery, the next day he found the base of the skull as well as parts of the brow and bony orbits in chunks of breccia that had already been blasted out. Broom set to cleaning off the matrix and was able to put all the fragments together. He was convinced that this individual represented the adult version of the Taung child, and said so in a note he sent to *Nature* that was published the same year.

The odd thing about Broom's conclusion was that it was based on very little comparative morphology. He couldn't compare the face of his Sterkfontein specimen with Taung because the former was distorted. He couldn't compare skull bases because in his specimen the encasing limestone matrix still obscured this region. He barely mentioned the endocasts except to say that the brain had been much wider, especially toward the front, in the Sterkfontein adult. Curiously, given his penchant for teeth, he did not compare the first of the two preserved upper permanent molars of the adult with its counterpart in the Taung child. Instead, he compared his specimen's first molar with that tooth in a specimen of a presumed fossil ape from an earlier time period that had been

 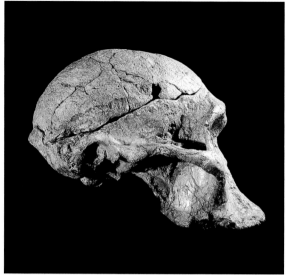

discovered in France. Broom thought that the configurations of the molar cusps of the fossil ape, called *Dryopithecus*, and his specimen were quite similar.

By the end of his note, Broom had gone from referring to the Taung specimen as humanlike to calling it an ape, and from extolling the near identity of this specimen and his from Sterkfontein, to emphasizing their unstated differences. Add to this his belief that the Taung child was geologically much older than his specimen, and you come to his totally unfounded conclusion: the Sterkfontein specimen might have represented the same genus as the Taung child, but was surely of a different species, *Australopithecus transvaalensis*. Two years later, in considering another specimen (the front of the lower jaw of a juvenile), Broom would place this species in its own genus, *Plesianthropus*. Given Broom's uncritical evalu-

ation of the Sterkfontein and subsequently other specimens, it is perhaps no wonder that the taxonomic lumping advocated by Mayr and Dobzhansky in the 1950s could have take in place so easily and without question.

In June 1938, Broom turned his attention to the site of Kromdraai, just up the valley from Sterkfontein. From Barlow, he had bought part of an upper jaw, and from a young schoolboy he purchased the four upper teeth that had once resided in this specimen. Upon being pressed for more information, the lad took Broom to

Kromdraai, not much more than a narrow fissure in the ground, where he had hidden a lower jaw with two teeth. Further snooping in the area produced bones of the lower part of the skull vault, the lower face, and upper jaw, as well as a reasonably complete mandible with premolars and molars that fit the upper jaw. [Figure 15]

Two features convinced Broom that this specimen was more humanlike than apelike. First, the right and left bony ear tubes were positioned below the plane of the cheek bones. In apes, these tubes are level with the cheekbones. And second, the foramen magnum was set as far forward as these bony tubes, which had to mean that this individual had a more erect posture than an African ape. Although it was larger overall, especially in tooth and jaw size, than A. transvaalensis, Broom thought that this more "robust" specimen was more humanlike because its face was flatter and because he believed that it had had a smaller canine.

In years to come, Broom's younger colleague, John Robinson, would make two contradictory arguments about this robust South African hominid. Because, he thought, it had waddled and had to sit and rest quite frequently, and thus couldn't have walked as efficiently as the more gracile and lightly built transvaalensis form, it was the less modern and less humanlike of the two. Yet its small canine made it look like a "good" ancestor for later hominids because living humans also have smallish canines. The situation was also complicated by the fact that the robust australopiths had smaller brains and larger cheek teeth than the gracile form. The robust australopiths were thought to have had smaller brains because their large cheek teeth suggested that, like a (dumb) cow, they had a diet high in vegetable matter. A more protein-rich diet, in contrast, would have led to a larger brain; and carnivory in the gracile australopiths was supposedly indicated by their larger canines. And to be efficient carnivores, the gracile australopiths had to be more proficient bipedalists than the waddling, grazing robust forms. What a complicated proposition! In such ways is the saga of how australopiths were taxonomically dealt with is riddled with whimsy and with a naïve approach to interpreting our potential ancestors.

When Broom announced his new Kromdraai hominid in 1938 in a note to Nature, the first thing he did was to change the genus of his Sterkfontein hominid from Dart's Australopithecus. Now he believed that whatever came out of Sterkfontein represented a different genus of hominid altogether. The name he gave it was Plesianthropus, meaning "near man." This Plesianthropus was not, of course, as humanlike as the Kromdraai hominid. Then, in 1946, with G. W. H. Schepers, he published a monograph on all South African hominids and declared that, because the Taung child and a youth from Kromdraai were similar, all of these australopiths equally represented "ape-men" that lay intermediate between apes and humans. Yet, intermediate or not, Broom kept the specimens from different sites in different genera: Australopithecus for Taung, Plesianthropus for Sterkfontein, and Paranthropus for Kromdraai. This classification of hominids would surely

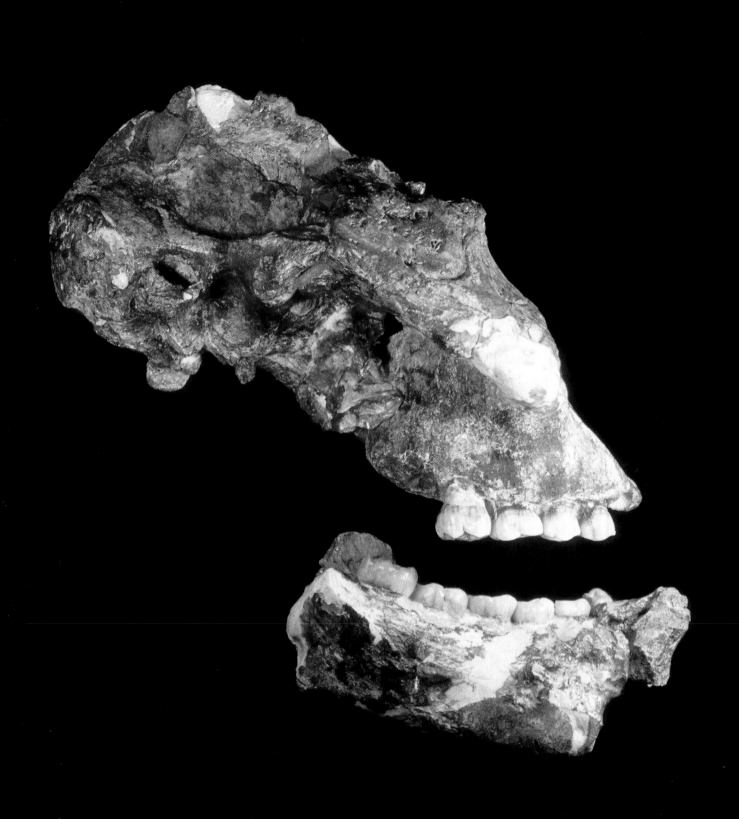

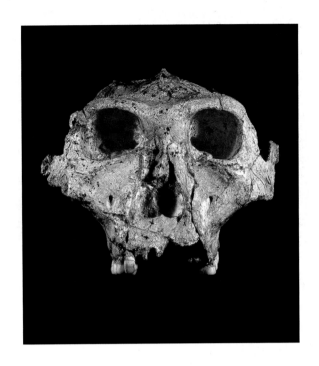

make one think that there had been quite a lot of diversity in the past. But a paleontologist or systematist seeing the "evidence" for it would be shocked. It's not inconceivable that one genus of hominid was represented at Sterkfontein and another at Kromdraai, but where was the scientific rationale?

In 1948, Broom opened a new site, called Swartkrans, which lay just across the valley from Sterkfontein. The first specimens forthcoming were a mandible and a few isolated teeth that were appreciably larger than those of Kromdraai's *Paranthropus robustus*. A note in *Nature* announced the discovery of a new "apeman," which Broom called *Paranthropus crassidens*. Excavations at Swartkrans during the next eight months or so uncovered three variably preserved skulls, of which one was essentially complete, lacking only the front of the upper jaw and small parts of the very top and bottom of the braincase. Now this really was a robust skull. [Figure 16] The brow was bulging and continuous. The face was broad, flat and almost vertical. And the jaw was deep, with huge chewing teeth. Thickened and scarred attachment areas on the bones attested to the gigantic set of muscles that had moved that jaw.

Continued excavations that year unearthed more pieces of skull, tooth, and jaw, as well as most of the right side of a pelvis larger than that from Sterkfontein. Broom now thought that the pelvic bones of *Paranthropus* and *Plesianthropus* were both humanlike in shape, indicating proficient bipedalism. But the front of the pelvis was also somewhat expanded, as in apes, rather than reduced, as in humans. And to some paleoanthropologists, including John Robinson, this suggested that neither hominid was quite as efficient a biped as a living human, and that, of the two, the more massive and clunkier *Paranthropus* was the less proficient.

While Broom was busy becoming South Africa's most visible paleoanthropologist, Dart lay back in the shadows. Although he had been informed of paleontological opportunities at the site of Makapansgat, which was mined from 1925 to 1935, he did not explore the area until 1947. When he did investigate Makapansgat, he concluded (wrongly, as it turned out) that many of the fossils (which included hominids) had been carbonized. This, he thought, meant that they had been burned by early hominids. The accumulated bones, jaws, horn cores, and antlers were, in Dart's eyes, evidence of bone cracking and manipulation and thus evidence of an "osteodontokeratic" (bone, tooth and horn) culture. Later that year, James Kitching, later to become a distinguished student of fossil reptiles, also recovered the rear of the cranial vault (with the back of the palate still attached) of an adult "humanoid."

Although in overall shape this specimen was pretty much a dead ringer for the most complete of the Sterkfontein skulls (Sts 5; *see* Figure 16), Dart chose to allocate his specimen to a new species, *Australopithecus prometheus,* after the god of fire. Perhaps this taxonomic recognition was motivated as much by the fact that the site of Makapansgat lay well to the north of Sterkfontein as by the novelty of finding what Dart thought was the first fire-using hominid. Of course, neither of these considera-

tions can take the place of comparative anatomy in pursuing a systematic analysis. But human evolutionary studies do have this history of invoking the bathwater as much or even more than the baby.

Thus, Dart not only openly thought that early humanoids were inventive tool makers, but he also concluded that they, or at least this species of them, had made fire as well. By his speculations regarding the Taung child, which led to scenarios of bipedalism and possibly even language, to the use of tools and even fire in the manipulation of the environment and perhaps even aggression, Dart located the foundations of both the good and the bad aspects of modern human behavior at the very base of our evolutionary beginnings.

The New Era

By the 1950s, australopiths—which included the robust form (*Paranthropus*) and the gracile form (*Australopithecus,* which had come to subsume *Plesianthropus*)—were sufficiently represented cranially, dentally, and skeletally that paleoanthropologists could argue from actual evidence about how proficient each was bipedally and which was our ancestor. Of course, at times they found it difficult to tease the two topics apart.

From Sterkfontein had come not only skulls and jaws, but also some important skeletal parts that had long been central to the anatomists' distinctions between bipedal humans and quadrupeds. There were, for example, two lower ends of right and left

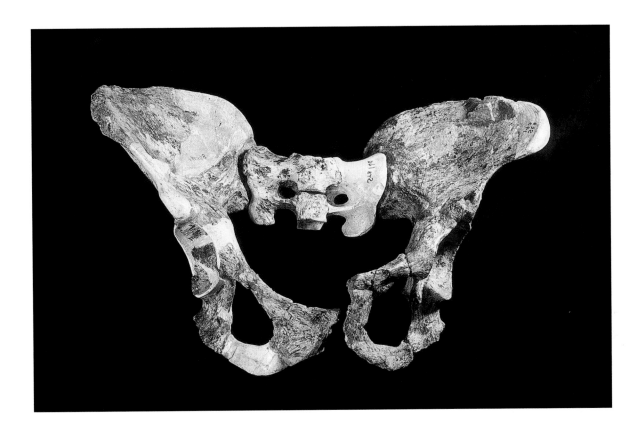

[Figure 17]

Most of a pelvis (and lower vertebral column)—collectively referred to as Sts 14—was recovered from Sterkfontein. The pelvis is distinctly humanlike in that the bladelike upper portions are expanded posteriorly, deep and strongly curved from front to back, and flared to the side; and the sacrum curves slightly into the large and heart-shaped pelvic canal. Photograph by Ron Clarke.

femurs. Although fragments, they clearly showed that in life the shaft of the bone had brought the knee right in under the body, as in modern humans. In an ape or a dog, for instance, the shaft of the femur comes straight down from the side of the pelvis. The angle implied that the early hominid had been a biped.

There was also most of a pelvis: the right and left sides and the sacrum. [Figure 17] The shape of the pelvic bone was similar to a human's with a bladelike upper portion that was short, deep from front to back, and expanded posteriorly. It was also strongly curved like the wall of a cup around the back toward the sacrum. The sacrum was slightly curved inward toward the large and heart-shaped pelvic canal—in agreement with the curve Blumenbach had described for humans and in obvious contrast to the straight sacrum and small pelvic canal of apes. The lower part of the vertebral column was represented by a number of vertebrae. When the vertebrae were put together as in life, they curved forward, toward the belly. This is what one sees in humans. This curve never appears in other animals, even if they are made to stand upright, as in circus acts. The upper part of a humerus was also preserved, and was more humanlike than apelike in the position of the groove for the biceps muscle's tendon.

Put these features together with the forward position of the skull's foramen magnum and what do you get? Because, as the argument went, these features are surely associated in living humans with upright bipedalism and the non-locomotory use of the arms, then they must also have served a similar function in any fossil that had them. But does the one interpretation naturally follow from the other? Just because we see modern humans walking and using their arms and hands in certain ways, and modern humans have skeletal distinctive features unlike those of other living animals, does this mean that early humans used their arms and legs and carried their bodies in exactly and only the same way we do? The assumption has been that features evolve for a particular reason. In the case of human bipedalism, our skeletal features, so clearly articulated by Blumenbach, are seen as the result of selection for the way in which we negotiate the world. If these features are also seen in the earliest humans, they had to have evolved for similar reasons.

But why? Just because we see an organism doing something in a particular way doesn't mean that this is the only behavior available to it—or, to its ancestors. Only if one thinks that a particular feature or behavior evolves slowly, as its bearers adapt to a particular situation, does this way of thinking make sense. But if, on the other hand, evolutionary novelty emerges rapidly through random mutations affecting the genes that regulate development, then adaptation takes on a different meaning. It may not be that natural selection is picking and choosing the better-adapted individuals, just as animal and plant breeders select individuals with the "best" kinds of features. Rather, as the late nineteenth-century and early twentieth-century geneticists were inclined to think, individuals may retain novel features for no better reason than that they don't get in the way of survival. Once there, however, these novel traits or behaviors can be exploited by their bearers.

Although many paleoanthropologists sought the origins of human bipedalism virtually intact from these early hominids, there was still the lingering need to put everything into the context of a smoothly transformational evolutionary continuum from ape to human. Thus, because there were also a few features in which australopiths differed from living humans, and because, collectively, australopiths were thought of as being intermediate between apes and humans, their abilities as bipedalists were thought of as being compromised in some ways. There was the less-than-modern-human expanded upper front part of the pelvic bone. The vertebrae, especially in the lower regions, were narrower from side to side, as in apes. The curve of the ribs suggested a more conical chest—again, more like apes than living humans.

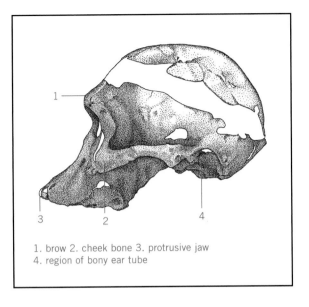

1. brow 2. cheek bone 3. protrusive jaw
4. region of bony ear tube

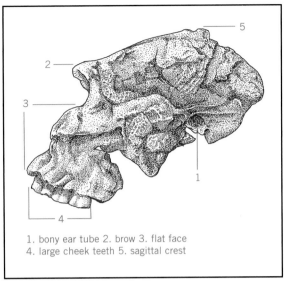

1. bony ear tube 2. brow 3. flat face
4. large cheek teeth 5. sagittal crest

[Figures 18 and 19]

Sts 5 (left) and Sk 46 (right) typify the "gracile" and "robust" early hominids from South Africa. In general, Sts 5 is a less bulky-boned skull, with a protrusive jaw, less developed brows, a more rounded brain case, thinner cheek bones, less prominent muscle scars and no crests, and probably relatively larger anterior teeth. The region of the bony ear tube lies level with the cheek bone. In SK 46, the bone is generally more massive and expanded, the brain case is lower and bears a central crest for muscle attachment, the brows (although of similar configuration to Sts 5 [see Figure 14a and b]) are larger, the face is broad, deep and vertical, and the cheek teeth are quite large compared to the front teeth. As in SK 48 (see Figure 16), the bony ear tube lies below the level of the cheek bone.
Drawings by Don McGranaghan and
Diana Salles, respectively.

While most of these features could be thought of as indicating the more apelike qualities of the australopiths, other features were not so easy to pigeonhole. For example, the upper end of the australopith femur was peculiar when compared to the femurs of both apes and living humans. The ball-like head was not large but tiny, fitting into a small socket on the pelvis;

and it was separated from the shaft of the femur by a long rather than a short neck. The orientation of the bladelike upper part of the pelvic bones was also odd. It turned outward, like the brim of an upside down hat, rather than being cuplike (as Blumenbach had noted in humans) or flat and vertical (as in most mammals). Nonetheless, because the australopiths were supposed to be transitional forms arising from something apelike, their small femoral heads and long femoral necks and oddly oriented upper pelvic bones were interpreted as part of a primitive-but-on-the-way-to-becoming-modern-humanlike stage of bipedalism.

But if you think about it, it would seem that in these features the australopiths actually stand out from all other "higher" primates, living humans and apes included. And because of this difference, the australopith femur actually signals that there was something unique about being an australopith. It is only when australopiths (or any fossils, for that matter) are interpreted within the constraints of an already accepted ape-to-human evolutionary continuum that their features, especially those that are so distinctive and different, have to be explained away. Thus, rather than being the pinnacle of an evolutionary sequence, the human femur (at least its upper end) is similar to that of apes because it hasn't changed very much since the time of their last common ancestor. But the australopiths' femur had changed. And this realization should, in turn, have led us to question whether we really can point to any australopith as an early but direct human ancestor. But because paleoanthropology has been focused on discovering ancestors, which requires having in place a notion of the points at the ends of a transformation series, the uniqueness of the australopiths are downplayed.

As for precisely which australopith—*A. africanus* or *P. robustus* (with which *P. crassidens* was lumped)—was on the "direct line" of human evolution, the majority vote lay with the former hominid. Although the upper jaw of *A. africanus* was more projecting and prognathic than that of the flatter-faced robust australopith, overall, the former was much less bulky—more gracile—in jaw and skull, its cranial vault more rounded and its tooth proportions more humanlike. Because the larger cheek-toothed robust australopith was supposed to be more herbivorous and the larger front-toothed gracile australopith more carnivorous, and the gracile form was, in turn, supposed to have had both smarter brains and fleeter feet, there appeared to be a strong argument for choosing the gracile

hominid as our ancestor. [Figures 18 and 19]

Most paleoanthropologists further supposed that a greater proficiency in bipedalism and superior cerebral abilities in the gracile form also suggested that *A. africanus* was a committed tool user, if not actually a tool maker, as evidenced in the crude quartz and chert artifacts that had been found at Sterkfontein and Makapansgat, both *A. africanus* sites. There was a big difference between being a tool user and being a toolmaker. Sea otters and Australian finches are tool users, if you consider the mammal's abalone-bashing stones and the birds' use of thorns to extract grubs from trees. But humans, as had long been known, *make* tools with which to manipulate their environment and, consequently, their own fate. Thus, the argument went, only a hominid that did more than just use objects as tools, that actually *made* tools, could be embraced as a direct ancestor of *H. sapiens*. In retrospect, it seems obvious that all hominids were potential toolmakers. But in the context of the history of paleoanthropology, in which human capacities were considered so special and unique, considerations other than just morphology took center stage in the debates on human ancestry.

The presence of stone tools at Swartkrans, a robust australopith site, thus posed a problem. But it was soon "solved" by such paleoanthropologists as C. Loring Brace and Milford Wolpoff, who proclaimed that there had only ever been one species of australopith, of which the robust form was the male and the gracile form the female. In parallel with Mayr and especially Dobzhansky's notions on hominid

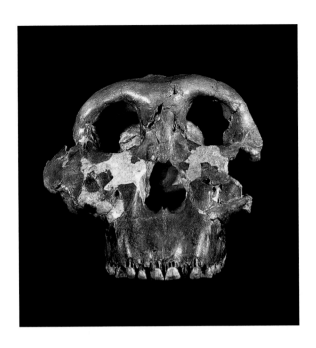

[Figure 20]

Olduvai Hominid (OH 5), to which Louis Leakey originally gave the genus name *Zinjanthropus*, is best regarded as a hyper-robust species of *Paranthropus*. In particular, OH 5, nicknamed "Zinj," is quite similar to, but more massive than, SK 48 (see Figure 16) in the development of its brow, face, cheek bones, and sagittal cresting; the cheek teeth are also larger and the anterior teeth minuscule. Photograph by Jeffrey H. Schwartz; courtesey of the National Museum of Tanzania.

when it came to the earlier hominids. But it remained a curious thing that, even while debates were raging about how many species there really were, their morphology was hardly being discussed at all. Species, or even separate genera, were decided more on the basis of where a specimen came from, or how old it was, than on what it looked like. For those who argued that all were just odd versions of the same species, neither time nor place nor morphology seemed to matter much.

Not Another Australopith! And Another?

The problem of "How many species?" was stretched to the limits of paleoanthropological credulity with the discovery in July 1959, by Louis and Mary Leakey, of a massive-jawed and big-toothed hominid that essentially looked like a larger and more robust version of the South African *P. robustus*. [Figure 20] This prize emerged from deposits at the Tanzanian site of Olduvai Gorge, which the Leakeys had first worked in the 1930s. During the 1930s the Leakey's had not only identified potentially fruitful localities but had also found stone tools, bones of various mammals, and the remains of a not-too-ancient human. Unfortunately, the political climate was such that the Leakeys had to leave East Africa for England before pursuing in-depth excavations. But the Leakeys' time in England was apparently not the smoothest either, and eventually they left England to return to Olduvai.

evolution, this "single-species hypothesis" was predicated on the belief that there could only be one toolmaking (that is, culture-bearing) hominid at one time. Although no vertebrate paleontologist would ever dream of making similar claims about two such morphologically disparate extinct mammals, the single-species hypothesis would long remain a contender against the multiple-species hypothesis in the debate about early human relatives.

Eventually, even those who embraced the single-species hypothesis would loosen up

Although Louis dubbed the new hominid *Zinjanthropus boisei* in his 1959 announcement in *Nature*, "Zinj" (catalogued as OH 5 to denote its status as the fifth hominid specimen from Olduvai) would remain its nickname. Because the tendency at the time was to follow Ernst Mayr in reducing the number of hominid genera, many paleoanthropologists thought that naming *Zinjanthropus* was too much, although it would do as a species of *Paranthropus*. But by the time that Phillip Tobias, Dart's successor at Wits and a collaborator of the Leakeys, published the descriptive volume on Zinj in 1967, the taxonomic tide had turned completely toward Mayr's opinion that the morphological differences among all australopiths were relevant only at the level of the species. So *Paranthropus robustus* became *Australopithecus robustus*, and thus Zinj became *Australopithecus boisei*. Subsequently the tide turned again, and nowadays not only are *Australopithecus* and *Paranthropus* up and running as distinct genera, but there are questions emerging about whether the species placed within each genus are particularly closely related to each other and even whether, collectively, australopiths constitute an evolutionary group.

One thing that would remain unassailable was the demonstration that humans had an antiquity never before imaginable. Up until excavations at Olduvai, none of the other hominid-bearing sites, including those in South Africa, had been dated by chemical or other means of determining exact geological age. They either could not have been, as at the difficult-to-date breccia caves of South Africa, or they had been excavated prior to the advent of relevant techniques. And Carbon-14 dating was only good for organic material that was younger than forty thousand years or so. At Olduvai, however, the lower levels of the sequence of geological layers (identified as Bed I to Bed V from the bottom up) were interspersed with volcanic materials that were becoming datable geochemically. The new technique used was potassium/argon (K/Ar) dating, which exploits the fact that an unstable potassium isotope, emitted with the volcanic rocks, will convert at a constant rate to stable argon. The ratio of potassium to argon in a rock is, therefore, a measure of the time since the volcanic rock began to cool. When Leakey and his collaborators first applied this method at Olduvai, human antiquity was generally supposed to go back only about half a million years or so. But rocks from the bottom of Bed I, whence Zinj came, produced the amazing age of approximately 1.75 million years (myr) before present. Hominids now had an antiquity that would have made Schaaffhausen, who had argued vociferously that the Feldhofer Grotto Neanderthal was not antediluvian, spin in his grave.

Study of the Zinj specimen itself clearly revealed that it had indeed been characterized by a number of distinctive features that were very reminiscent of the South African robust australopith. The hyper-robustness of this specimen was emphasized when a lower jaw from Peninj, a site near Lake Natron, which is not too far from Olduvai, was found to be a near-perfect fit for the Zinj skull. Ron Clarke, who was then working for the Leakeys, used the Peninj

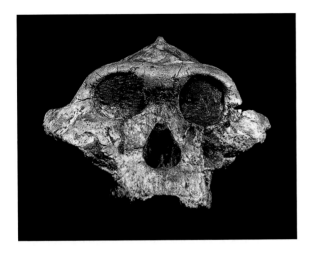 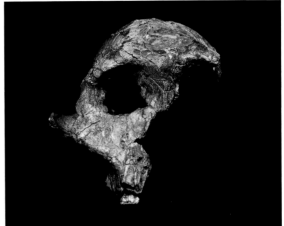

[Figures 21 and 22]

Among the specimens of hyper-robust early hominid discovered at Koobi Fora, Kenya, KNM-ER 406 (left) and the much smaller KNM-ER 732 (right) are among the most complete. They are of great interest because, in spite of the size difference, they display many similar features, such as the configuration of the brow, face, upper jaw, cheek bones, and neck-muscle attachment areas on the base of the skull. The difference in size between the two and the presence of the sagittal crest in 406 are consistent with the larger specimen being a male and the smaller a female of the same species. Photographs by Jeffrey H. Schwartz; courtesey of the National Museum of Tanzania.

mandible to make a model of how Zinj's lower jaw probably looked. The teeth of the Peninj mandible were also of similar proportions, and the enamel of the third molar was curiously wrinkled. What is interesting to us about these features of robust and hyper-robust australopiths is that they are so clearly distinctive and easily distinguished from any gracile australopith and, certainly, any hominid assigned to the genus *Homo*. You can pick up a specimen and know immediately that it's from this robust/ hyper-robust group. These peculiarities should

signal that there is something evolutionarily different about these early hominids. But because the fossils were interpreted within the continuum of human ancestry—and because the gracile australopiths seemed to look more like modern humans, or more so than the robust/forms—the robust australopiths were thought to be the more primitive, apelike, and, by implication, "less evolved," australopiths. In reality, however, it is becoming clear that the robust and hyper-robust forms are actually quite derived in many morphologies, whether compared with apes, to gracile australopiths, or to species of *Homo*. And, as such, they should be thought of as not in our direct ancestry, not because they aren't "evolved enough," but because they are "more evolved" than we in various features.

In 1966, while Phillip Tobias was putting the finishing touches on his Zinj volume, an international team of paleoanthropologists— the American F. Clark Howell, the Frenchman Yves Coppens, and the Kenyan Richard Leakey, son of Louis and Mary—embarked on a project in the lower Omo River valley, which lies in southern Ethiopia, just north of its border with Kenya. Their efforts were rewarded. For one thing, they established an antiquity for toolmaking that had been lacking—an incredible 2.5 myr for the earliest tools in the archeological sequence. But the hominid specimens represented a less clear-cut arena of interpretation. Some paleoanthropologists thought that there were two types of hominids at the site: huge and extra huge. Coppens and collaborators did not. They thought that these were the remains—primarily mandibles with teeth—of a hominid so huge and robust in jaw and massive in cheek tooth size that it was deserving of its own genus and species, for which they coined the name *Paraustralopithecus aethiopicus*. But this "new" hominid would quickly lose its identity. First, the genus name never really caught on. And then the specimens were lumped into the species "*boisei*," which had come to be *the* accepted East African robust australopith. Eventually, Richard Leakey and colleagues' discovery in the 1980s of a skull somewhat similar to, but not exactly like, the robust and hyperrobust australopiths would lead to the revival of the species *aethiopicus*. At some point the dam would have to break. For, how much longer could paleoanthropologists follow Mayr's dictum of unilinear human evolution and keep putting skulls and jaws into the same wastebasket of a species before someone was bound to say, "Hey, these don't look like the same thing"? And fortunately, thanks in large part to the

work of Richard Leakey and his collaborators, the specimens that continued to be discovered kept adding to the improbability that Mayr had been correct about hominids. To the contrary, it seemed, the human fossil record—at least the older and less threatening part of it—was a record of diversity. The question was, and continues to be, how one goes about sorting it out.

Richard Leakey did not remain with Howell and Coppens because during an aerial survey of the region around Lake Turkana (then still called Lake Rudolf), Kenya, into which the Omo River flows, he discovered his own fossil localities. And, from Richard Leakey's first season in 1968, these locales have proven to be a paleoanthropologist's gold mine. Among the first discoveries, from the Koobi Fora area on the east shore of the lake, was the fairly complete but thoroughly matrix-filled skull of what surely represents a male robust australopith. Catalogued as KNM-ER 406 (for Kenya National Museum, East Rudolf, the 406th vertebrate fossil found), it was not too long thereafter paired with a smaller skull (KNM-ER 732). [Figures 21 and 22]

Although only about one-half of the right side of the smaller skull, KNM-ER 732, is preserved, it had the same essential features as the larger 406. Given its smaller size, some areas—such as the swollen area where the bandlike neck muscle attaches—appear to be even more massive than in 406. If 732 and 406 represent, respectively, the female and male of the same species (which seems a reasonable conclusion because female and male gorillas are comparable in their similarities and dissimilarities), then we would expect that these attributes missing in 732 were the same. But is this species the same as *A. boisei*, or is it yet another species of australopith? This is not an outlandish question in light of the apparent fact that some of the specimens from Koobi Fora that Bernard Wood, their monographer, assigned to *A. boisei* actually differ considerably from one another. The problem has been that there are lots of massive jaws and the teeth of many are worn. Thus they give the impression of looking like the same thing. But when you study the jaws and teeth of juveniles and other individuals with less worn teeth, as we did for the first time a few years ago, you can see that there are differences, sometimes quite remarkable differences, in dental morphology.

The implications of these differences for understanding the australopiths as a group and as potential species within that group are intriguing, especially when you consider that among the various femurs from Koobi Fora, at least one is similar to the South African australopith femora, with a small head and a long, narrow, compressed neck. Maybe, then, a number of these early hominids diversified in features of skull, jaw, and teeth, but shared an ancestry that is indicated by similar australopith postcranial features. This suggestion is not so far-fetched in light of a skull that Richard Leakey and his colleagues discovered at a site on the west side of Lake Turkana. [Figures 23a and b] Catalogued as KNM-WT 17000, this specimen is nicknamed the Black Skull because it mineralized almost as dark as coal. It has gen-

erally been accepted as a robust type of australopith, although which kind is another matter altogether. At 2.5 myr old, this specimen is as old as the stone tools at Omo and older than any other robust type. It has been reconstructed by Alan Walker, one of Richard Leakey's and his wife Meave's longest-standing collaborators, as having an essentially flat cranial base. The cranial base of other australopiths varies from bent to considerably bent. As reconstructed, the lower face and upper jaw of 17000 protrudes quite forward, in obvious contrast to the flat and sometimes vertical face of other robusts. If these configurations are indeed anatomically accurate, then, as many paleoanthropologists see it, 17000 is primitive relative to other australopiths.

Because the base of the skull and the face really are a jigsaw puzzle of pieces that would tax the best among us in putting them back together, we think the jury is still out on the position of the lower face and the configuration of the cranial base. It seems, from our study of the specimen, that the face could be positioned differently, lower down relative to the cranial vault. By doing so, the cranial base would become more flexed. The palate, although without teeth, is intact, and it is huge compared with the upper face. In this regard, some at least of the Omo mandibles that had been assigned to the species *aethiopicus* make appropriate companions for such an upper jaw. The 17000 palate certainly differs from the upper jaw of South African robusts, Zinj, and KNM-ER 406 and 732; it is very rounded at the front with long sides, and broader at the front than at the back. But in 17000, the eyes and brain

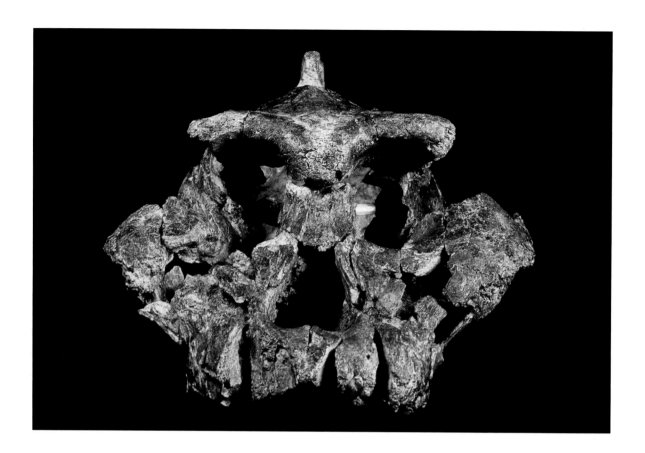

case were relatively small and the brow was much thinner than in other robusts. In fact the brain case was so small that the huge chewing muscles ran out of room and provoked the development of a large bony crest atop the head for much needed attachment space. Among some of the odd features of 17000 were its chunky cheek bones, which bowed forward to an even greater extent than in Zinj.

The Black Skull certainly seemed to throw a wrench into the works. Up until its discovery, paleoanthropologists were having a hard enough time trying to sort out the relationships of *"africanus," "robustus,"* and *"boisei,"* a task

[Figures 23a and b]

As reconstructed, the "Black Skull," KMN-WT 17000, differs from other East African robusts in having a projecting face and a flat cranial base. It looks, however, as if the face could be reoriented, which would make it less prognathic and a bit flatter and have some flexure of the cranial base. KNM-WT 17000 certainly does differ from the other robusts in having much thinner brows, more forwardly facing and arced cheek bones, and a huge sagittal crest.
Photographs by Jeffrey H. Schwartz; courtesey of the National Museums of Kenya.

made even more difficult because, following Mayr's lead, they were trying to use the age of the specimens in their deliberations. Now things became more complex yet.

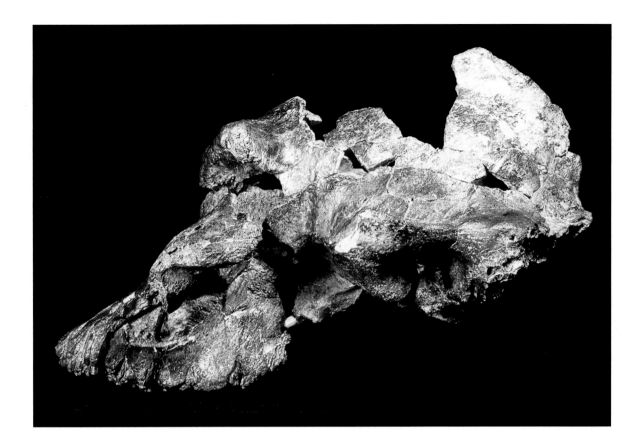

The Age of Discovery

Because the history of paleoanthropology has largely been one of extending the perception of what features constitute *H. sapiens*—indeed, what is supposed to be special about being a highly variable, culture-bearing hominid—into the past, it is no wonder that, in approaching the present from the past, paleoanthropologists should have embraced a stratigraphic approach to assigning evolutionary positions and taxonomic categories. Because of this, the ages of fossil hominids, which it is obviously necessary to know if your intention is to line up speci-

mens from older to younger, have implicitly or explicitly been considered more revealing than their morphology. As a result, the species to which fossils are assigned have varied as new techniques have changed their dating. It is altogether extraordinary how debates over the taxonomy and relationships of the australopiths have depended so much on the ages of the sites.

Yet, even despite the obvious dilemmas and contradictions that arise when using a stratigraphic or time-based approach to sorting out fossils and their presumed evolutionary relationships, once you're in the grips of it, it's hard to get out. So when problems in sorting fossils into seemingly neat time packages arise, the tendency is to think that if only the stratigraphic context of the specimen or age of the deposit were better known, the difficulty would disappear. Clearly, this would seem to a case of the tail wagging the dog. But tradition is hard to break, and it certainly had its impact on how the australopiths were interpreted.

As presently reconstructed, Sterkfontein, Makapansgat, and Taung have yielded the oldest of the accepted triumvirate of australopith species (*africanus*, *robustus*, and *boisei*), coming in with a time span of about 3 to 2.4 mya. From oldest to youngest, the different stratigraphic layers at Sterkfontein have been identified as Members 1 to 6, with the greatest number of specimens coming from Member 4, which could be as old as 2.8 myr; (we shall soon discuss the intriguing specimen from Member 2, which is older than 3 myr). Although there has been some suggestion that the Member 4 hominids vary too much from one another to be considered a single species, the general consensus is that all belong to the same species, *A. africanus*. Stone tools have not been found in Member 4, but simple artifacts have turned up in the younger Member 5, which has also yielded some "gracile" fossils that have been assigned to the presumed descendant of *A. africanus*, *H. habilis*. Five members have also been identified at Makapansgat, with most of the fossils assigned to *A. africanus* coming from the lower part of Member 4 (at least 3 myr old) and one specimen from higher up in this section (younger than 2.8 myr). As for Taung, mining destroyed the exact location where the child's skull was found, but associated monkey fossils place the hominid at over 2 myr.

The age of Kromdraai, the type site of South African *robustus*, is difficult to determine. The hominid fossils may be as old as 2 or as young as 1 myr. At Swartkrans, a messy depositional history was painstakingly worked out by Bob Brain, who retired not too long ago as head of the Transvaal Museum in Pretoria. Hominid fossils from this site probably date between about 1.8 and 1.5 myr; most of them have been identified as *robustus*, but (interestingly) some specimens have been identified as *H. erectus* (more on that in a later chapter). Stone (and some bone) tools also occur in the hominid levels.

Stratigraphy has been used to suggest that *africanus* was ancestral both to *robustus* and to the first member of a *Homo* lineage, *H. habilis*. This scheme has been embraced by some paleoanthropologists because it retains the general notion of *A. africanus* as a likely candidate for the ancestor leading to the more gracile *Homo* lineage, as well as a form from which the more robust South African australopith could have evolved. In this scheme, of course, what one sees in *A. africanus* is primitive, or less evolved, than in *Homo*. So, *Homo* could have evolved from *A. africanus*, and the robust australopiths could also have descended from this species without changing their postcranial skeleton. However, the situation becomes less clear-cut when the East African robusts are included.

To recap, the East African hyper-robust Zinj from Olduvai comes with an approximate age of 1.75 mya. "*aethiopicus*" from Omo, which many paleoanthropologists lump with *boisei*, could be as old as or even slightly older than 2.5 myr. But even at 2.3 myr, it's still old. The youngest hyper-robust australopith specimens from Omo are approximately 1.5 myr. From Koobi Fora, the hyper-robusts, such as the male KNM-ER 406 and female 732 (*see* Figures 21 and 22), may be the same age or slightly older than Zinj (*see* Figure 20), but not older than 2 myr. The Peninj mandible and other isolated hyper-robust specimens (such as from Chesowanja) are somewhat younger.

When the geological sequence was translated into an evolutionary sequence, the scenario that emerged was that the hyper-robust form gave rise to the less robust form. Even back in the 1970s and early 1980s, when this notion was being touted as fact, we couldn't embrace it. For one thing, the age of a fossil doesn't tell you the relative degrees of distinctiveness (or derivedness) versus primitiveness or (commonality with other species), of its morphologies. On purely morphological grounds, the hyper-robust form—being "more" developed in features of jaw and face as well as tooth size and enamel wrinkling—would seem to be the natural "extension" of the specific morphologies established in the smaller robust form, which, of course, is comparatively more robust than its gracile contemporaries. It is the very suite of distinctive robust and hyper-robust australopith features that from the outset points to the real situation. If you're different enough to be easily distinguishable, then there is something unique, or derived, about you that sets you

apart from others, whether the comparison is at the level of specimens, species, or even genera.

But if sorting out specimens that at first glance appear to be generally similar into potential species is not a simple matter, it is perhaps even more difficult to figure out the evolutionary relationships of species that are very similar to each other. This is because it doesn't matter how many similarities any two species share if other species also have those features. As we pointed out in Chapter 2, when making morphological comparisons, it is important to search for those features that only two species share. Then we can seek out other features that these two species share uniquely with a third, and yet other features that these three share uniquely with a fourth species, and so on. It's the derived features that give the systematist clues as to which species may form a clade. Hence, although the gracile australopiths may look more like *H. sapiens* than robusts do, with their large front teeth and rounded brain case, it doesn't mean that the gracile australopith was ancestral to the *Homo* lineage. Most fossil and living apes, as well as many Old World monkeys, also have the same dental proportions and cranial shape.

The discovery of the Black Skull (KNM-WT 17000) (*see* Figure 23a and b) from the Nachukui Formation on the west side of Lake Turkana didn't help matters much, either. Dated at approximately 2.5 myr, this skull certainly predated almost everything else that had been thought of as a robust type of australopith. So the question was, "How do we fit it into a stratigraphic scheme?" Although easily distinguishable from the Zinj and KNM-ER 406 types of robusts, KNM-WT 17000 was, and still is, thought of by some paleoanthropologists as being only an early variant of the East African "*boisei*" robust, which, because of its antiquity, was still regarded as ancestral to the South African robust. Even among those who appreciate that the distinct differences between 17000 and all other robust australopith skulls warrant recognition at the species level, there is still a tendency, because of the time sequence, to view *aethiopicus* as having been ancestral both to *boisei* and to *robustus*. What's more, some paleoanthropologists prefer to keep *africanus* as the ancestor of the robust group. In a more radical scenario, in which *aethiopicus* may or may not be regarded as distinct from *boisei*, the South African australopiths are considered part of a lineage in which *africanus* gave rise to *robustus* as well as (possibly) to the *Homo* lineage. And in an even more extreme evolutionary construct, some of the South African gracile australopiths are primitively retained in *A. africanus*, which is seen as ancestral to a *boisei-robustus* group, whereas other gracile australopiths as well as *aethiopicus* are regarded as species of *Homo* (with *H.* "*aethiopicus*" giving rise to *H.* "*africanus*," which, in turn, gave rise to *H. habilis*).

But this is hardly the whole story. The muddle of human evolution that was produced by putting stratigraphy in charge became even messier with the discovery of the famous *A. afarensis*, and has not been improved by even more recent fossil finds.

The Making of a Hominid

All the bigwigs of paleoanthropology were in attendance at a 1974 conference on human evolution that Cliff Jolly had organized at New York University. There was also a newcomer, who took more than twice his allotted time to talk about his new site in Ethiopia, presenting slide after slide after slide of this fossil elephant, and that fossil pig, until he finally showed the last slide: the lower end of a femur and upper end of a tibia of a fossil hominid, with the knee joint of a chimpanzee on the left and the knee joint of a modern human on the right for comparison. Mary Leakey, for one, was quite outraged at this upstart's taking so long to introduce the knee joint of what was clearly an australopith—of obviously similar morphology to those known already from South Africa. But this was only the beginning for Donald Johanson, who, with his collaborators, would return with dazzling results to the site of Hadar, which lies in the Afar depression of Ethiopia.

The Afar depression, or triangle as it is also called, had been well known to geologists because it is an area where three tectonic plates meet. The famous partial skeleton that was nicknamed Lucy came from a locality of Hadar (A.L. 288) that dates to 3.2 myr. The remains of at least 13 individuals from the A.L. 333 locality date to about 3.4 myr, and other specimens are slightly older. The Lucy skeleton has been assigned to the species *A. afarensis*. Although this might be the most famous of the specimens of this species of early hominid, neither it nor the other specimens from Hadar are its oldest representatives.

When Johanson, in collaboration with Tim White and Yves Coppens, formally introduced *A. afarensis* in their publication of 1978, they chose a specimen from a different site as the type specimen of their new species. This site, Laetoli, is situated in Tanzania, well over 1500 kilometers to the south of Hadar. Laetoli is perhaps most famous for the trails of footprints that have been attributed to *A. afarensis*. But Laetoli has also yielded a considerable number of hominid fossils, and Johanson, White, and Coppens used one of them—a virtually complete lower jaw with its teeth preserved—as the type specimen of *A. afarensis*, in part to demonstrate how geographically widespread this hominid had been. With a time span of 3.46 to 3.76 myr, the Laetoli members of the *afarensis* family are older than those from Hadar, which date from about 3.4 to 3.0 myr. *A. afarensis* has also been identified at the Ethiopian sites of Belohdelie (a frontal bone), Maka (the upper end of a femur), and Fejej (isolated teeth). Belohdelie and Maka are more or less contemporaneous with Laetoli, whereas Fejej may be 4 myr old. Inasmuch as the Maka femur is generically australopith in its preserved morphology, and the other specimens have been identified as *A. afarensis* primarily because of their ancientness, who these fossils really represent is still unknown. It's not completely evident that they should be *A. afarensis*. Indeed, even the Hadar and Laetoli specimens have not been exempt from controversy.

One of the first debates had to do with the number of species represented in the sample. There are very large and very small individuals.

At first, Johanson was inclined to believe that the large individuals represented one species, and the small ones represented another—a position that some paleoanthropologists have continued to maintain. But, largely through the efforts of Tim White, Johanson was swayed to the viewpoint that the differences in size between specimens, although greater than between males and females of any living primate, the gorilla and orangutan included, could be accommodated in a single species. From then on, Johanson promoted the hypothesis that Hadar and Laetoli bore evidence of a single, hugely sexually dimorphic species. In retrospect, as we will discuss momentarily, he probably should have held to his first impression.

As for the morphologies of the collective *afarensis*, they, too, presented a mixture of enigmas. The morphology of the variously represented regions of the *afarensis* skeleton—from the pelvic bones, to sacrum, femur, tibia, vertebral column and the foramen magnum position—was essentially the same as the comparable parts of South African and other East African australopiths. But the skull and mandible were another matter. The brain case was much smaller than expected while the jaws and teeth were huge. Clearly, it seemed, bipedalism had not appeared synchronously with brain enlargement, as many had expected. If *afarensis* was the key, then the evolution of bipedalism occurred long before the expansion of the brain and the diminution of the face and jaws. And in specific details of skull and tooth, *afarensis* was equally clearly more apelike than any other hominid.

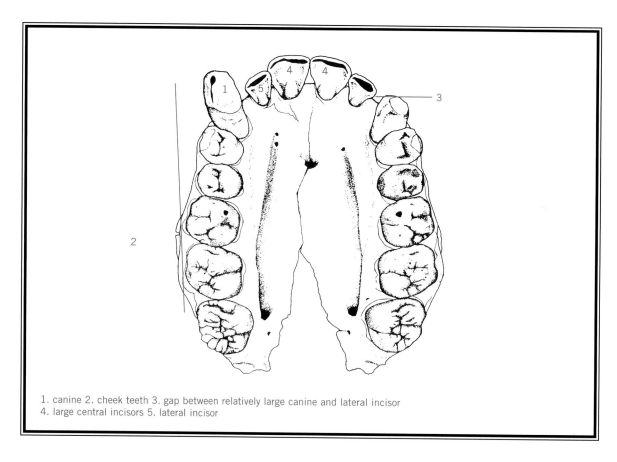

1. canine 2. cheek teeth 3. gap between relatively large canine and lateral incisor
4. large central incisors 5. lateral incisor

Thus, as Blumenbach had pointed out in living humans and apes, the upper canine of *afarensis* was tall and separated from the incisor in front of it by a gap, which would have received the large lower canine. [Figures 24a and b] The upper canine of *afarensis* was much taller than in other australopiths. A. *afarensis* was also seen as being more apelike—actually chimplike—in having very tall and broad upper central incisors. And all upper incisors were somewhat forwardly inclined. But Johanson and his colleagues really focussed on one dental feature in particular as quintessentially ape-like: the presence of a single cusp on the lower

first premolar, or, as it's incorrectly called, bicuspid tooth.

The reason that so much weight was put on the presence of a single cusp on this so-called bicuspid is that, decades earlier, the British paleoanthropologist Sir Wilfred LeGros Clark had declared that this was a major distinction between humans and apes. Humans have a true bicuspid, whereas apes have a single-cusped lower first premolar. This distinction was historically important because it was LeGros Clark who, in the 1940s, helped to establish the hominid status of the then-known australopiths, in part by claiming that they were

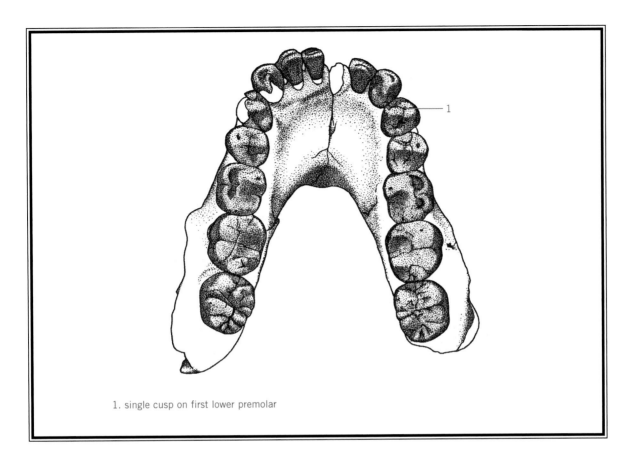

1. single cusp on first lower premolar

similar to *H. sapiens* in having a bicuspid lower first premolar. Although this is not true of *H. sapiens* (all of us can verify by looking in the mirror that our lower first premolar is essentially a single-cusped tooth, with only some individuals having what appears to be a small second cusp) the myth lingers.

From our perspective, however, the similarities between *afarensis* and other hominids are broadly shared and, thus, primitive. They do not indicate any particular relationship beyond suggesting that all are members of the same but larger-than-just-hominid evolutionary group. And the presence of two well-developed cusps on the lower first premolar of non-*afarensis* australopiths would seem, along with the features of the pelvic bone and femur, to distinguish the non-*afarensis* forms even further from other hominids.

Under pressure to justify the argument that *afarensis* could be ancestral to other hominids, it seemed imperative that the list of close comparisons between the fossil hominid and apes should be as comprehensive as possible. And comprehensive it was, going from the backward slope of the front of the lower jaw and the forehead to the somewhat triangular snout and the broad-based but low brain case with inwardly tilted sides. The top of the brain case even bore a distinct sagittal crest onto which large chewing muscles had attached.

A. afarensis appeared apelike in its skull, and jaws. It was apelike in some aspects of its teeth; and it also had the skeletal features that were associated, in other australopiths, with a primitive level of bipedalism. It thus seemed to serve well as the ancestor of all other hominids. But although much of the morphology of the skeletal bones of *afarensis* had already been known in the South African australopiths, there were some unanticipated twists.

Arboreal Bipeds?

As reconstructed by Johanson's colleagues, particularly Owen Lovejoy and Bruce Latimer, *afarensis* had been a fully committed biped, with all the imaginable morphological trappings. The often-illustrated reconstruction of the skeleton of *afarensis* depicts a striding individual with a non-opposable big toe; a roughly spindle-shaped rib cage; a rather vertical pelvic bone; not-too-short legs; and not-very-long arms, toes, and fingers. The position of the big toe in alignment with the other toes comes from the interpretation of the footprints from one particular track at Laetoli, where it appears that two individuals were walking together side by side in a field of volcanic ash that had become muddy during the rainy season. [Figure 25] Some paleoanthropologists who have looked at these prints see the impression of a big toe, with those of the other toes to its side. Ron Clarke, however, thinks that the big toe is slightly divergent and that the footprints have other ape-like characteristics as well—a conclusion recently confirmed by his French colleague Yvette Deloison.

Peter Schmid also entered a dissenting opinion for other areas of the *afarensis* skeleton. In his reconstruction, the rib cage is quite conical, narrow at the top and fans out considerably at the bottom. [Figure 26] But he didn't base this reconstruction on sorting out the ribs by themselves. He looked first at the shape of the pelvic girdle, which he also reconstructed in manner different than that of Lovejoy and his colleagues. In Schmidt's reconstruction, the *afarensis* pelvis is much broader from side to side and more turned out above the hip joints. Because the shape of the rib cage has to be coordinated with the shape of the upper part of the pelvis, and because sets of back muscles course between them, it had to follow that the bottom of the rib cage was going to be more expansive than the

[Figure 25]

The most famous set of footprints at Laetoli, Tanzania, depicts what appear to be two tracks, of a larger and a smaller individual walking bipedally next to each other. The impressions certainly look as if there is a big toe and four small toes. But, according to Ron Clarke, because of the way in which chimpanzees walk on their hind feet, these apes leave similar depressions on damp soil—which could mean that the makers of the Laetoli footprints did not have a humanlike foot. Photograph by Craig Chesek, courtesy of Department of Library Service, American Museum of Natural History.

humans and virtually all other mammals face up, are oriented to the sides. The *afarensis* pelvis, therefore, is less bowl-shaped than it is like a broad, upside-down, wide-brimmed hat. Thus, if the pelvic girdle is broad, as it was in *afarensis* (and, as we mentioned earlier, in other australopiths), then so also must have been the lower part of the rib cage. The upper part had to be narrow because that's how the preserved skeletal pieces would go together.

The reconstruction of a broad pelvic girdle also has significance for the femur because the two articulate together. The broader the pelvic girdle, the more strongly the shaft of the femur will angle inward if the knees are positioned directly under the torso. And, indeed, this is precisely what you see in *afarensis* and other australopiths—much greater angling of the femur at the knee joint than in anything attributed to the genus *Homo*. So, is this a primitive stage in the evolution of modern human bipedalism, or is it evidence of something specific to being an australopith? If you hold to the view that "older" equates with "more primitive," then you are forced to interpret the uniquely configured femur of australopiths as being a stage "on the way" to becoming human—and

upper part. Ergo, the *afarensis* rib cage was probably quite conical.

In Schmid's reconstruction of *afarensis*, the bladelike pelvic bones are turned severely outward, so that their top margins, which in

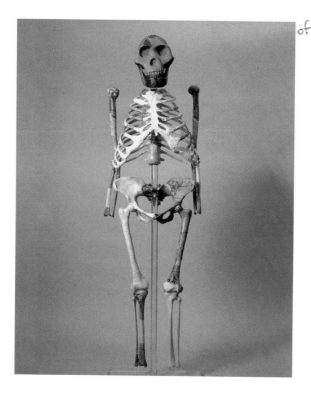

[Figure 26]

Peter Schmid's reconstruction of "Lucy's" skeleton is quite different from that of Owen Lovejoy, who had worked with Johanson on the fossil. For instance, in the Schmid reconstruction the bladelike portions of the pelvis are oriented much more horizontally, giving a wider and shallower appearance to the structure as a whole. Since major back muscles attach from the bladelike parts of the pelvis to the lower ribs, it makes sense that the lower end of the rib cage would also have been quite wide—which means, in turn, that the rib cage would have tapered upward quite strongly. In keeping with Lucy having had long and strongly curved finger and toe bones, as do chimpanzees and orangutans, Schmid's reconstruction also emphasizes the long arms typical of an arboreal hominoid. Photograph courtesy of Peter Schmid.

of the australopith femur stands out as distinctive of the group consisting of *afarensis, africanus, aethiopicus robustus,* and *boisei* (we don't have the femur of *aethiopicus*). Which in turn suggests that none of them could be ancestral to the *Homo* lineage because an ancestor should be more primitive, not more derived, than its presumed descendants. If we think about who has the uniquely two-cusped lower first premolar— *aethiopicus, africanus, robustus,* and *boisei* then we can think of them as an evolutionary subgroup of australopiths.

As for the other parts of the skeleton, the expectation prior to the discovery of the *afarensis* skeletons was that, if australopiths had been fully committed bipeds, then they would have had proportions of arm and leg as in humans: relatively short arms, very long legs. With the discovery of enough pieces of arm and leg to engage in debate, the question regarding *afarensis* has been: are the arms long or are the legs short? Well, even if the relative proportions of the arms are more humanlike than apelike (the lower arm is much longer compared with the upper arm in chimpanzees and especially the full-time arborealists—orangutans and gibbons)—the arms of *afarensis* were still quite long. Less debatable is the fact that the legs of *afarensis* were quite short. As for the fingers and toes, they were quite long, and the shafts of these bones were curved (as in orangutans and gibbons), in contrast to humans and even to the terrestrial gorillas (in which these bones are relatively short and their shafts rather straight). In addition, the groove along the backside of the lower end of the outer lower leg bone, the fibula, through which the tendon of a muscle

this would include the lower as well as the upper end, with its oddly small head and long neck. If, on the other hand, you equate uniqueness with derivedness, then the configuration inserting on the sole of the foot passes, is not only deeper than in humans, but also deeper than in chimpanzees. And this, in turn, suggests that the larger muscle of *afarensis* would have been better able to stabilize its foot, as when being pressed against a vertical support, than in any human or chimpanzee. Put these *afarensis* features together and, according to Randy Susman and colleagues at SUNY-Stony Brook, you have an australopith that was probably more committed to life in the trees than on the ground. In fact, the Stony Brook group concluded, many features that had come to be associated with bipedalism may very well have been useful to *afarensis* (and, by extension, other australopiths) for shinnying up and down trees. Only when these hominids had to travel between arboreal habitats would they find themselves walking bipedally, "forced" to do so by their own anatomies.

If true, this is a very neat story. But even if it is not, it should serve to remind us that features do not necessarily evolve to perform a certain function. The ways in which we see organisms dealing with their daily circumstances need not be the result of natural selection molding morphology for a specific purpose. Some morphologies may permit a number of avenues of exploitation.

Take, for instance, the case of the mongoose lemur, which is found on various islands in the Indian Ocean. On some islands, this prosimian primate forms large groups, tends to be most active during the day, spends considerable time traveling on the ground, and subsists primarily on the leaves and shoots of plants. But on other islands, this same animal—identical as far as we can tell in tooth, skull, and bone with those with the other islands—forms small groups, tends to be more active at night, spends its time in the trees, and hangs from its hind feet to reach flowers from which it harvests pollen and nectar. If you were to see these animals first in the wild, you would never guess that you couldn't tell them apart skeletally or dentally.

We take the case of the mongoose lemur as an important lesson about just how far one can go in inferring behavior from skeletal remains. Just because living humans use their skeletons specifically and in certain ways for getting around does not mean that other hominids were restricted only to this kind of locomotion. Morphology may be the arbiter in determining phylogenetic relationships, but it is not an infallible reflection of behavior.

Earliest Ancestors?

The picture of human evolution as proceeding in a more or less straight line toward those features we hold most dear in *H. sapiens* was shaken up further with the discovery in 1995 by Meave Leakey and her colleagues of fossils they assigned to a new species of *Australopithecus, A. anamensis*. The first specimen of this species had been discovered almost twenty years earlier by the paleontologist Bryan Patterson as he was surveying this region west of Lake Turkana for potential fossil sites. In one area, Kanapoi, Patterson found the lower end of a humerus. In collaboration with his Harvard colleague, the physical anthropologist W. W. Howells, Patterson published an article in the journal *Science* about how humanlike this lower humerus, was—a conclusion later reinforced by the comparative metrical and statistical analyses of Howells' student Henry McHenry and his collaborator, Rob Corruccini, and later again by the French paleontologist, Brigitte Senut. In these studies, the computer programs plotted the Kanapoi humerus in the group with the human humeri on the basis of similarity in shape.

Of further interest in McHenry and Corruccini's analysis was the fact that although the other fossil hominid humeri in the sample—one from Kromdraai and the other from Koobi Fora, and both supposedly robust types of australopiths—didn't plot out with the Kanapoi humerus, they weren't grouped together either. Whereas the Kromdraai lower humerus plotted in between the human and chimpanzee groups, the Koobi Fora lower humerus did not group with humans, apes, or the Kromdraai hominid. And although though the Koobi Fora specimen didn't even seem to be hominid, the Kanapoi lower humerus grouped right in there with the modern human sample! This is not what you would expect from the general way in which human evolution is portrayed.

When Meave Leakey and her colleagues worked Kanapoi and another locality, Allia Bay, they found parts of upper and lower jaws as well as a few more parts of the postcranial skeleton. Patterson's fossil humerus and Leakey's postcranial specimens had come from the Upper Kanapoi sediments, which were thought to be more or less contemporaneous with the section at Allia Bay, which was dated to about 3.9 myr ago. The jaws came from the Lower Kanapoi, dated to about 4.2 myr. The pieces of skeletal bone are large and robust whereas the jaws seem to come in two sizes, large and small.

As for the jaws and their preserved teeth, they were essentially like those of *afarensis*, especially the smaller individuals. In contrast with the australopith tibia, in which the upper articular end of the bones sits atop the shaft like a flat mushroom cap, the Upper Kanapoi tibia was said to be like a modern human's in that the shaft of the bone flares out like a trumpet bell to meet the margins of the upper articular surface. And although we wouldn't have described the Kanapoi tibia as being excessively trumpet shaped, the disparity between the top and the shaft is not quite as severe as in australopiths.

When Leakey and her collaborators lumped all of the Kanapoi and Allia Bay specimens together into the species *Australopithecus anamensis*, they created an animal that was very primitively hominid in its jaws and teeth but humanlike in its knee and elbow joints. Whereas *afarensis* had been primitive in both craniodental and postcranial morphology, *anamensis* would seem to have taken that extra evolutionary "step" toward the modern human condition.

But Peter Andrews of the Natural History Museum in London, who is best known for his work on fossil apes, didn't think it proper to lump the Lower Kanapoi jaws and teeth together with the Upper Kanapoi/Allia Bay postcranials. Because the type specimen of *anamensis* was from the Lower Kanapoi specimens, he concluded that it is with this assemblage that the species should be associated. And because the specimens of tooth and jaw that would then be attributed to *anamensis* were more apelike than humanlike, Andrews suggested that *anamensis* might actually have been a kind of extinct ape rather than a primitive hominid. With these specimens removed from the sample, Andrews felt that the Upper Kanapoi and Allia Bay skeletal bones, with their chronologically associated jaws and teeth, provided evidence of a real hominid from these two localities. But this unnamed hominid would still be an enigma because it had a *Homo*-like elbow and knee but was more *afarensis*-like than not in its jaws and teeth.

Most recently, Leakey and her colleagues have reported the redating of these sites, which indicates that the Upper Kanapoi is not much younger than the more than 4-myr-old Lower Kanapoi. They have also discovered more postcranial bones that are definitively hominid morphologically. But however you slice it, the fossils from Kanapoi and Allia Bay do not provide us with a simple picture of early hominid evolution. Rather, if everything allocated to the species *anamensis* goes together, then we have a hominid that chronologically preceded *afarensis*, but was *afarensis*-like from the neck up and *Homo*-like from the neck down. This certainly adds to the picture of early hominid diversity as more like a bush than a sparsely branched tree. If Andrews is correct, and all these specimens do not come from the same species of hominid—and even if we just allow the possibility that not all specimens assigned to *afarensis* belong to the same species—then the early part of the human evolutionary bush becomes even more complicated.

Tim White and his colleagues recently announced the discovery of a new species they attributed to *Australopithecus*, *A. garhi*. As with *anamensis*, this species, approximately 2.5 myr old, presents a combination of the unexpected: very primitive in skull, jaws, and teeth, but is surprisingly *Homo*-like in its skeletal bones. This "species," if it all goes together, is younger than *anamensis* and *afarensis*, so White and his colleagues have argued that it is the ancestor of later hominids. But it might equally well be another twig of the bush, another evolutionary experiment achieved by the random activation of some and deactivation of other of the genes that regulate development that we, as hominids, all share.

On the other end of the spectrum comes the recent discovery by Ron Clarke of four foot bones from Member 2 (3.3 myr old) of Sterkfontein. These specimens go from the bone right under the tibia (the talus) to the preserved back end of the metatarsal for the big toe. Clarke coauthored an article with Phillip Tobias on this set of bones, which were collectively nicknamed Little Foot. In the article, Clarke pointed out how the joint between the first metatarsal and the tarsal bone right behind it would not have fixed the big toe in alignment with the other toes. Instead, the joint would have permitted motion of the big toe away from the other toes—perhaps not quite as far as in an ape, but certainly much farther than any human

Extinct Humans

[Figure 27]

The skull and left humerus of StW 573 *in situ*. As Ron Clarke has reconstructed the foot bones of this specimen, which he and Phillip Tobias assigned to a species of *Australopithecus,* the big toe would not have been in line with the other toes, as it is in ourselves. Rather, as in apes and other primates, the big toe, like the thumb, would have been somewhat divergent. Photograph by Ron Clarke.

(Darwin's claims of opposable big toes in "primitive" living humans notwithstanding). [Figure 27]

What a shocker. At 3.3 myr old, Little Foot had a foot more similar to an ape (at least at the front; behind it was more humanlike) than conventional wisdom held for early hominid bipeds. Could Ron Clarke and Yvette Deloison be correct, then, about the real nature of the Laetoli footprints? That the weight had been borne on the outside of the foot, as in an ape, for example, and that the prints reflect other arboreal capabilities too. To check this out, Clarke recruited two circus chimps to walk bipedally over wet sand. The prints made by one of them were remarkably similar to those from Laetoli!

What, then, defines a hominid? Not, as Aristotle and Blumenbach would have predicted, the foot, unless it is in a few minor bumps on the talus bone at its rear. Nor the shape of the rib cage or the relative lengths of the arm, leg, and finger and toe bones. Nor the details of the skull or teeth, either. Instead, the critical features would seem to be in some aspects of the pelvic bones and sacrum and angle of the lower end of the femur, in the curvature of the lower spine, and in having twin depressions on the upper end of the tibia, where the femur sits. [Figures 28, 29 and 30]

It had been thought for quite some time that having a layer of thick enamel on the cheek teeth, especially the molars, was another hominid characteristic. That was until it was discovered that a number of ape-related fossils, some being as old as 18 myr and others as young as 0.5 myr, also had thick molar enamel—as does the orangutan. Given the widespread distribution of this feature, it thus does not help to define hominids. But, because hominids, many fossil "apes," and the living orangutan have thick molar enamel, it is likely that this feature characterized their last common ancestor. Consequently, it would be as a primitive retention from this ancestor that hominids would have thick molar enamel. Or is this the case?

In 1994, Tim White, Gen Suwa, and Berhane Asfaw announced the discovery in the Awash region of the Afar triangle of an even older human ancestor, which they dubbed *Australopithecus ramidus.* Dated at 4.4 myr, this would certainly make it the earliest known hominid—if it is a hominid. However, later that year, White and his colleagues published a correction, a change of mind about the taxonomic allocation of their human ancestor. *Australopithecus* was dropped, and a new genus, *Ardipithecus,* was substituted. Could this mean, on second thoughts or new, unpublished discoveries, that this is not a hominid after all?

White and his colleagues based their claims of hominid status for *Ardipithecus* on only a few features. They pointed to the elliptical shape of the upper end of the humerus, the extremely far-forward position of the foramen magnum, and the shape of the first of the teeth that the premolars replace, the milk molars, which they likened to *afarensis*. Otherwise, especially in the teeth, this "hominid" was like an ape: primitive. And not only were the shapes of all other teeth unhominid, but the enamel covering them was thin. So, if this *was* an ancestral hominid, thick molar enamel has developed multiple times among groups of fossil apes as well as in a common ancestor of hominids that postdated this Awash species. Also unusual about *Ardipithecus* is the fact that its foramen magnum is situated farther forward—in front of the plane of the bony tubes of the ear region—than in any other hominid.

Ardipithecus may seem to make a good hominid ancestor because it is so primitive compared with the rest of the bunch. But, first,

[Figure 28]

Left: When humans stand erect, their knees lie underneath the body because the shaft of the femur angles in from the hip to the knee joint creating a wider angle on the inside than on the outside of the knee. In other living quadrupeds, the lower end of the femur forms a right angle with the tibia at the knee joint. Drawing by Bridget D. Thomas.

[Figure 29]

Middle: As a human matures and becomes a more proficient biped, the vertebral column becomes clearly curved in its various sections: the neck or cervical vertebrae and the lower or lumbar vertebrae curve inward and the thoracic vertebrae in between curve outward, as do the fused sacral vertebrae of the pelvic region. Drawing by J. Anderton, with permission.

[Figure 30]

Right: In humans, the twinned and rounded lower ends of the femur sit in twin depressions on the upper end of the tibia. In apes for instance, there is only one concave depression on the tibia; the other area of articulation is convex. Drawing by Bridget D. Thomas.

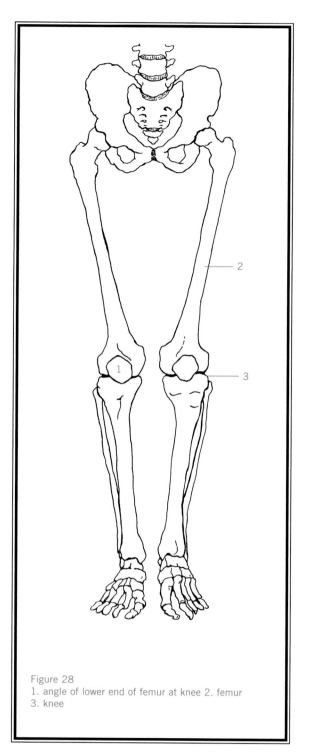

Figure 28
1. angle of lower end of femur at knee 2. femur 3. knee

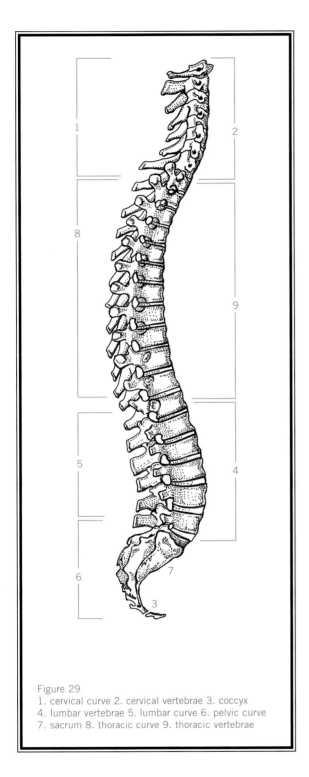

Figure 29
1. cervical curve 2. cervical vertebrae 3. coccyx
4. lumbar vertebrae 5. lumbar curve 6. pelvic curve
7. sacrum 8. thoracic curve 9. thoracic vertebrae

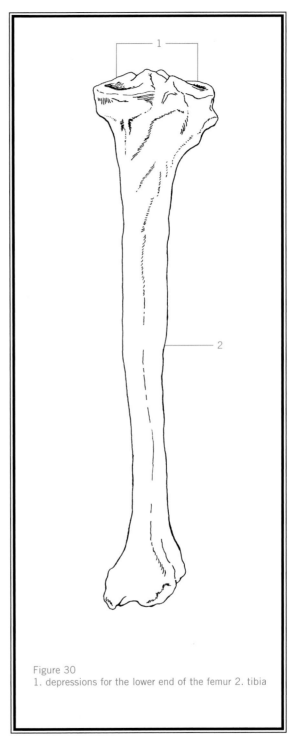

Figure 30
1. depressions for the lower end of the femur 2. tibia

one would have to argue convincingly that it is the closest relative of everything else that's considered to be a hominid. And at present, this isn't a very easy thing to do. Even if *Ardipithecus* were to have shared a common ancestor with hominids, the position of its foramen magnum is so uniquely derived compared with every one of its presumed descendants that it couldn't have been ancestral to any of them for the simple reason that an ancestor cannot be more specialized or derived than its descendants! How much easier things would be if time truly were the arbiter of hypotheses of evolutionary relationship, and older really was synonymous with primitive and, thus, ancestral.

What to Do with Australopiths?

Although there is now undeniable evidence that early human evolution is dominated by a diversity of a markedly variable and differently "packaged" species—perhaps even more than are currently recognized in the literature, we still cannot ascertain their potential evolutionary relationships using the language of taxonomy. As long as these species are kept in the same genus there will always be the tendency to think that these species form a natural group. That's just the way it is. It may be that taxonomists claim that classifications are only tools for communicating. But, in reality, most of us are bound by these classifications. For it is reasonable to think that a named taxonomic group is the same thing as an evolutionary group. As students we are forced to memorize classifications,

and that's how we often continue to conceive the evolution of these organisms. Hominids are just the worst example. With only two genera typically in use—*Australopithecus* and *Homo*—it is difficult to combat the notion that the history of human evolution has not been very complex. Although (with the exception of *Ardipithecus*) many of our colleagues continue to lump all African early hominids into *Australopithecus*, the obvious uniqueness of the robust species cry out for their recognition as an evolutionary group. This group, in turn, could be embraced taxonomically by the genus *Paranthropus*. But if *P. aethiopicus*, *P. robustus*, and *P. boisei* do constitute a potential evolutionary group, does that mean that, by default, the species that would still remain in *Australopithecus*—*afarensis*, *anamensis*, *africanus*, *garhi*, and yet another but poorly known species from Chad, *bahrelghazali*—are themselves very closely related species? Probably not.

Let's look again at the broader picture with regard to the *Paranthropus* group and the better known "leftover" species of *Australopithecus-afarensis*, *anamensis*, and *africanus*. This entire collection of species may be united with those placed in the genus *Homo* by such features as the broadened and shortened upper part of the pelvic bone and sacrum, lower spinal curvature, and double impressions on the upper surface of the tibia. The australopiths emerge as an evolutionary group because of their skeletal particularities, such as of the pelvic girdle and femur. Within this australopith group, *A. africanus* and *Paranthropus* would be distinguished on the basis of having two cusps on the lower first pre-

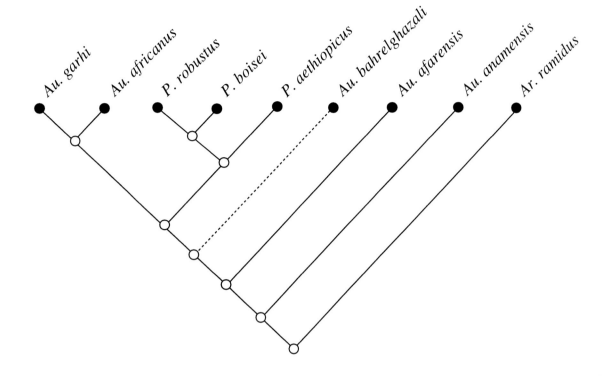

Au. garhi *Au. africanus* *P. robustus* *P. boisei* *P. aethiopicus* *Au. bahrelghazali* *Au. afarensis* *Au. anamensis* *Ar. ramidus*

[Figure 31]

Cladogram summarizing the possible relationships among the various species of *Australopithecus/ Ardipithecus/Paranthropus* discussed in this chapter. These relationships are highly tentative and are subject to reinterpretation with better species characterizations and analyses of the distributions of derived characters.
Cladogram by Ian Tattersall / art by Bridget Thomas.

molar. And, of course, the species of *Paranthropus* certainly should be considered a distinct group. One of the consequences of this hypothesis is that *afarensis*, as proposed by Johanson and his colleagues, is separated from *africanus* because *africanus* is evolutionarily closer to the *Paranthropus* group. According to very strict rules of classification, the species *africanus* has to go with the genus *Australopithecus*, which would certainly be an "unnatural" grouping if *afarensis* were kept in that genus, too. [Figure 31]

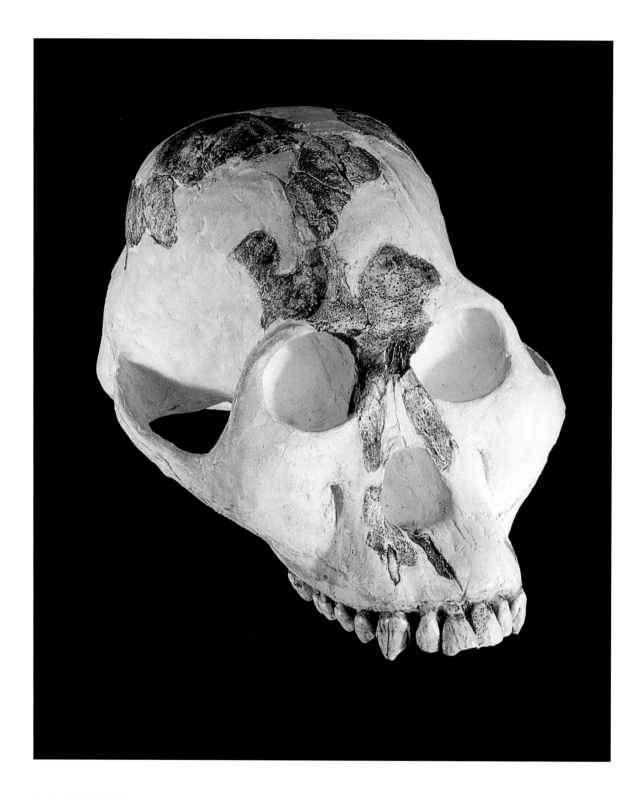

Extinct Humans

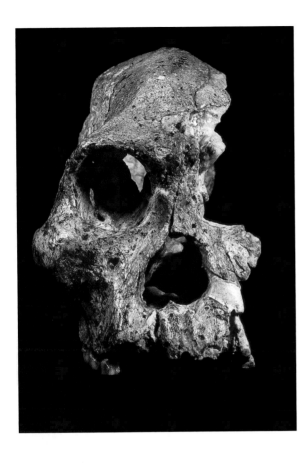

[Figures 32, 33, and 34]

Reminiscent of orangutans, StW 252 (left) has, for example, a more forwardly projecting upper jaw, more marked disparity in size and shape between the upper central and lateral incisors, and larger and more morphologically detailed upper canines than Sts 52 (above). StW 252 and Sts 52 also differ in details of upper molar morphology as well as in third molar size. The teeth of Sts 71 (next page) are either very worn or missing, and so is detail of tooth morphology, but this specimen is similar to Sts 52, and different from StW 252, in having, for example, a relatively flatter lower face and a third molar that is smaller than the second. Photographs by Jeffrey H. Schwartz (Sts 52 and Sts 71) and Ron Clarke (StW 252).

We can just hear some of our colleagues muttering, if not fuming, at the suggestion that we should recognize more hominid genera. But if we were dealing with an organism other than a hominid, nobody would bat an eyelash at this proposition. Fortunately, after we wrote the first draft of this book, colleagues, such as Bernard Wood at George Washington University, have begun to consider similar conclusions.

But before we get too caught up in wrangling about how many genera we should name, we have first to make certain that we have sorted out as reasonably as possible the situation at the species level. Have we recognized all the species that are potentially lurking in known collections? Probably not! Take, for instance, the specimens attributed to the species *africanus*. These specimens have been described as exhibiting an amazing amount of variability that ranges from the totally wild and dentally very "female orangutan-like" specimen from Sterkfontein (catalogued as Sts 252), to the shorter-faced specimens (such as Sts 71 and 52). If you show photos of these specimens to students who have not yet been inculcated into the dogma of paleoanthropology, they can't believe that these things represent merely different versions of the same species. [Figures 32, 33 and 34] It is probably the grouping together in *africanus* of different species—not different kinds of individuals of the same species—that is behind this "remarkable" situation. And the same goes for other situations, such as the East African robust sample. From the differences we have already noted among the teeth to the outrageously long-faced Black Skull, who knows how many species are

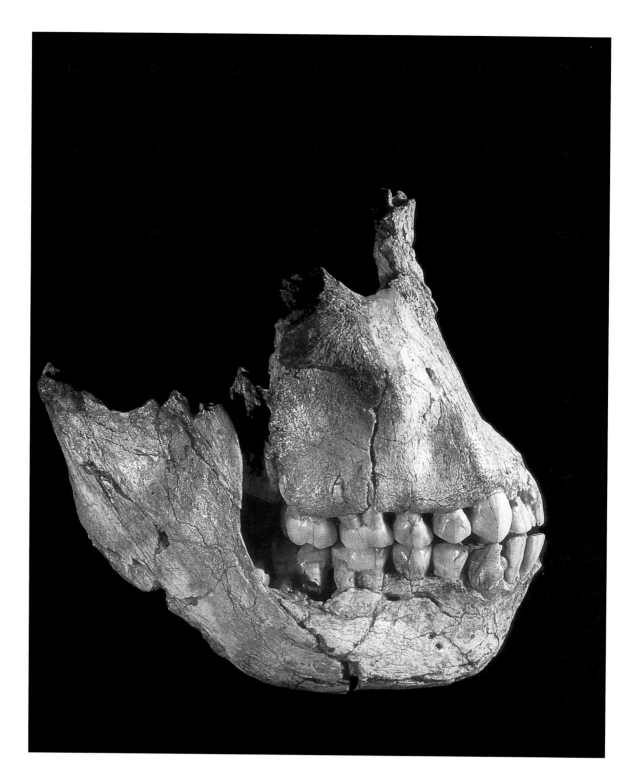

Extinct Humans

really represented in this collection? Even *afarensis* and *anamensis* should be rescrutinized. And, to the extent that Johanson's initial suspicion that two hominids are present in the sample of *afarensis* is justified, and that Andrews' concerns about lumping all Kanapoi and Allia Bay specimens together into *anamensis* are well founded, then we are probably looking at an incredibly interesting picture of early hominid diversity that began with the very origin of the group.

Although we are still in the midst of our study of the entire human fossil record, we are increasingly impressed by how much the picture of human evolution defies the constraints that Mayr and Dobzhansky imposed upon it. It is not a sea of unfathomable variability streaming toward the present. Rather, like the evolutionary history of most other organisms, it is astonishing in its diversity. As corny as it might sound, we do our extinct relatives better justice by referring to our collective evolutionary group as a "family bush" rather than a "family tree"— especially when that tree is primarily trunk.

CHAPTER 4

The Mysterious
Homo habilis

The Mysterious *Homo habilis*

Despite Louis and Mary Leakey's long-awaited success at Olduvai in 1959, the 1960s' dawned upon a human fossil record that had yet to take on anything remotely resembling the shape familiar today. Our current perceptions of human origins are so strongly conditioned by our knowledge of an eastern African record that then barely existed, that it takes a conscious mental effort nowadays to reconstruct the intellectual and fossil milieux into which the Leakeys dropped their next bombshell, *Homo habilis*. As we've seen, by the time the 1960s rolled around, paleoanthropology had fallen firmly under the spell of the Evolutionary Synthesis, whereby virtually all evolutionary phenomena could be ascribed to the gradual action of natural selection within lineages of organisms. Attention was fixed on *transformation*, both in species and the anatomical characteristics of individuals, and the intellectual fashion was strongly against the recognition of new species. By reinforcing the mindset already entrenched via the Great Chain of Being, this tendency created its own burden, of which we'll be seeing more. However, the Synthesis did achieve a very necessary clearing-out of a vast collection of old names that had been more or less randomly assigned, and that were obscuring the actual pattern of human evolution.

Thus it was that in 1964, when *H. habilis* was named, the newly enlightened practitioners of paleoanthropology were deeply reluctant to clutter their science with any new names whatsoever. Their outlook was firmly linear. Essentially, South African *Australopithecus africanus* had somehow given rise to eastern Asian *Homo erectus* (which in turn spawned *Homo sapiens*). This much was unquestioningly accepted, although between *A. africanus* and *H. erectus* there yawned a huge gulf that begged to be filled. One might, naively, have expected that an early species of *Homo* in exactly that slot would have been widely welcomed. In the event, things were very different, and it will take a little background to explain how.

Olduvai

As the pace of work at Olduvai picked up thanks to the munificent support attracted by the Zinjanthropus discovery, new hominid finds there began to accumulate rapidly. A site right at the base of the exposures in the Gorge, and thus marginally older than the Zinjanthropus locality, produced a partial braincase and a broken lower jaw, plus some hand bones and most of a left foot. The braincase, jaw and hand bones were together given the number OH (Olduvai Hominid) 7, and the foot became OH 8. Louis

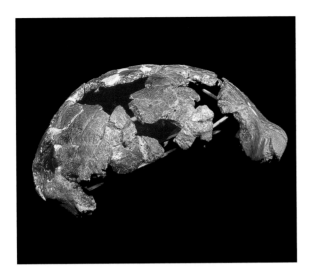
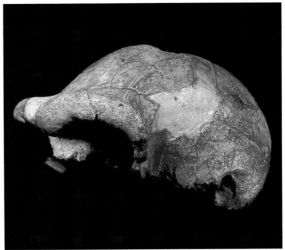

[Figures 35 and 36]

Two hominid crania from Bed II, Olduvai Gorge, Tanzania: the lightly built OH 16 skullcap (left), and the dramatically different and more robust (as well as much larger) OH 9 braincase. Photographs by Jeffrey H. Schwartz; courtesy of the National Museum of Tanzania.

Leakey concluded in 1961 that all these bits belonged to the same species. This species was not only less specialized than his Zinj, but was also "a remote and truly primitive ancestor of *Homo*." According to Leakey, it was this primitive ancestor, not Zinj, who had made the crude stone tools that had attracted the Leakeys to Olduvai in the first place. All this was pretty compelling; but his colleagues had barely had time to begin digesting these pronouncements when Leakey and two geologist colleagues came up with the next surprise, which we've already briefly mentioned. This was the first radiometric date ever obtained on a truly ancient fossil hominid. K/Ar dating from ashfalls closely associated with the hominid sites at the bottom of the Gorge produced an average age of about 1.75 myr. This was truly a revelation, for Leakey's own earlier estimate of the age of Olduvai Bed I had been 600 thousand years (600 kyr). And even this had been widely felt to be a little over-enthusiastic.

Following the dating triumph, which to Leakey had the advantage of making huge amounts of time available in which to transform his hominids into later humans, discoveries continued to be made at Olduvai. These included OH 13, a partial braincase and associated upper and lower jaws from the middle part of Bed II, and OH 16, a highly fragmented cranium from near the bottom of Bed II. Both fossils contrasted strongly with a braincase of a much larger and more heavily built hominid, OH 9, that had been recovered at the top of Bed II, and were considered by the Leakeys to be groupable with their "pre-Zinjanthropus" specimens from Bed I. [Figures 35 and 36] Finally, in 1964, Louis Leakey joined with his colleagues Phillip Tobias and John Napier to describe the more lightly built hominids from Olduvai Beds I and II as representatives of a new species of *Homo*. In acknowledgment of their view that it was this hominid, not Zinjanthropus, that had made the stone tools of lower Olduvai, the group called it *H. habilis*, or "handy man." They pointed out that, at some 640 ml, the brain volume estimated from the OH 7 specimen was significantly larger than the australopith average of about 500 ml, and thus "on track" toward modern *Homo*. They also found some *Homo*-like proportions in the premolars and front teeth, which were otherwise part of a rather gracile-australopith-like dentition.

Yet beyond these characteristics Leakey and colleagues were hard put to find any really convincing reasons for including *habilis* in *Homo*, and it is difficult not to conclude that they did so largely because they subscribed to the idea of "Man the Toolmaker." This notion, whereby the making of stone tools was the fundamental innovation that introduced humanity, had been gathering influence in paleoanthropology over the decade or more since the London Natural History Museum's Kenneth Oakley had published his book of that name. In the long term, the result of all of these various influences was to remove careful morphological analysis from discussion of "early *Homo*," of which there is still no satisfactory morphological definition. In the shorter term it was, of course, predictable that the rather shakily based notion of *H. habilis* should encounter considerable turbulence—especially after Leakey went so far as to declare that his *H. habilis* was directly ancestral to mod-

[Figure 37]

The 1.9 myr-old KNM-ER 1470 cranium from Koobi Fora, Kenya. This large-brained (and apparently quite large-toothed) fossil played a major role in convincing paleoanthropologists that *Homo habilis* was a genuine entity; ironically, it is now widely regarded as representing the species *Homo rudolfensis*. Photograph by Jeffrey H. Schwartz; courtesy of the National Museums of Kenya.

ern humans, whereas the entrenched Asian *H. erectus* was nothing more than a side branch.

All in all, then, *H. habilis* did not arrive in the paleoanthropological literature at the most intellectually propitious of moments. And it has to be admitted that the new hominid itself consisted of no more than a couple of handfuls of fragments that could be interpreted in several different ways. One frequently expressed view was that the Bed I specimens were not really distinguishable from *A. africanus*—a notion that was sometimes linked with the assignment of all the Bed II hominids to *H. erectus*. Some paleoanthropologists had problems in principle, and were—bizarrely—heard muttering that there was not enough "morphological space" between gracile australopiths and *H. erectus* to admit a third species. Almost every possibility was explored. But in the end it has to be admitted that on the basis of the Olduvai material alone, sorting out the affinities of *H. habilis* was a tricky problem indeed. A wider variety of fossils was clearly needed to place the issue in perspective. Yet, after three decades in which the human fossil record has grown by leaps and bounds, we still have no totally convincing answer. This suggests that part of the problem, at least, has lain in how paleoanthropologists have approached the question. We'll return to this in a moment.

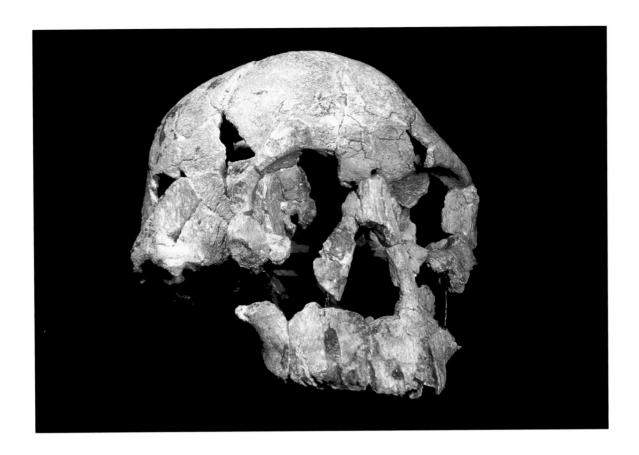

East Turkana

It was thus a desultory debate that continued over the status of the Olduvai finds. Soon, these came to include a badly crushed cranium, OH 24, that was found low in Bed I in 1968. But as time passed the notion of *H. habilis* itself became more familiar and thereby somehow more acceptable, although it remained hard, as it were, to put a face to the new species. Until, that is, the Leakeys' son Richard began to make remarkable finds in northern Kenya, on the eastern shores of Lake Turkana. Beginning in 1968, a team under Richard Leakey's direction

began work in this harsh and remote region of eroding badlands. Almost immediately, the team made major hominid finds. The 1969 season produced not only a complete if toothless cranium of a robust australopith, but stone tools lying within a volcanic ashfall. This deposit (known as the KBS tuff) was promptly K/Ar dated at 2.6 myr, although it was later redated after much argument to a firm 1.9 myr. Many more hominid fossils followed, perhaps the most famous of them being the partial cranium, known by its catalog number, KNM ER-

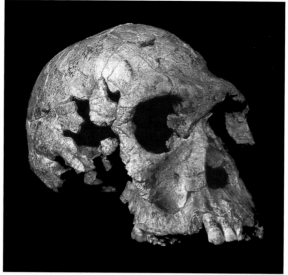

1470, which was found in 1972 in sediments that lay just below (and were hence fractionally older than) the KBS tuff. [Figure 37]

The 1470 specimen was found in hundreds of fragments, but careful reconstruction showed that much of the braincase and face was preserved. The contact between these two areas of the skull was rather tenuous, and all of the tooth crowns were gone. What was immediately evident, however, was the large size of the brain. This was initially estimated at 800 ml, although it was later scaled back to about 750 ml. But even the latter estimate was significantly greater than the 640 ml of OH 7. On the other hand, the face was pretty flat, with forward-facing cheekbones. (*see* Figure 43) Further, the palate was short and broad, and what was left of the tooth roots suggested that the crowns would have been rather large. All these observations put Leakey in mind of various australopiths, although how strong this resemblance was depended partly on the arguable angle at which the face was glued to the rest of the cranium. Debate thus ensued. Some authorities emphasized the resemblance of 1470 to australopiths, but although Richard Leakey was happy to assign the specimen to a species of *Homo* because of its large brain size, he hesitated to place it in *H. habilis*. Partly this was because of its much greater cranial capacity. But perhaps more importantly it was because he believed at the time that 1470 was very much older than the Olduvai specimens. For paleoanthropologists at large, however, 1470 offered a practical solution to the problem of *H. habilis*. Here at last was a distinctive hominid that could give an identity to the fragments from Olduvai. This was hardly an example of the highest standards of paleontological analysis within paleoanthropology But back in the early 1970s, as we've already hinted, what passed for analysis in paleoanthropology was more a matter of intuition than of rigorous inquiry. Indeed, even today, with a much stronger theoretical basis for phylogenetic reconstruction available, standards of morphological analysis within paleonthropology are not yet what they might be.

It was not long before the plot thickened yet further. In 1973 continuing work at East Turkana turned up two more crania, ER 1805 and 1813. [Figures 38 and 39] ER 1805 was rather fragmentary, and was covered in a tough matrix that was hard to remove. Once cleaned up it proved famously hard to interpret, and it has been assigned at one time or another to almost every conceivable species. Most recently, it has been compared closely with Olduvai *H. habilis*. The 1.9-myr-old 1813 was another kettle of fish entirely. A broken but exquisitely preserved small cranium with some teeth present, this specimen immediately reminded Richard Leakey of South African *A. africanus*. This was probably mostly because it had a very small brain of not much more than 500 ml volume.

Although the comparison with *A. africanus* did not garner a great deal of support, most other commentators did feel that such a small brain ruled the specimen out of membership in *Homo*. This notion ruled the day until the influential paleoanthropologist Clark Howell opined that the small 1813 was plausibly a female *H. habilis*. Once Howell had taken the plunge, oth-

ers were prepared to follow in this attribution, which effectively confirmed the status of *H. habilis* as an all-embracing "wastebasket" species into which a whole heterogeneous variety of fossils could be conveniently swept. Richard Leakey, let it be noted, was never comfortable with this, and once the 1813 specimen had been firmly redated to about 1.9 myr along with the KBS tuff, he pointed to resemblances with OH 13 from Olduvai Bed II. In his view, neither of these specimens represented *H. habilis* (a species whose identity depends on the OH 7 fragments), but he suggested that 1470 might. All in all, the finding of a lot more 1.9-myr-old fossils had done nothing much to elucidate the identity of *H. habilis*.

The Transvaal

While all this was going on in eastern Africa, work was steadily continuing at the South African australopith sites. At Swartkrans, John Robinson had long ago noted that a few of the hominid fossils were much more lightly built than those of the massive *Paranthropus* that dominated the site. What's more, he was impressed by the presence of stone tools in the breccia deposits. In response to the naming of *H. habilis* by Louis Leakey and his colleagues, he had suggested that the genus *Homo* should be divided into two successive species: *H. transvaalensis* for the earliest toolmakers, and the larger-brained *H. sapiens*. Because Robinson believed that all gracile hominids, including *A. africanus*, lay in a single evolving lineage, he did not expect any of these species to be sharply definable. He was, indeed, content to accept cultural innovation as the critical factor in recognizing the earliest *Homo*, and to abandon the generic name *Telanthropus* that he had previously applied to the gracile fossils from Swartkrans. Still, Swartkrans *Homo* remained a handful of rather anonymous bits until 1970. In that year, Ron Clarke realized that a palate that had been assigned to *Telanthropus* actually joined with two other fossils—part of a face and a braincase fragment—that had previously been thought to represent the robust australopith *Paranthropus*. [Figures 40a and b]

Once reassembled, these pieces, now known as SK 847, made up part of the left side of a cranium that all agreed belonged to a species of *Homo*. Just what species remained obscure, however, until Clarke pointed out a resemblance to the newly discovered KNM ER-3733 (*see* Figure 55) cranium from East Turkana, then assigned to *H. erectus*. Because the Member 1 Swartkrans deposits from which SK 847 came are generally considered to be somewhere in the range of 1.9 to 1.6 myr old, whereas ER-3733 is about 1.8 myr old, this seemed quite reasonable. However, a recent photographic reconstruction of SK 847 by Fred Grine has emphasized certain differences between the two specimens that have again thrown open the species affiliations of the Swartkrans specimen—thereby joining an increasing number of early *Homo* specimens that are merely referred to as *Homo* sp. (unspecified species of *Homo*).

Sterkfontein, too, produced stone tools, from the deposits known as Member 5. These

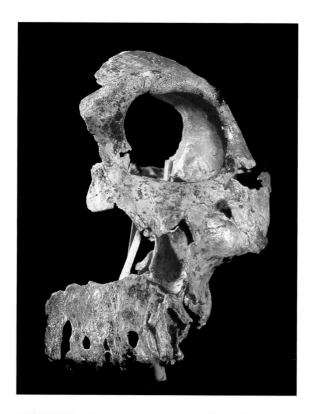

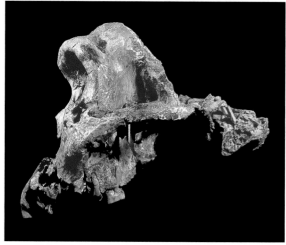

[Figures 40a and b]
The SK 847 cranium, now assigned to the genus *Homo*. Its individual components had earlier been identified as both *Paranthropus* and *Homo*. Photograph by Jeffrey H. Schwartz.

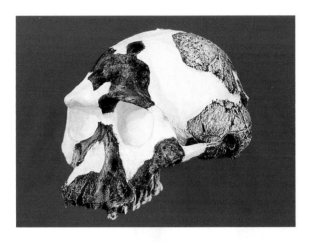 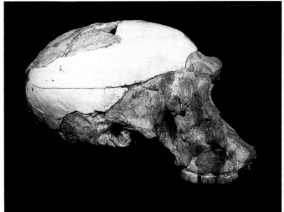

[Figures 41 and 42]
Left: the Stw 53 cranium from Sterkfontein, South Africa. This specimen is highly fragmentary, but has been described as a South African *Homo habilis*. Right: side view of the reconstructed OH 24 cranium from lower Bed I, Olduvai Gorge, also generally referred to *Homo habilis*. Despite these attributions it should be noted that, morphologically, this species is very poorly defined. Photographs by Ron Clarke, and Jeffrey H. Schwartz respectively; courtesy of the National Museum of Tanzania.

sediments, as we've noted, are probably around 1.5 myr old, and thus about a million years younger than the Member 4 deposits that produced *A. africanus*. It was from Member 5 that, in 1976, Alun Hughes reported the recovery of a partial cranium that was given the number StW 53. [Figure 41] The specimen was too incomplete to provide an immediate estimate of brain size, but clearly the cranial capacity had not been notably large. Nonetheless, its describers opted for an allocation to genus *Homo*, and they compared StW 53 closely with Olduvai *H. habilis*. The comparison became even closer later on, when a reconstruction by Ron Clarke came out quite closely resembling his own reconstruction of

OH 24, at least in general proportions. [Figure 42] In the minds of most paleoanthropologists StW 53 thus became a southern African *H. habilis*. It remained fairly evident, though, that the principal underlying reason for classifying the specimen in this way was not morphology, but that it was thought (wrongly, as it turned out) to come from the stone tool-bearing Member 5.

Back to Olduvai

In 1985, Don Johanson and colleagues began fieldwork at Olduvai Gorge, which by then had lain fallow for several years. In the following summer they found the badly fragmented remains of a hominid skeleton, OH 62, in deposits right at the bottom of the Gorge. The specimen was so badly shattered that even after several hundred individual fragments had been recovered it was only possible to reconstruct the palate and parts of the right arm and legs with any accuracy. Still, what was reconstructed turned out to be surprising indeed. The palate, containing several teeth, appeared very similar to that of Stw 53. This, of course, helped to confirm Stw 53 as *H. habilis*, the classic gracile hominid of Olduvai. So far so good. But at the same time the limb bones turned out to be extremely archaically proportioned, with relatively long arms and short legs. Indeed, the body skeleton of the tiny but adult (and presumably female) OH 62, who would have stood only barely over three feet and who would have had to look up into the eyes of the tiny "Lucy," showed more similarities to ape skeletons than did Lucy. This has turned out also to be true of a rather broken-up *Australopithecus africanus* skeleton recently described from South Africa's Sterkfontein; but it was emphatically not what was expected of *H. habilis*. In the event, though, the dental resemblances to Stw 53 won the day for *Homo*.

This complication arose at a time, the mid-1980s, when some paleoanthropologists were beginning to distance themselves from the standard view of *H. habilis* as an intermediate "stage" between *A. africanus* and *H. erectus*. Instead, they were starting to inquire instead whether a variety of hominids might not be present under the umbrella of the catch-all "*habilis*." In 1984, for example, the anatomist Bernard Wood cited evidence for "at least three non-australopithecine taxa" in the early Pleistocene of East Africa. And a couple of years later a careful review by the English paleoanthropologist Chris Stringer found evidence for "at least three Plio-Pleistocene [about 2 myr-old] species of 'early *Homo*'" in eastern Africa. The result of this change in perspective was a subtle shift of emphasis away from the notion of the species *H. habilis* and toward the even vaguer concept of "early *Homo*." To the extent that wastebasket species, such as *H. habilis* had become, are a true impediment to understanding the complexities of the fossil record, this nomenclatural change (for it was nothing more than that) was to be welcomed. But on the other hand, every specimen must belong to a species, and nothing is gained in the long run by evading the problem of to which species individual fossils should be allocated.

Nonetheless, such evasion is undeniably convenient, and in proof of this there has been a recent trend to refer to the most ancient fossils considered to belong to *Homo* simply as "early *Homo*" or "*Homo* sp." Often this is done with the admirable aim of avoiding rushing to judgement in a preliminary publication, for very often such temporary appellations simply stick. But often it becomes simply an excuse for avoiding the tough realities of deciding what the known fossil record actually represents. There is, thus, still no agreed-upon morphological definition for the genus *Homo*. The early *Homo* specimens make a motley assortment. Among them, for instance, is a 2.4-myr-old temporal bone from near Lake Baringo in Kenya that has been referred to *Homo* sp. (though our own examination of this fossil suggests strongly that it is in fact a robust australopith). More securely positioned as a member of *Homo* is a slightly younger (2.33-myr-old) partial palate discovered at Hadar, Ethiopia, in association with crude stone tools. This is the earliest association of a hominid with stone tools recorded from anywhere. Another 2.4-myr-old *Homo* fossil, this time a lower jaw, is known from Uraha, in Malawi, but this one *has* been assigned to a species: *Homo rudolfensis*. We explain below.

Unraveling *Homo habilis*

It was becoming evident by the end of the 1980s that not only had the creation of a new *Homo* species at Olduvai by Louis Leakey and colleagues been justified, but that the one species *H. habilis* was insufficient to accommodate the variety of morphologies that had developed subsequent to the emergence of the genus *Homo* at perhaps 2.5 myr ago. It was clear that it was at last time to grasp the bull by the horns, and to ask what exactly the structure of this complex was. Among the first to respond to this challenge was Bernard Wood, the monographer of the hominids from East Turkana. In broaching the question of *H. habilis*, Wood's initial task was to examine the Olduvai specimens to determine exactly what was present at the Gorge. In the end, he decided that the gracile Bed I and Bed II materials could all be allocated to the single species *H. habilis*—which had to embrace even the archaic OH 62. In contrast, when he compared the large numbers of Turkana fossils with each other, Wood found that he needed at least two species to accommodate the early *Homo* in his sample. Some East Turkana fossils, including the crania 1805 and 1813 (*see* Figures 38 and 39), could be allocated to the Olduvai species, and called *H. habilis*. Others, including 1470, were clearly different. And a

name was already available for this second species: *H. rudolfensis*, based on a species of Pithecanthropus that the Russian anthropologist V. P. Alexeev had created in 1975 to contain the 1470 cranium (*see* Figure 37). This species, like *habilis*, was represented by numerous fragmentary bits of upper and lower jaws. Further, because of its similarity to an East Turkana mandible that Wood had assigned to the same species as 1470, the Uraha fossil from Malawi also received the designation of *H. rudolfensis*.

Associating upper and lower jaws in the absence of positive evidence (such as an articulating skull and mandible) is tricky enough. Where you mostly have nothing but a fragmentary scattering of individual body parts, associating elements of the cranial and body skeletons is even trickier. Furthermore, not very many limb bones are known from East Turkana. But a couple of thighbones are larger and more modern-looking than their counterpart in OH 62, whereas a partial skeleton called KNM ER-3735 is more archaic in proportions, with long arms that recall OH 62. Wood concluded that the evidence of the postcranial bones reinforced the two-species notion he had arrived at on the basis of the cranial fossils. Two early forms of *Homo* were present at East Turkana 1.9 myr ago. One was the small and rather primitive-bodied *H. habilis*. The other was the larger-bodied (and larger-brained) *H. rudolfensis*, with rather more modern body proportions.

Although Wood had been a loyal member of his East Turkana team for many years, Richard Leakey opted for a different interpretation. He saw OH 62 as morphologically distinct from the other gracile Olduvai specimens, which were the true *H. habilis*. Thus there were two kinds of gracile hominid in the Olduvai record at 1.8–1.9 myr ago, just as two kinds were exemplified at East Turkana at that time—but perhaps not the same two. Very confusing. But can we conclude that, at least in East Turkana, we have at this time straightforward evidence of a small, primitively proportioned *H. habilis* and a larger, postcranially more modern *Homo rudolfensis*? Apparently not. Ron Clarke has noted that a recently found Olduvai *H. habilis* palate called OH 64 almost perfectly fits the eroded upper jaw of 1470 from East Turkana. If this match is appropriate, and if OH 64 is indeed properly associated with the OH 7 *H. habilis* type specimens, then it is 1470 among the East Turkana specimens that properly represents *H. habilis*. *Homo rudolfensis* disappears, and instead we must seek another name (or names) for the form represented by OH 62 and the postcranially archaic specimens from East Turkana. Indeed, we must decide whether these fossils are properly classified as *Homo*.

The possibilities are rampant, and practically the only thing that cannot be denied in all of this is that the only two decently preserved and reasonably complete specimens at the center of this debate, ER 1470 and ER 1813, are so dramatically different in morphology that they cannot conceivably belong to the same species. What's more, in light of the fact that 1470 had an impressively large brain and 1813 an almost equally impressively small one, it is tempting to assume that 1470 lies somehow closer to ancestry of later *Homo* than 1813 does. Yet the morphology of the temporal bone, a complex skull component that paleontologists have traditionally found to be highly informative about relationships among mammal species, suggests to us the exact reverse. The temporal mophology of ER 1813 is relatively *Homo*-like, whereas that of ER 1470 remains more like that of a remoter ancestor.

Obviously, we can't solve the conundrum of *H. habilis* and its rivals in this work. Making sense of this mass of fossils will require painstaking and exhaustive restudy of the specimens already known, preferably augmented by the recovery of more complete fossils, especially at Olduvai where work continues. Yet the general pattern is already clear. In the million years or so after the 2.5-myr mark there is no simple linear transition from one species of gracile *Australopithecus* to a successor species of *Homo*. Instead, there is evidence for a period of wild evolutionary experimentation in the hominid family. There is a history of numerous speciations and extinctions, during which competition among a diverse hominid species influenced the future direction of hominid evolution. Elisabeth Vrba suggests that this pattern in the hominid record at about 2.5 myr is a part of a larger "turnover pulse" of mammal species in general, caused by a major climatic cooling and aridification that caused the expansion of open environments at the expense of forests (see below).

We don't know exactly how many hominid species participated in this ferment (although at East Turkana alone, in the period centering on 1.8 myr ago, it's generally agreed that there were at least four). Nor do we have anything resembling a complete idea of what even one of those

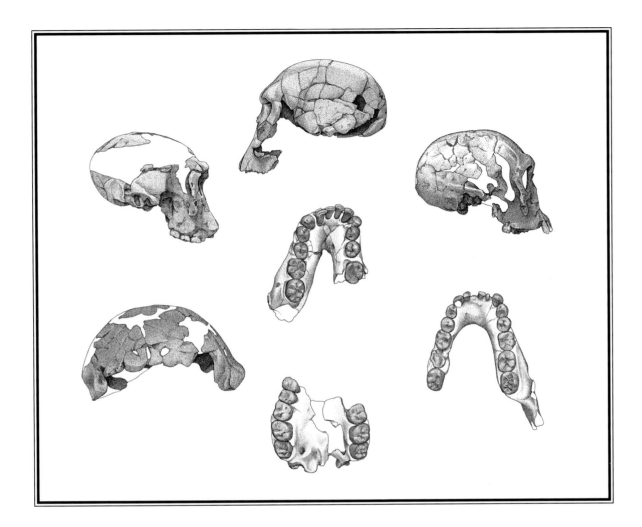

species was like biologically, or of how many of them made and used stone tools. But among all this uncertainty, one thing is dazzlingly clear: once again the evolution of our own lineage, in this crucial period of its emergence, has turned out to be no exception to the pattern of diversity and experimentation that has marked the general history of life. [Figure 43]

[Figure 43]

Some of the many fossils that have at one time or another been ascribed to *Homo habilis*. They make a rather odd assortment, with a variety of morphologies and brain sizes. The type mandible OH 7 from Olduvai Gorge is in the center; clockwise from center top are KNM-ER 1470 and KNM-ER 1813 from northern Kenya, the mandible and maxilla of the paratype OH 13 from Olduvai; and the partial crania OH 16 and OH 24 from Olduvai. The most distinctive of these specimens is ER 1470, which most paleoanthropologists would nowadays allocate to the species *Homo rudolfensis*—ironically, since it was this specimen more than any other that finally convinced scientists that *Homo habilis* was a real biological entity. Drawings by Don McGranaghan.

The Influence of Climate

Humans are tropical animals. Our birthplace was the continent of Africa, and the first three-fifths at least of the evolution of the human family took place solely there. Early on in the history of geology it was recognized that the landscape of Europe had been scoured by glaciers in the not too distant past, and that at such times the climate had been substantially colder than it is now. From these observations was developed the notion of the Ice Ages (more technically known as the Pleistocene geological epoch). This was a period, beginning about 1.8 myr ago, during which ice sheets waxed and waned as northern climates shuttled between the severely cold and the temperate. In contrast, however, it was assumed until quite recently that tropical climates had remained much more stable than this, providing a more consistent ecological arena for human evolution. This assumption, it turns out, is wrong.

Some of the best evidence for major climatic vicissitudes on the African continent comes from studies of the fossil animals that lived there. This is because climate change is tracked closely by the vegetation cover, which in turn determines which animal species will live happily in a particular region. Any major environmental oscillation will thus rapidly be reflected in the fossil record as a change in the animal species represented at a given locality. In this way, at around 5 myr ago, the African fauna began to take on the aspect familiar today: an event that that took place in concert with a worldwide episode of drying and cooling that saw forests contract while grasslands grew. It is highly unlikely to be coincidental that it was probably at about this time that bipedal hominids first began to move out of the deep forests into the woodlands at their fringes. And many paleoanthropologists agree with Vrba in considering it significant that at about 2.5 myr ago, when the first forms called *Homo* show up in the fossil record, another major faunal change is also recorded. In this dramatic event, forest antelopes became rare (some 29 species at least became extinct in the 2.8–2.5 myr period), to be replaced in fossil faunas by antelope species that specialized on open grasslands. Although the details are debated, it is clear that around this time an increase in aridity and seasonality of rainfall converted a substantial proportion of Africa's remaining forests to grassland—although true open Serengeti-style savannas still lay in the future. What might have propelled this change?

As it happens, geological studies in the northern hemisphere indicate that a major polar glaciation was beginning at almost exactly this time. As the ice cap expanded, it finally reached the Atlantic shores, where its extremities calved off in the form of icebergs. Cores taken from the seafloor sediments of the central North Atlantic ocean are witnesses to this event. Normally, seafloor deposits laid down far out in the ocean contain only fine clays, derived from windborne dust. But some Atlantic cores oddly contain coarse, heavy sand grains. How did they get to the middle of the ocean? One sole mechanism is known. The sands can only have been dropped where they were found by melting icebergs, as those ice islands finally relinquished the sediment load they had accumulated while grinding across the continent on their way to the sea. The earliest such sand grains have been dated to almost exactly 2.5 myr ago, and they announce the beginning of a series of glacial cycles that has continued up to the present. Over the past 2 myr or so, powered by variations in Earth's orbit that have affected the planet's uptake of energy from the Sun, climates have swung from maximally cold (glacial) to maximally warm (interglacial, as now) at intervals that have latterly stabilized at about 100 kyr. Along with swings in mean annual temperatures went variations in humidity and other factors, and it is important as well to bear in mind that transitions between colder and warmer conditions were not smooth. For there were numerous minor oscillations within each major climatic cycle.

The inauguration of the Ice Ages thus ushered in a period of unsettled climates and ecologies, worldwide. Not only did this process produce a constant stream of ecological changes locally, but it profoundly affected world geography. During cold times, when much of the world's water became "locked up" in expanding polar and mountain ice sheets, sea levels dropped. Land was exposed along the continental edges, and what had previously been islands were joined to the continent. Conversely, in warmer periods sea levels rose, cutting off what had been contiguous land masses. At the same time, the process of warming and cooling moved vegetation zones up mountains and down, respectively, creating and removing ecological barriers. Such processes inevitably involved the isolation and recoalescence of small populations of animals, including hominids. And both of these phenomena are essential ingredients in the evolutionary process.

Because of the "genetic inertia" of large interbreeding populations, evolutionary novelties become properly established only in small isolated populations. And it is, in turn, competition between species with similar ecological requirements but small differences that gives rise to some of the larger-scale patterns that we see in the evolutionary record. Putting all these considerations together it is easy to see that, in the entire four-billion-year history of life on Earth, conditions must rarely have been more propitious for evolutionary innovation and diversification than they have been since the beginning of the Ice Ages. Turnover pulses and similar theories are dramatic reminders that Earth's climatic system is an integrated whole, and that hominids are—or have been until very recently—integral parts of the larger ecosystems in which they have lived.

Early Toolmakers

The earliest stone tools inaugurate the archaeological record in eastern Africa at about 2.5 myr ago, almost exactly as we begin to find the earliest fossils generally accepted—not, as we've seen, always for the best of reasons—as *Homo.* Unfortunately, the 2.33-myr-old association at Hadar of a very fragmentary early *Homo* palate with stone tools is the only such co-occurrence yet known in the first half-million years or more of stone tool manufacture. Given the poor definition of species in the early *Homo* record, the upshot is that we have absolutely no idea exactly *who* made the first stone tools, even in terms of that hominid's most general physical attributes. Cognitively, however, the story is different; for although the first stone tools themselves are rather crude and superficially unimpressive, making them was actually a fairly complex business.

Broadly speaking, the earliest stone tools are classified as "Oldowan," for Olduvai Gorge whence implements of this kind were first described. Oldowan implements consist of small cobbles and simple flakes struck from them using a hammerstone. [Figure 44] Early on it was believed that the primary implements were the "shaped" cobbles. However, experiments have shown that although such "cores" may have been used for various purposes, the toolmaker's object was principally to obtain the sharp flakes. A tiny flake an inch or two long may seem like a pretty rudimentary tool. But when made out of a suitable material, flakes of this kind bear very sharp and durable edges and make remarkably functional implements. Indeed, experimental archaeologists have butchered entire elephants using nothing more elaborate.

With fuller knowledge, it is quite common nowadays for paleoanthropologists to describe the australopiths as "bipedal apes." This is probably not too inaccurate, although the lack of an associated archaeological record leaves us with few ways of assessing their behavior directly. And apes have trouble making stone tools, as

experiments with a young bonobo called Kanzi have shown. After Kanzi gained some fame as a star in communications experiments, the archaeologists Nick Toth and Kathy Schick conscripted him as a student of stone toolmaking, and frankly didn't get very far even after intensive coaching. To obtain a sharp flake you first have to choose a cobble of the right type, and then you have to hit this core with your hammerstone hard, and at precisely the right angle. It takes a fair bit of cognitive sophistication to figure all this out, and even after repeated demonstrations over many months, Kanzi never really got the idea. Regardless of who made the first stone tool, and what these toolmakers looked like, they were showing cognitive abilities way beyond those of apes purely through the act of making tools. An increased sophistication is reflected in other aspects of their behavior, as well. For the record indicates strongly that early stone toolmaking was not simply an opportunistic process, carried out as necessity demanded. The Oldowan toolmakers not only knew how to identify the kinds of stone that would produce sharp flakes when struck, but they also anticipated needing those flakes, and carried cobbles of the appropriate kind quite long distances before making them into tools as required. Such planning and foresight

---

[Figure 44]

An Oldowan "core" tool made from volcanic rock. More commonly used as cutting tools were the small sharp flakes detached by sharp blows from such cores. In the background is glimpsed the Hadar, Ethiopia, landscape in which many such implements have been found. Photograph courtesy of Institute of Human Origins.

goes well beyond anything yet observed or inferred among living apes, even those that use rudimentary tools (stones for cracking nuts, twigs for "fishing" termites, etc).

So we know that, whatever they looked like, in reasoning power the earliest toolmakers had advanced well beyond the "bipedal apes" from which they were descended. What can we say about their lives? The sites at which Oldowan tools are found are simple. They are merely points on the ancient landscape at which there is evidence of early human activity, mainly in the form of the stone tools themselves, and of animal bones that show traces of cutting and bashing. And although cutmarks on mammal bones are clear evidence that animals were butchered by hominids, it is remarkably difficult to say much beyond this with any confidence. Were the toolmakers hunters, or did they simply scavenge the remains of animals that had died natural deaths or were killed by predators? Archaeologists used to favor the idea that the early toolmakers had hunted small- and medium-bodied mammals, using guile to compensate for their slowness and small body size. And indeed, in view of the fact that some populations of chimpanzees, at least, are known to indulge in cooperative hunting of small mammals such as monkeys or young bushpigs, it does seem likely that some hunting of small prey was carried out not only by the first toolmakers, but by their predecessors as well. Nonetheless, archaeologists nowadays tend to doubt that hunting was a significant component of the early hominid behavioral repertoire, Much more likely, most butchered skeletons

represent the results of scavenging activities, especially because many of them are the remains of rather large animals. Whatever the case, the frequency on the landscape of sites where cut bones and stone tools occur together strongly suggests that the processing of animal carcasses was a common behavior, even an habitual one, among early *Homo*.

Most early archaeological sites are associated with grassland and woodland habitats. Such exposed environments would, of course, have been dangerous places for relatively slow, small-bodied and vulnerable primates such as the first toolmakers. And this would have been especially true in the vicinity of animal carcasses, which invariably attract the avid attention of predators and scavengers of all kinds. It is no easy task competing with lions and hyenas for juicy animal remains, and this may in fact account for the unexpectedly high proportion of limb bones often found at stone tool sites. It seems very likely that, acutely aware of the hazards they faced away from the forest, the early toolmakers took advantage of their newfound ability to cut through tendons and ligaments to rapidly detach limbs from carcasses encountered at random spots on the savanna. These body parts could then be carried to safer places, often revisited, for further processing and consumption. One reason to conclude that carcasses thus dismembered were generally scavenged rather than hunted is found in the hominids' treatment of such bones. The shafts of limb bones show an unusual kind of fracture when pounded with rocks. Such fracturing exposes the fat-rich marrow, which would not only have been a valuable nutritive resource for the early hominids, but was also the one most likely to have been left behind once large predators and scavengers with preferential access had removed the internal organs and flesh.

It would, of course, be a mistake to assume that, simply because of their newfound cutting and pounding capacity, the diet of the early toolmakers became one centered on animal protein. The overwhelming probability is that these hominids were opportunistic foragers who roamed the landscape in small groups of perhaps a dozen individuals, and who probably rarely strayed very far from the woodlands and forest fringes and out on to the open savanna. On their wanderings they would have encountered many different sources of vegetable foods, such as berries, fruits, seeds, tubers, and so forth. Indeed, it is virtually certain that such foods contributed the bulk of their diet. They probably exploited carcasses simply as and when they encountered them, although it seems very likely that as time passed they became expert at reading indirect signs of where carcasses lay, such as vultures wheeling in the air above. The very earliest of the toolmakers, although of course bipedal when on the ground, unquestionably retained quite archaic body proportions, with relatively long arms and short legs, narrow shoulders, and long extremities. These attributes would have lent them facility in the trees, in which they are very likely to have foraged and sheltered at night, just as their forebears had done. Poised between forest and savanna, this lifestyle clearly had major advantages, for it was a stable adaptation that had endured for millions of years before the invention of toolmaking, and continued for a long time after. It was, evidently, a lifestyle that was only modestly disturbed by the invention of stone tools, although this innovation would radically influence later human evolution. This should not surprise us, for any innovation has to take place within a pre-existing species, since there's no other place it can do so.

Significantly, it is only coincident with the 1.8-myr climatic shock, which yet further reduced the amount of forest (and, probably more importantly, forest fringes) in Africa, that hominids of essentially modern body form finally appeared. These were beings who were truly emancipated from the woodlands, and were at home far out on the pitilessly sun-drenched savanna.

The mystery of *H. habilis* thus persists. The ancestry of later hominids is presumably represented somewhere within the large and miscellaneous aggregation of fossils that have at one time or another been called *H. habilis*. But for the time being there is no agreement on exactly how many hominid species are included in this assemblage. Indeed, we don't even know how many major hominid body plans existed at this crucial juncture, when our ancestors were leaving the forest fringes. One thing is clear, however. Sorting out this mess (and we make no apologies for the term) to everyone's satisfaction is very unlikely to occur as long as linear notions of human evolution linger in paleoanthropology.

CHAPTER 5

The Emergence of the Modern Body

The Emergence of the Modern Body

East Side Story

For some years now, Yves Coppens, France's most renowned paleoanthropologist—who is so famous that he is even a character in a popular cartoon strip—has taken great pleasure in publicly lecturing on his pet scheme concerning the diversification of early hominid species. A superb raconteur, who can word play as well in English as in his native French, Coppens entitled his theory "East Side Story" to capture what he envisioned as the important events in human evolution that occurred in East Africa during the Pliocene, the geological epoch that lasted from about 5.5 to 1.8 myr, and the Pleistocene, which spanned the period of 1.8 myr to about 10 kya. But it is quite likely premature to root an entire theory of human origins on the specimens that have emerged from one region of the world. What happens, as it did, when an unexpected fossil is found in a totally unexpected locale? This is precisely the case with the recent discovery 2500 kilometers to the west, in Chad, of an enigmatic jaw of a hominid attributed by none other than Coppens and colleagues to *Australopithecus bahrelghazali.* Is it now "West Side Story"? And if this kind of speculation is dubious, it is even more problematic to allocate specimens from one part of the world to the same species as specimens

from almost halfway around the world not because of what they look like, but because of their contemporaneity. However, this is exactly what has happened in the case of specimens from Asia that were the first-discovered representatives of the species *Homo erectus,* and later-discovered specimens from East Africa of apparently similar age. But what else would you expect given the stranglehold that Mayr and Dobzhansky's pronouncements of a single-evolving human lineage had on paleoanthropology, wherein the only players are *Australopithecus, Homo habilis, Homo erectus,* and *Homo sapiens*? Even with increasing acceptance of diversity during human evolution being the rule rather than the exception, it is hard to shake off long-held traditions.

When East Meets the Far East

By 1975, the paleoanthropological world had probably been exposed to as much new discovery as it could bear. What with multiple species of *Australopithecus,* plus *H. habilis, H. erectus,* and all the differently configured specimens (not just Neanderthals and extant humans) that been crammed into the species *H. sapiens,* it was getting harder and harder to keep the idea of a single evolving lineage alive. Even, however, with grudging acceptance of the possibility of some diversity early on in human evolution, there was still pretty much a consensus that, at least within the genus *Homo*, there was a continuum proceeding from *H. habilis* to *H. erectus* to *H. sapiens*. But, then, in 1975, one of Richard Leakey's "hominid gang" of fossil hunters, Bernard Ngeneo, discovered the skull of a hominid that would be only the tip of the iceberg of what lay in store for paleoanthropology. This particular skull, KNM-ER 3733, was pretty complete, missing parts of the face and, unfortunately, all but one molar tooth. But it was unexpectedly very fragile because, although the skull itself was relatively quite large and had a rather massive face and protrusive brow ridges, the bone itself, at least of the face, was quite thin. The bone of the brain case turned out to be thin, too, but originally you couldn't tell, because the whole thing had been filled to the brim of the foramen magnum with the hardest matrix imaginable. Even Alan Walker's chiseling didn't make a dent, at first. But after several tries, with different chisels, Walker split the skull open, which made it possible for him to clean out the interior of the brain case and then glue it back together. [Figure 45]

At 1.8 myr old, 3733 took many people by surprise. For those who had dearly held onto the single-species hypothesis there was a lot of backpedaling to do, because this specimen was unquestionably contemporaneous with specimens of *Paranthropus boisei* from many East African sites, including the same area of East Turkana. It was also a bit of a surprise because it could more easily be embraced by various paleoanthropologists, including Walker, as a representative of *Homo* than could the other non-*boisei* specimens—such as 1470—that the East Turkanan deposits had yielded just a few years earlier. So, what to do with it?

Although it seemed pretty obvious to us from the beginning that this is a great specimen of noteworthy and distinctive morphology, such was not the general conclusion among paleoanthropologists. When Alan Walker sat down with the specimen to clean it and then take notes on it for publication with Richard Leakey, he thought it looked like the cast of the "Peking Man" (actually "Peking Woman") skull, representative of Chinese *H. erectus*, that the German paleoanthropologist Franz Weidenreich had put together from various bits and pieces from the Zhoukoudian site. As we now know, however, and discuss in the next chapter, it is possible to make a more realistic reconstruction of what Peking Man may have looked like cranially. But putting this point aside for the moment, beyond vaguely general similarities of skull shape, there weren't any particular details that Walker cited as unique to 3733 and the Chinese *H. erectus* as reconstructed by Weidenreich— just a sense that the two might represent different versions of the same thing.

More than two decades after Walker and Leakey's description of 3733, another paleoanthropologist, Philip Rightmire of the State University of New York at Binghamton, produced an article in which he reiterated the conclusion that there is no reason to regard this specimen as belonging to a species other than *H. erectus*. In this study, Rightmire's *H. erectus*

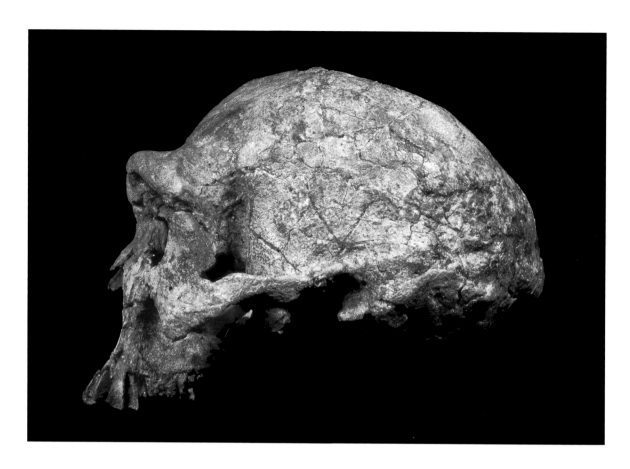

[Figures 45 and 46]

Although various paleoanthropologists have lumped KNM-ER 3733 from Kenya (above) and Sangiran 17 (right) from Java (right) together in *Homo erectus*, their morphology suggests to us that the two specimens represent different species. To be sure, the lower face of Sangiran 17 has been crushed upward, compressing the nasal opening, but it is clear that there are real differences between the two, such as in the configuration of the brow, the shape and orientation of the cheek bone, the size and shape of the eye sockets, the verticality and length of the lower face, and overall face-to-cranial vault proportions and orientation. Photographs by Jeffrey H. Schwartz; courtesy of National Museums of Kenya.

of comparison was one of the Javanese specimens, which would make sense as the first specimen of *H. erectus* did come from Java.

Unfortunately, Rightmire's specimen of choice—Sangiran 17—was squashed a bit during fossilization, which resulted in the upper jaw being pushed into the nasal region. In addition to shortening the face, this produced a nasal opening that is so tiny that it's hard to imagine how the individual would have breathed had it really looked this way in life. Nevertheless, Rightmire's measurements and statistical analysis pointed to this specimen and 3733 being similar in various ways. And, because *H. erectus* is *the* hominid of Java, it seemed a reasonable conclusion that the East African specimen represented this species, too. [Figure 46]

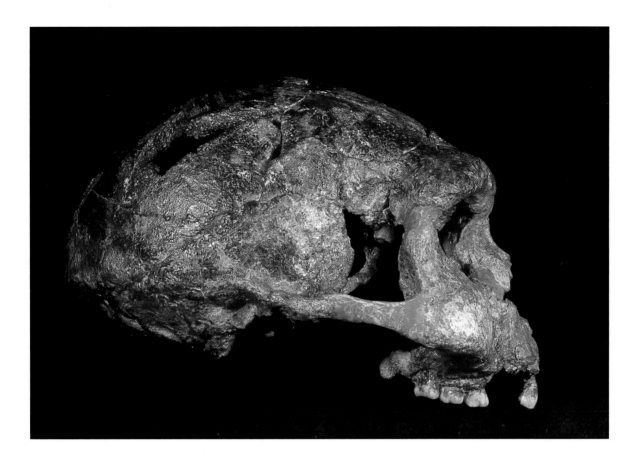

The general resemblances between 3733 and various Asian fossils aside, are there easily recognizable similarities between 3733 and *H. erectus*—a species that, as we'll see in the next chapter, has an almost iconic significance for paleoanthropologists? Well, it's hard to make exhaustive comparisons because most *erectus* specimens from Java, including and importantly the type specimen that Eugene Dubois discovered, lack the face. The only relatively complete specimen is the one from Sangiran—Sangiran 17—that Rightmire chose. But, to us, this specimen differs markedly from 3733 in many features. [Figures 47 and 48] For

instance, the brow ridge of Sangiran 17 is thick, forwardly and downwardly prominent, and is almost straight across. The brow of 3733 is thin, arced above the orbits, and upwardly and forwardly protrusive. The cheek bone of Sangiran 17 is forwardly placed and puffed outward. In 3733 it is angled back and down, and set back. The eye sockets of Sangiran 17 are small and almost rectangular, in contrast to the large and almost round orbits of 3733. And the overall cranial profile of Sangiran 17 is long and low, whereas the forehead rises sharply in 3733. Because of crushing during fossilization of the Sangiran specimen we can't compare the nasal

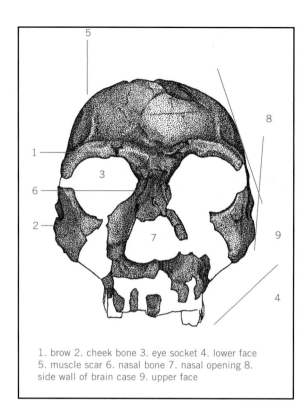

1. brow 2. cheek bone 3. eye socket 4. lower face
5. muscle scar 6. nasal bone 7. nasal opening 8.
side wall of brain case 9. upper face

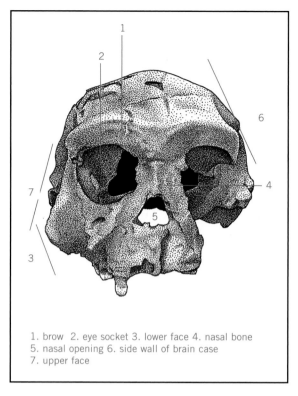

1. brow 2. eye socket 3. lower face 4. nasal bone
5. nasal opening 6. side wall of brain case
7. upper face

[Figures 47 and 48]

From the front, differences between KNM-ER 3733 I(left) and Sangiran 17 (right) are seen in the shapes and orientations of the brow, cheek bone, and lower face, the size and positioning of the eye sockets, the degree of development and course of muscle scars, the verticality or slope of the sidewall of the brain case, and the overall shape and elevation of the brain case. Although the nasal opening of Sangiran 17 was compressed upward during fossilization, it would probably have been smaller than in KNM-ER 3733. Drawings by Don McGranaghan.

regions, but the lower face is preserved and even that is different in the Javanese specimen: it is quite long and bowed outward, in contrast to 3733 in which it is short and almost vertical. Although a modern human skull might turn up with one or other of the configurations of forehead of Sangiran 17 or 3733, or of the cheek bone of 3733, we've yet to come across any human that has all of the features of one of these fossil specimens. Modern humans may be variable in their features, but so are the members of any species.

Despite such manifest anatomical differences, however, for some paleoanthropologists the "case" for regarding 3733 as merely a variant of Asian *Homo erectus* has been cemented by recent redating of some Javanese specimens. If these results are to be believed, some of the Javanese *erectus* date to over 1.7 myr. As far as geological dating goes, this is close enough to the 1.8 myr date of 3733 for these specimens to be considered contemporaneous. And as contemporaries, according to tradition, this makes

3733 and Asian *erectus* taxonomic bedfellows, regardless of what they looked like and the fact that they existed almost half a world apart from one another.

Another East African *Homo erectus*?

Almost 10 years after the discovery of 3733, the leader of Richard Leakey's hominid gang, Kamoya Kimeu, took himself out for one last survey of the area around the site at which he and his group had been camped at Nariokotome, on the east side of Lake Turkana. The search for fossils there had been relatively good for vertebrates in general, but not for hominids. Before moving on to a different locale, Kamoya thought he'd check out an area that hadn't been scrutinized, primarily because it was where no one expected to find anything. There were lots of black lava pebbles and organic debris. This landscape did not provide the kind of surface where paleontologists are accustomed to finding fossils. Usually fossils are found in badlands where the weather exposes and eventually erodes them out of the rocks.

But it not for nothing was Kamoya the head of his illustrious group. Almost immediately upon reaching this unpromising patch, he found a small fragment of a hominid's skull. After being contacted by Kamoya, Leakey and Alan Walker flew up to the site from Nairobi to pitch in on the search for more fragments of hominid. Little did anyone know that, by the time they'd finish at Nariokotome in 1988, they would collect more parts of any pre-Neanderthal skeleton than had ever been known before, the Lucy skeleton included. And, fortunately, this time, Leakey and Walker would finally come up the skeleton of a basically healthy individual.

A few years before, the hominid gang had found another skeleton of what was called *Homo erectus*. But this skeleton showed signs of a disease that thickened the walls of its bones. Walker thought that it might have been a case of too much vitamin A, which is crucial to normal bone development. Walker even speculated that the source of too much vitamin A, or avitaminosis A, was liver. Perhaps, he wondered, had this individual been special in some way? For, in various human societies, such as the Inuits, the leaders, or others deemed important, get first dibs on the best parts of the kill. And the liver is one of the most sought-after parts of an animal. Unfortunately, because liver is high in vitamin A, too much of a good thing can be bad for your bones. And this, Walker suggested, was the case with this particular individual.

On the basis of a few cranial fragments, Walker immediately concluded that he was on the trail of *Homo erectus*. Just from looking at the brow region when the relevant pieces of the skull were discovered, Walker was convinced that this was a *H. erectus*. As he and his wife, Pat Shipman, described it, what impressed him the most were the brow ridges. They were large, and large size also characterizes specimens of Asian *H. erectus*. When the geophysicist Ian MacDougall and the geologists Frank Brown and Craig Feibel completed the dating and stratigraphic analyses, and came in with an age of older than 1.5 myr, which is not much younger than 1.7 mya *H. erectus* from Java, the fate of the Nariokotome specimen seemed to be sealed: what else could it have been if it wasn't *H. erectus*? What else existed during this time period that was not an australopith or *H. habilis*? Although it is truly remarkable just how much of a single individual's skeleton could be recovered, this amazing find also presented a dilemma because, *H. erectus* or not, most of it couldn't be compared with anything else closely related to it because the comparable parts weren't known!

When, in the 1890s, Eugene Dubois concluded that all of the specimens that he had excavated from the site of Trinil in Java represented the same species, *Anthropopithecus erectus* (which later he changed to *Pithecanthropus erectus*, which later Ernst Mayr and others lumped into *Homo erectus*), he had two molar teeth, one premolar, one skull cap, and a bunch of femurs, of which only one was complete from top to bottom. Since then, with the dozens of specimens of *Homo erectus* uncovered in the fields near the city of Solo, only two (of which Sangiran 17 is the most widely known—we haven't yet been able to see the second skull but have plans to do so within the year) were preserved with their faces still attached to the skull cap. Otherwise, there are in essence only skull caps, some pieces of jaw, and numerous isolated teeth.

Although facial fragments were excavated from the Chinese *Homo erectus* site of Zhoukoudian along with skull caps, parts of mandibles, and isolated teeth (though we've recently discovered that many of these supposed hominid teeth are actually the teeth of extinct orangutans and some others are from pandas), the originals were all lost during the Sino-Japanese war. Despite the survival of casts that were made by Franz Weidenreich, detail that can only be discerned in original specimens is gone forever. And that is what we have in terms of fossils to compare with the Nariokotome specimen: a lot of skull caps, various fragmented skulls and jaws, a number of isolated teeth, and one intact femur. The other complicating factor is that the Nariokotome individual was a juvenile when it died. This means that most of the features of the fossilized skeleton might have changed in some way had the individual continued to grow and mature physically. This doesn't mean that the Nariokotome juvenile would have been transformed to look like something entirely different. That's pushing too far the old-fashioned physical anthropologist's saw of form following function—that, almost in Lamarckian fashion, an individual can totally transform itself by what it's doing or eating. Any systematist worth her or his salt knows that many of an individual's species-specific features are established early on in life. Thus, growth changes in the Nariokotome juvenile would mostly have involved the exaggeration of those characteristics that were already there by the time of death. Any similarities or dissimilarities between this specimen and others have to be evaluated with this fact in mind.

A Glimpse at the Life History of the Nariokotome Youth

As it aged, the Nariokotome youth would have kept growing. [Figure 49] You can tell this by looking at the ends of the long tubular bones of the limbs. At birth, every mammal has a plate of cartilage separating the ends of each long bone from the main shaft of the bone. Longitudinal growth takes place at the region of this cartilaginous plate. Growth ceases when these ends fuse to the shaft. Sometimes abnormal amounts of growth hormone prevent the ends from fusing to the shaft, in which case an individual will grow to become a giant. In other instances, insufficient amounts of growth hormone will cause the ends of the bones to fuse at too early an age. The result is a midget. If the ends fuse at the correct time, but growth hormone is again produced afterward, the only way the bones can grow is in girth. Broad hands, feet, and cheek bones, and a protruding "lantern" jaw, are signs of this anomalous condition. Fortunately, all indications are that the Nariokotome individual was basically a normal, growing individual when it died. And it still had

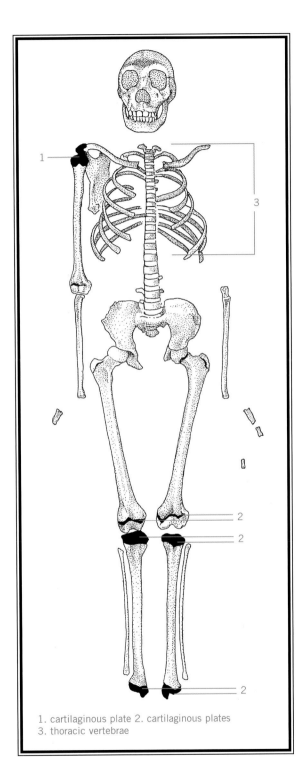

1. cartilaginous plate 2. cartilaginous plates
3. thoracic vertebrae

[Figure 49]

The Nariokotome boy, KNM-WT 15000, died before his skeleton had reached its full size, as is indicated by the fact that the ends of many of the long bones of the arms and legs were still not fused to the shafts of these bones. Plates of cartilage, represented in black in the reconstruction, would have separated the ends of long bones from their shafts. The small size of the Nariokotome boy's vertebral canals, through which the spinal cord had passed along the back, suggests that, even though the areas of his brain associated with speech were probably developed, the nerves necessary for intricate patterns of breathing were not. Complex sound production in human speech depends on subtleties of breathing. Drawing by Diana Salles.

some way to go before it would have been deemed an adult skeletally.

Similarly, one can tell if an individual has reached skeletal adulthood by looking at the sutures between the platelike bones of the brain case. In adult mammals, cranial sutures close up and coalesce after brain growth has ceased. But they were still pretty open when the Nariokotome individual died, from whatever causes. It's unlikely that we will ever know the exact cause of death because such evidence rarely ends up being recorded in the bones. This may seem odd, because there is a tendency to think that the crummier the bones look, the more they will have been ravaged by a lifetime of disease and damage. But it's actually the other way around. An individual whose skeleton has the scars of having lived obviously survived these assaults. Most of the serious things—such as a lethal virus, food poisoning, a wound to soft tissue and organs—leave no clues about themselves. Basically, it's cancers, such as primary bone cancer or secondary cancers from breast or prostate cancer, that let you live long enough to leave their marks on bone before they kill you. So, if you find a "clean" skeleton, such as the Nariokotome individual's, its fatal condition had killed it before the bones had become involved.

The teeth, too, gave clues as to the age of the Nariokotome individual. In humans, the last teeth to erupt in the jaws are the wisdom teeth, or third molars, and the second-to-last teeth to erupt are the second molars. In apes, the last teeth to erupt are the canines, and, especially in males, the upper canines. In the case of the Nariokotome youth, both the canines and second molars had erupted, but not the third molars. In the olden days, direct comparisons with humans would have been made to determine the age of this individual at death—as Raymond Dart had done in aging the Taung child. But we now know that this is not an appropriate form of comparison.

So, how old was this individual at death? We'll never really know, but the dental anthropologist Holly Smith, enlisted by Alan Walker to tackle this problem, calculated an age-at-death of perhaps 9 or 9.5 years, 11 years at most. If this had been a modern human, the teeth alone would have yielded an average age of 12 years, because that's when the second molar often erupts in this hominid. We can't, however, assume that other hominids had the same rates of growth. After crunching the data in various ways, Smith concluded that the Nariokotome youth had the growth rate neither of a chimpanzee, in which the teeth erupt at much earlier ages, nor of a modern human. Its growth rate was somewhere in the middle. It had matured more rapidly than a modern human, but not as rapidly as a chimpanzee. So, at 9 or so years, this youth was actually equivalent in terms of its predicted life span to a 12- or 13-year-old modern human. Clearly, the extrapolation is that its life span would have been shorter than a living human's, but certainly longer than an ape's.

Walker asked his Johns Hopkins colleague, Chris Ruff, who had already established himself as an expert in this line of reconstructive research, to help determine the Nariokotome youth's height and weight. Surprisingly, Ruff's estimation of height came out at around 5 feet, 4 inches. Not too tall, you think? Remember, however, this is supposed to be a 9-year-old individual. Ruff's prediction of the Nariokotome youth's stature at maturity was 6 feet, 1 inch, with a possible range of 5'10" to 6'4." But at his tender age the youth would not have been very heavy: perhaps 106 pounds, increasing to maybe 150 pounds in adulthood. Tall and lanky would be the description—just the kind of body build you see in people of desertic countries people, such as the Dinka from the Sudan and the Turkana and Masai from Kenya. In these folks, the great surface area of skin afforded by being tall and thin plays a critical role in the dissipation of body heat. The opposite is true of cold-dwelling individuals, such as the Arctic Inuits, who are short and stocky. Their great body volume and minimized surface area act to reduce the loss of body heat. Although any generalizations about body sizes and volumes are relevant to the discussion of adapting to different climates—the same conditions hold true for other animals, such as Arctic versus Saharan hares—they shouldn't be taken as indicating anything about evolutionary relationships.

Could it then be, as Walker concluded at one point, that some of the features of the Nariokotome individual were specific adaptations to hot and arid environmental conditions? After all, East Africa had been becoming more savanna-like. Or alternatively, as Walker suggested at another time, was the Nariokotome youth's height and lankiness representative of *H. erectus* in general? For, after comparing the femur of the Nariokotome youth with casts of the less complete *Homo erectus* femurs that Dubois had found, Walker concluded that all of the femurs had been of broadly similar length. However, the problem here is that conclusions of this kind can only be reached after you have shown that all of the specimens involved are from individuals of the same species. Otherwise, all you've demonstrated is that two or more different species have pretty much the same femur length. And because femur length, just like any other metrical comparison, doesn't capture the morphology of the structure, it shouldn't be used as primary evidence in allocating specimens to one species or another. Otherwise, for example, one might actually conclude that short humans and tall humans belonged to different species. When push came to shove, Walker came down on the side of the Nariokotome youth's being a hot climate-adapted hominid.

On the basis of the reconstructed height and build of the Nariokotome youth, Walker and Ruff concluded that, because the youth was adapted to tropical conditions, this individual had sweated like a modern human. This indicated that he (yes, the individual was believed to have been male, based on the shapes of some parts of the pelvis—assuming that the same criteria used to sex the skeletons of modern humans had obtained 1.5 myr ago) had been less hairy, probably by a lot, than any previous hominid. And because this youth had lacked a coat of hair, he probably had dark skin, because dark pigmentation is believed to be a protective adaptation against the harsh rays of the sun.

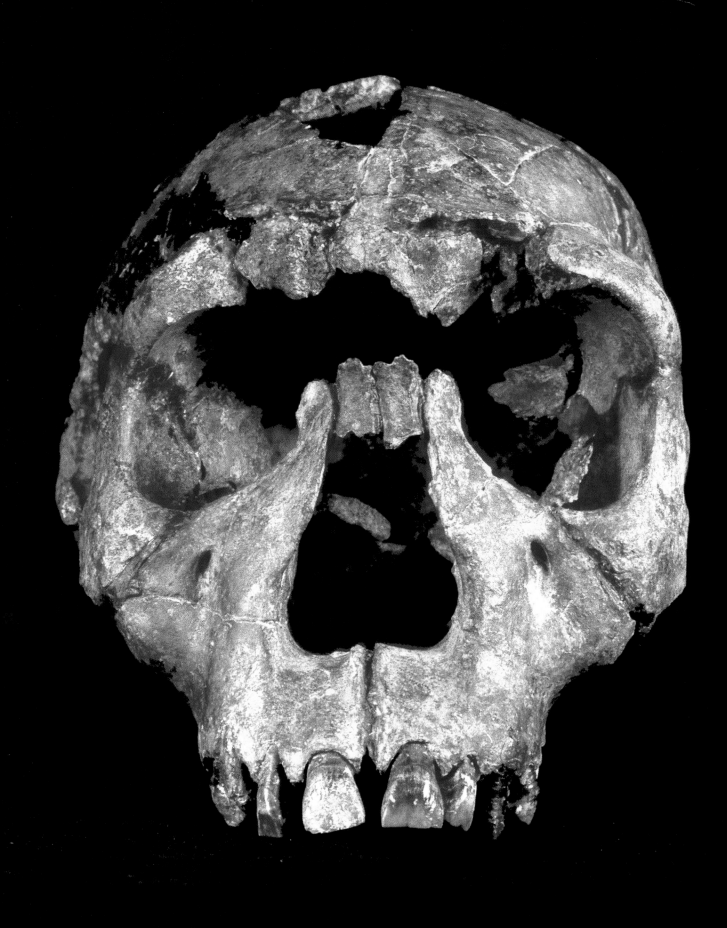

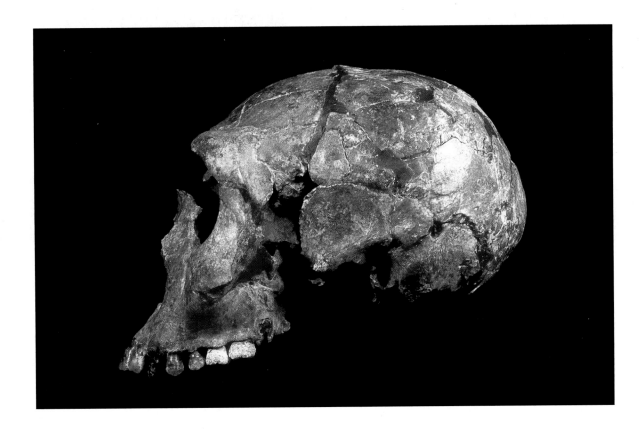

Back in 1970 Ron Clarke and colleagues had pointed out that the nasal region of SK 847 was quite prominent, and now Walker noted that the Nariokotone youth probably also had a projecting, human-type nose, because his nasal bones actually stood a bit away from the plane of the face. [Figures 50a and b] In apes, aus-tralopiths, and *H. habilis*, the nasal bones lie in the same plane as the facial region. As seen in living apes, this means that the fleshy nose is low on the face and the nostrils lie right at the front edge of the nasal cavity. But a projecting fleshy nose would put some distance between the nasal cavity and the portals through which incoming and outgoing air would travel. And, from the point of view of respiratory function, this projecting nose would mean that there would be a greater expanse of mucous mem-brane present in the nasal region. As Walker and others suggested, mucous membranes serve the functions of both heat and moisture exchange. *Homo erectus* (as represented by the

Nariokotome youth), had thus acquired a heat and moisture-capturing nasal region! It is interesting that the 3733 skull that we discussed at the very beginning of this chapter also had projecting nasal bones—more projecting than in the Nariokotome youth. (*see* Figure 45) And if 3733 is not *H. erectus*, then we're looking at a feature that evolved in another hominid, who had lived at a different time and perhaps in a different place and environmental situation, and who had preceded all other hominids with projecting noses.

For all of its presumed adaptations, the Nariokotome youth, although obviously capable of making sounds, apparently could not engage in articulate speech as we know or conceive of it. At least this is what is suggested by Ann MacLarnon's ingenious study of the vertebral column and the bony canal through which the spinal cord passes as it courses from the skull down to the end of the sacrum. The larger the canal, the larger the spinal cord, and the greater the number of nerve fibers that can emanate from it to service muscles in the nearby regions. It was by such reasoning, for instance, that the primate anatomist Friederun Ankel-Simons, who studied the size of this canal in a variety of primates, concluded that an approximately 18-myr-old Miocene fossil from Europe that was supposed to be related to the large-bodied apes, had actually possessed a tail. The spinal cord canal on this fossil remained large throughout the length of the sacrum, which meant that there would have been an abundance of nerve fibers available for the musculature attendant to the tail. In contrast, apes and humans lack a tail, and thus the sacral canal becomes narrower toward its end. As for the Nariokotome youth, the size of the vertebral canal was very restricted, beginning as high up as the cervical vertebrae in the neck region. In modern humans, the vertebral canals are quite large in the neck and on down through the back into the thoracic and lumbar vertebrae. It is as we near the sacrum that the vertebral canals become severely diminished. The difference between the Nariokotome youth and living humans (and Neanderthals, for that matter) suggested to MacLarnon that, beginning high up in the neck, the Nariokotome youth's spinal cord was not as rich in nerve fibers as in modern humans. Consequently, there were fewer fibers available to exit the spinal cord and innervate skeletal and other musculature. What this indicated in turn was that this individual had lacked control over the fine movements of the muscles that were associated with his vocal apparatus and his breathing. A critical muscle here is the diaphragm, which is the only involuntary-voluntary muscle in human bodies, and the muscle that living humans manipulate when producing articulate speech. Although Broca's area of the brain, which is implicated in configuring language, was reportedly visibly developed on the Nariokotome youth's brain (as seen on an endocast), he was probably unable to speak as living humans do—at least in terms of the intricacies of breathing and its impact on the production of sound.

Will the Real *Homo erectus* Please Stand Up?

One of the colleagues Alan Walker invited to participate in the analysis of the Nariokotome skeleton was Joan Richtsmeier, who had been in the forefront in the application of sophisticated mathematical analyses to the study of cranial shape. Walker's idea in taking this analytical route was to reconstruct the growth trajectory of the *Homo erectus* skull and face, from the young Nariokotome individual to the adult. The adult they chose to use was the 3733 skull, which they believed represented a female individual. Because they wanted to compare male with male, they used data on how male and female chimpanzees differ from one another to reconstruct what a male adult *H. erectus* would have looked like. Their conclusion: the Nariokotome youth already had the facial proportions of what was to be expected for an adult male.

Well, as much as we appreciate the high-tech aspects of this kind of analysis, as skeptics at heart we are a bit wary of placing huge amounts of faith in fancy morphometric studies (which is what using measurements to try to capture shape is called). Having worked together on diverse projects for over 25 years, we have found little occasion to resort to the use of calipers. Not, of course, that we think no one should measure anything. But it's been our experience that, until you sort out the nature of the morphologies, it's hard to know what to measure and why you should measure it. In keeping with this thought, we also feel that measurements alone do not definitively provide

the data upon which you should delineate species. To the contrary, the only way to collect measurements is to have decided what groups to measure. Then you can measure away and develop statistics that tell the parameters of each group, how they differ quantitatively from one another, and how individuals within each group differ metrically from each other. To use measurements, you have to begin with an assumption, which then you can quantify accordingly. Even the grand old maven of morphometrics, the physical anthropologist W. W. Howells (of Kanapoi humerus fame), who studied hundreds of human crania of populations from around the world, assumed that all specimens belonged to the same species, and only then dealt with the nuances of shape.

On that note, we must remember a very simple but extraordinarily important rule of taxonomy: the type specimen of a species is the reference against which you make all subsequent assignment of specimens to that species. And in this case, as our colleague and curator of the original *Homo erectus* skull at the natural history museum in Leiden, The Netherlands, John de Vos, always reminds us, the type specimen of *H. erectus* is the skull cap that Dubois discovered. [Figures 51a and b] Although this specimen lacks the facial skeleton, it still has notable features. To begin with, the brain case is very low and quite wide. When you pick it up and look at it from behind, you feel like you're holding a hamburger bun. In profile, there is almost no rise from behind the brow ridges to the back of the skull, which looks like a wedge or sideways "V." The muscle scars along the side of the

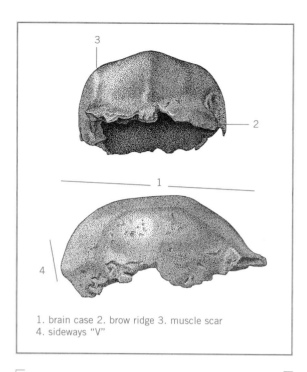

1. brain case 2. brow ridge 3. muscle scar
4. sideways "V"

[Figure 51]

As it is the type specimen of *Homo erectus*, the morphologies of the Trinil skull cap are vital in assessing which other specimens might belong to this species. Particularly telling is that the brain case is very low and, for its small size, somewhat long and yet very wide from side to side, and the frontal region slopes gently away from the thin, relatively straight, laterally flaring brow. In side view one can see how low the skull cap is and that the occipital region in the back is quite distended and "V" shaped. The very faint muscle markings lie on the side of the brain case. Drawings by Don McGranaghan.

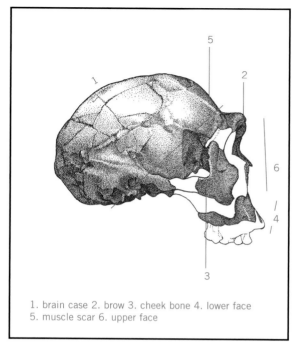

1. brain case 2. brow 3. cheek bone 4. lower face
5. muscle scar 6. upper face

[Figure 52]

In contrast to the Trinil skull cap, KNM-ER 3733 has much thinner brows that not only arc over the eye sockets, but also protrude both upward and out, creating a gully between them and the rather steeply rising forehead. The muscle scars are discrete crests that course up and somewhat toward the midline of the skull, which is somewhat high rising with a strong curve to the back. However, it is neither low nor extraordinarily broad. Drawing by Don McGranaghan.

skull where chewing muscles attached are very faint and delineate the slightly puffy side wall of the brain case. At the top of the skull on either side of the midline, there is a slight depression that makes the area between them appear to bulge a bit. And the brow ridges, which go almost perfectly straight across, project forward as a thin and somewhat laterally expanded ledge that flows smoothly into the long, inclined forehead.

In the brain case and brow, neither 3733 nor the Nariokotome youth can be described in the same terms as the type specimen of *H. erectus*. [Figures 52 and 53a and b] The back of the skull of 3733 may be a bit angular, but its brain case is quite inflated, and its brow is configured in a totally distinctive manner. It is thin and primarily upwardly tilted, which creates a deep gully between its back side and the very steeply rising

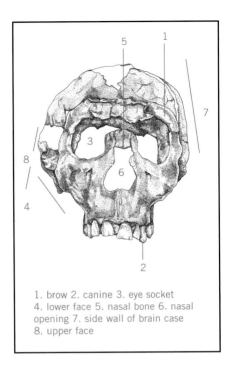

1. brow 2. canine 3. eye socket
4. lower face 5. nasal bone 6. nasal
opening 7. side wall of brain case
8. upper face

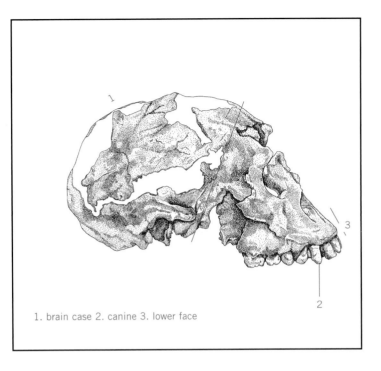

1. brain case 2. canine 3. lower face

[Figures 53a and b]

In contrast to both the Trinil skull cap and KNM-ER 3733, the brows of the Nariokotome boy WT 15000 are minimally swollen and flow upward into the somewhat rising frontal. Were this individual going to have prominent and barlike brow ridges, as in chimpanzees, gorillas, and baboons, for instance, they would have begun to develop noticeably at a much earlier age. In profile, the somewhat short and tall but not very broad brain case curves rather smoothly down to and around the back. In the shape and relative size of its eye sockets, nasal opening, nasal bones, and lower face, the Nariokotome boy and KNM-ER 3733 differ quite markedly. Of further importance is that the preserved upper molar of KNM-ER 3733 is morphologically distinct from its counterpart in the Nariokotome boy and those in specimens from Java we regard as representing *Homo erectus*. Drawings by Bridget D. Thomas.

forehead, and it arcs over each eye socket. In addition, the muscle scars on the side of the skull are raised and ridgelike and course high up and then down along the unexpanded side wall of the brain case. The Nariokotome skull is also quite distinct from the type specimen of *H. erectus,* but in different ways from 3733. Its brain case is relatively short and fairly highly rounded, the curve of the profile continuing smoothly around and down the back of the skull. The forehead rises moderately steeply directly from the tall but essentially unprojecting upper margins of the eye sockets. These differences strongly suggest that neither specimen represents *H. erectus.*

Similarly, when we compared 3733 and the Nariokotome youth, we found it hard to convince ourselves that the two were adult and juvenile versions of the same species. Their brows are completely different. The shapes of their skulls are different. The relative sizes of the upper and lower faces are different. The shapes of the opening of the nasal region are different, as are the shape, orientation, and degree of projection of their nasal bones. Had the Nariokotome youth survived until adulthood, we believe, it would have exaggerated the configurations already established, rather than converging with 3733.

As systematists at heart, who cut our academic teeth on studies of fossil and living apes and lemurs and an array of non-hominid primates, we've tried to bring the same (hopefully) dispassionate eye to our study of the human fossil record. It's tough to do this at times, partly because these *are*, after all, our relatives. And as hard as one tries to treat them just like any other animal, every once in a while you catch yourself being caught up in the aura of staring at a skull that, in overall size and shape, gives the impression of being more like you than a lemur or an ape—even though you know that it really doesn't look very much like you in a variety of details. But support of our initial conclusion that 3733 and the Nariokotome youth were not the same hominid also came when we studied the configurations of their preserved teeth.

Most mammal fossils consist of isolated teeth or of jaws with a few teeth in them. So, given that this is what you most commonly have to work with, you have to become—willingly or not—expert on the details of tooth morphology. And although the comparison between 3733 (with only a single upper molar preserved) and the Nariokotome youth is meager, it is very revealing. For the teeth are totally different from one another. In 3733 the molar crown is very high and its chewing surface relatively flat with low cusps. Strikingly, a cusp at the back and

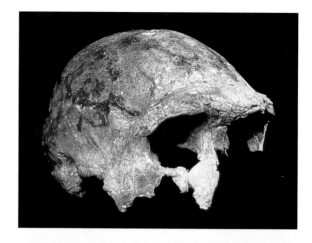

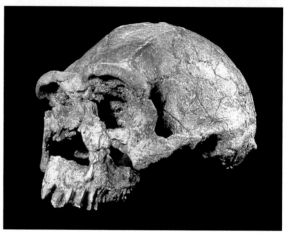

[Figures 54, 55, and 56]
Although paleoanthropologists have tended to group KNM-ER 3883 (top) with KNM-ER 3733 (bottom, and *see* Figure 45) and KNM-WT 15000 (*see* Figures 50a and b) as either *Homo erectus* or *H. ergaster*, KNM-ER 3883 differs from the other two East African specimens, as well as from the type specimen of *H. erectus*, the Trinil skull cap (*see* Figure 58), in obvious ways. Its brow is thicker and continuous from side to side; it is most protrusive over the nasal region, but it thins laterally and is not uniformly thick throughout. The forehead slopes steeply back, reaching its greatest height quite posteriorly. And, at least in contrast to the other East African specimens, the cheek bone is puffy and becomes expansive lower down. Interestingly, another partial cranium, KNM-ER 3732 (right), resembles KNM-ER 3883 more closely than any other specimen we have seen so far in our studies. Photographs by Jeffrey H. Schwartz; courtesy of the National Museums of Kenya.

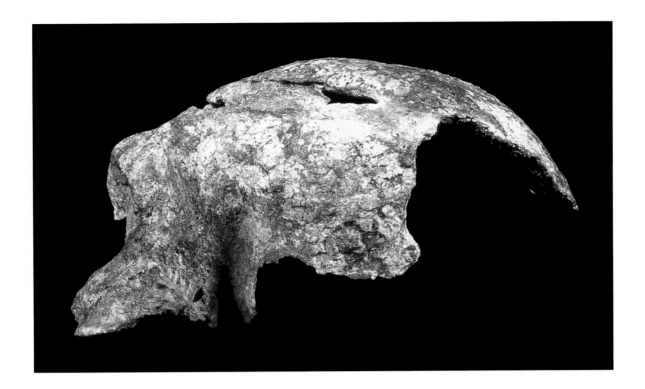

tongue side of the crown—the fourth cusp—is almost non-existent. In addition, the enamel surface is wrinkled. The equivalent tooth in the Nariokotome youth is lower-crowned, and the cusps and crests of the chewing surface are more distinct because the valleys between them are deeper. The fourth cusp is quite large and the enamel is not wrinkled.

What to do? Well, as we've suggested, these specimens are not, we think, *Homo erectus*. This is not a new interpretation. Other colleagues have ventured a similar opinion, including the mammalogist Colin Groves and his Czech colleague Vratja Mazak, who came up in 1975 with a new species name for these supposedly *erectus* African specimens: *Homo ergaster*. Until we had the opportunity to study the actual specimens,

we went along with this school of thought, which included 3733, the Nariokotome youth, and one other skull, KNM-ER 3883, in this other species. But having seeing the original specimens, we can no longer embrace that simple an interpretation. It's too restrictive. KNM-ER 3883 is as different in its own features from both 3733 and the Nariokotome youth as 3733 and the Nariokotome youth are from each other. When we came to this conclusion in the museum in Nairobi, we wondered if the heat was getting to us, until we found another specimen (3732) that belongs to whatever species 3883 represents. [Figures 54, 55 and 56]

But even this isn't the whole story. When Colin Groves established the species *ergaster*, he didn't use any of these skulls. Instead, he chose

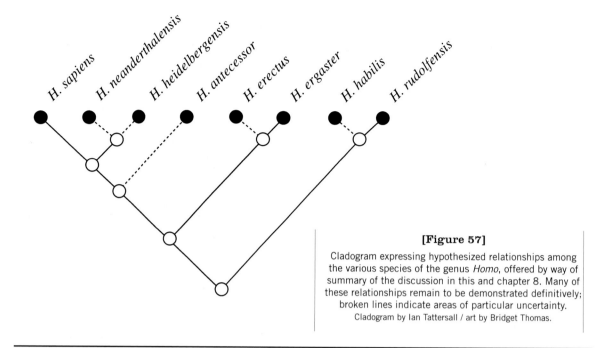

[Figure 57]

Cladogram expressing hypothesized relationships among the various species of the genus *Homo*, offered by way of summary of the discussion in this and chapter 8. Many of these relationships remain to be demonstrated definitively; broken lines indicate areas of particular uncertainty.

Cladogram by Ian Tattersall / art by Bridget Thomas.

a fairly complete (although broken in the midline) lower jaw, KNM-ER 992, as the type specimen. And it turns out that, once more, the teeth of this lower jaw are quite different morphologically from the lower teeth of the Nariokotome youth. Yet, in order for the Nariokotome youth to be considered a specimen of *ergaster*, it would have to be comparable in dental morphology with the type specimen, 992. It isn't. To make 3733 an *ergaster*, we would have to have the dental trail go from the lower teeth of 992 to the lower teeth of the Nariokotome youth (which it doesn't) and then from the upper teeth of the Nariokotome youth to the upper tooth of 3773 (which it doesn't). So, the trail of real *ergaster* appears to begin and end with the type specimen, 992. Further, because the skulls of 3733, Nariokotome, and 3883/3732 are all so remarkably different, we find it hard to go along with the notion of lumping them all together in the same species *ergaster*, even if this taxonomic act goes far beyond making them merely a very variable African version of the otherwise Asian *Homo erectus*. Some of our colleagues haven't liked this suggestion when we've presented it at meetings. But the obvious conclusion is that, as radical as separating a species *ergaster* from *erectus* has been thought to be, it's only the beginning in sorting out the details of just how many species there might have been—even in this one part of the world, during this rather short period of time. [Figure 57]

Lifestyles

One of the most striking patterns to emerge from the analysis of the hominid record is that innovations in culture and biology tend not to appear in concert. And this is certainly what we see with the presumed *ergaster* specimens.

For about a quarter of a million years after the time of 3733 (from 1.5–1.8 mya) the stone tools found in the East African record continued to be exclusively Oldowan in character. Only at about 1.5 myr ago, or even a little less, were such utensils joined by a new kind of tool, one made to a "mental template" held in the mind of the toolmaker. This new tool type was the Acheulean handaxe. Larger than the simple flakes of the Oldowan, the teardrop-shaped handaxes were consciously shaped to a standard form and were symmetrical in all three dimensions. It is hard to say what the functional advantage was of this visually impressive tool type over the simple sharp-edged flakes that continued to be manufactured alongside it; but handaxes were evidently highly attractive to the hominids who made them, because they continued to be produced in Africa for the next million years, sometimes in staggering quantities.

Exactly what impact this technological innovation had on the lifestyles of the *"ergaster"* hominids is equally cryptic, because other than that of the tools themselves there is not much reliable evidence. The little evidence there is suggests that lifeways did not change much from Oldowan to early Acheulean times. Almost invariably, sites bearing evidence of early human activity in the Turkana Basin lay originally along water sources of various kinds, where vegetation, thus shelter and plant foods, would have been most readily available. The few Acheulean sites in the Basin tend to be found away from the margin of the ancient lake, in places where larger lumps of suitable stone were to be found. Exactly what this implies remains obscure, as do the butchery sites where no artifacts were found, the implements used evidently having been carried away by their users. All in all, the indications are of purposive movements across the ancient landscape by small groups of early hominids who most likely scavenged the remains of larger mammals they encountered. Sometimes the hominids left evidence of having returned to a particular spot, but there is as yet no convincing evidence of "home bases" in the sense of favored places repeatedly revisited or semi-permanently occupied. Indeed, when we put together everything we know about the *ergaster*-group, the dominant impression is of mobility rather than of sedentariness.

How many different species of mobile hominid were there and how did they impact the landscape? At present, we are only beginning to scratch the surface of this topic. But, even if we don't know how many species existed beyond *ergaster* or how that species spread out, one things seems to be clear. The acquisition of modern body proportions, as especially evidenced in the Nariokotome youth, appears to have been followed very rapidly by vigorous expressions of human wanderlust.

CHAPTER 6

Homo ergaster and *Homo erectus:* The Great Diaspora

Homo ergaster and *Homo erectus:* The Great Diaspora

Until quite recently it was believed that hominids exited Africa for the first time only at around a million years ago. The earliest hominids known outside the confines of this continent were representatives of *Homo erectus*, recovered from sites in Java and China. And although these specimens were for the most part poorly dated, the best estimates placed the oldest of them at no more than a million years or so. Because they were discovered early on, and in keeping with traditional linear thinking, the Java Man and associated fossils, although recovered in far-flung eastern Asia, have become widely regarded as the "mainstream" hominids of the period around a million years ago. Yet as we will see, this placement is looking increasingly improbable. Not only were the first émigrés from Africa not *H. erectus* (rather, they must have been *H. ergaster* or a related species), but *H. erectus* itself appears to have been a local, and ultimately terminal, eastern Asian development.

As we've already intimated, new datings of early hominids and stone tools from Asian sites now suggest that human precursors had reached as far as Java and China by as much as 1.8 myr ago. It is interesting to note that this date comes hard on the heels of the acquisition of essentially modern human body form in Africa, but before the invention of carefully shaped tools. It thus seems that it was not any technological innovation that made possible the extraordinary mobility that humans have shown ever since. Instead, it was the physical emancipation of hominids from the forest fringes. And once early humans were definitively out on the savannas, a whole new range of possibilities was open to them, with profound consequences for ecologies and competitors worldwide as, indeed, for Hominidae itself. We have seen that the human family had already become highly diverse in the period of its confinement to Africa, with numerous species being spawned despite a presumed relative uniformity of body plan among most of them. Once outside the continent of origin, however, a host of new ecological opportunities awaited, and were rapidly seized as local radiations of hominids evolved in newly occupied regions. In this chapter we look at the first human colonization of the world beyond Africa, and at the background that lies behind our current understanding of it.

Java Man

By the middle 1880s, the notion was already well entrenched among European scientists that humanity had an evolutionary past. Yet until 1886 (when two more Neanderthal skeletons were found at the site of Spy, Belgium), the entire human fossil record consisted of parts of three Neanderthal individuals (one of them yet to be recognized as such), a toothless lower jaw (the affinities of which are not clear even today), and a handful of *Homo sapiens* skeletons associated with extinct Ice Age mammals and dating from the last glacial period. At this time, most felt that the Neanderthal specimens were simply pathological oddities, or that they represented an extinct "barbaric" form of *H. sapiens*. The barbaric interpretation clung on with considerable tenaciousness, even as terminology was softened. Some scientists of the time were not greatly concerned by the slenderness of the empirical evidence for the human evolutionary past; they believed that it was possible to establish humanity's place in nature purely on the basis of comparative anatomy and embryology. When appropriately analyzed, such data can indeed reveal degrees of propinquity among species. Other scientists, however, felt strongly that humanity's evolutionary origin could be firmly demonstrated only by evidence from the fossil record, such as already existed for many other groups of animals.

Nobody cleaved to this idea more enthusiastically than a young Dutch anatomist, Eugene Dubois. In 1887, Dubois unexpectedly quit his job at the medical school of the University of Amsterdam, and signed on as a medical officer in the Royal Dutch East Indies Army. He sailed for Java with the avowed intention of finding the fossils of early man. It was widely believed that humans had evolved outside Europe, prob-

ably in the tropics where their closest relatives, the great apes, lived. Further, the tropical East Indies were the home of one of these relatives, the orangutan, and were also conveniently close to India, whence fossil apes had recently begun to be reported. Most importantly, however, the impecunious Dubois needed outside financial support for his researches; and how better to obtain it than as a persuasively articulate government servant, in the jewel of the Dutch Empire?

Still, Dubois' move to the East Indies was a huge gamble, and it's truly remarkable that it should have paid off at all. Indeed, to begin with it didn't. Dubois focussed his attention initially on limestone cave deposits on the island of Sumatra: deposits similar to those that had yielded hominid fossils back in Europe. But although—in appalling field conditions—his team of convict workers found enough fossil bones of species still living in Sumatra to interest the colonial government in supporting his work, these finds were too recent for the tastes of an aspiring paleoanthropologist. Dubois thus transferred his attentions to Java, where a fossil human skull—now known not to be very old—had turned up in a rockshelter at Wadjak, on the eastern end of the island. Finally, Dubois turned to open-air deposits, and in November 1890 he discovered a large fossil fauna, including a famously inscrutable fragment of human lower jaw, at a place called Kedung Brubus.

In 1891, Dubois began investigating sediments on the banks of the Solo river near the village of Trinil. Here his crew of convicts dug a vast pit that eventually reached 50 feet in depth.

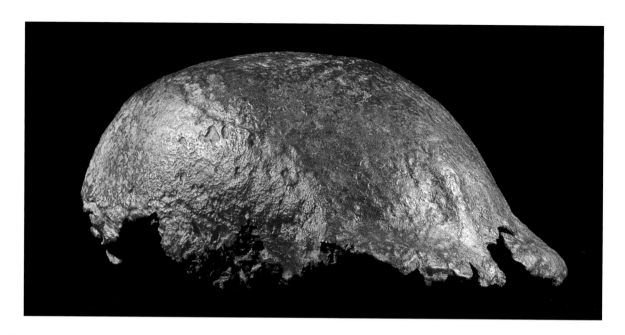

[Figure 58]

The Trinil skullcap reported by Eugene Dubois from Central Java in 1891. This long, low skullcap with inwardly sloping sides is the type specimen of *Homo erectus*. *(see* Figures 51a and b) Photograph by Jeffrey H. Schwartz.

The pit that yielded huge numbers of fossil bones of mammals and other vertebrates. In September 1891 a single hominoid molar tooth was found, and in the next month a skullcap. [Figure 58] Work was soon suspended with the beginning of the rainy season. But when excavation restarted in 1892 a thigh bone was found in an extension trench, reportedly at the same stratigraphic level as the skullcap and tooth but several meters away. Dubois had initially compared the skullcap and tooth most closely with those of chimpanzees. The thighbone, however, was very humanlike. Once his reappraisal of the long, low skullcap had shown it to have a brain capacity (about 940 ml) considerably larger than that of any ape, Dubois concluded that he held in his hands evidence for an apelike man, rather than a manlike ape. For this creature he had first proposed the name *Anthropopithecus* ("man-ape"), but he soon changed the designa-tion to *Pithecanthropus erectus*, "upright ape-man." From the accompanying fauna he estimated an age for this hominid that lay somewhere in the early Pleistocene epoch, or late in the Pliocene epoch that preceded it. Exactly how old that was, of course, nobody at the time knew; all geological dating was rela-tive—older than this, younger than that.

In 1895, Dubois arrived back in the Netherlands with the message that, during the late Pliocene (as we now know, 3–2 myr ago) or the early Pleistocene (2–1 myr ago), there had lived in Java a small-brained but upright-walk-ing being that could be classified neither as ape nor as human. Reactions were mixed. Many savants questioned the association between the skullcap and the thighbone, and this uncertainty widely impeded early acceptance of Dubois' conclusion that here was evidence for an evolutionary intermediate between apes and humans. A few scientists were prepared to listen. In the five years after his return to Europe, Dubois energetically lectured and showed off his rather meager fossils at meetings and international congresses. And it has recently been shown that he was much more successful in convincing his colleagues of his interpretation than legend allows. Unfortunately, the more his interpretations were accepted by his colleagues, the less his fossils remained his own unique intellectual property. Thus ultimately, in 1900, Dubois reclaimed his proprietorship by sequestering *Pithecanthropus* from his colleagues. But although the fossils remained inaccessible to others for almost a quarter-century, the genie was already out of the bottle.

Ironically, or perhaps inevitably, the colleague who most greatly annoyed Dubois by expounding at length on "his" fossils was the German anatomist Gustav Schwalbe, the leading *Pithecanthropus*-booster of the first decade of the twentieth century. Schwalbe accepted the association of skullcap and thighbone, and saw evidence for a simple linear sequence leading from *P. erectus* through *Homo primigenius* (his name for the Neanderthals), to *H. sapiens*. Schwalbe's views were influential in the years right after the turn of the century, but in the second decade of the century new entrants on the scene distracted attention away from *Pithecanthropus*. Thus France's Marcellin Boule, monographer of the famous La Chapelle Neanderthal skeleton, saw fit to almost entirely ignore *Pithecanthropus* in his discussion of the course of human evolution (dismissing it as a giant gibbon). And in England it was naturally in the interests of the champions of the fraudulent Piltdown "fossil" (still over forty years away from final exposure) to play down the significance of Java Man as much as possible.

Although paleoanthropologists of the period played no role whatever in the development of general evolutionary theory, it is probably significant nonetheless that this decline in the fortunes of *Pithecanthropus* coincided with the chaotic period of debate and disagreement about the mechanisms of evolution that followed the rediscovery in 1900 of the principles of inheritance, and the consequent birth of genetics as a science. Certainly, it took the establishment of a consensus among evolutionary theorists, decades later, to put *Pithecanthropus* back at center stage in debates about human evolution.

Peking Man

As long as *Pithecanthropus* consisted of hardly more than a skullcap and a femur whose age and association remained in doubt, it was perhaps natural that many paleoanthropologists preferred to suspend judgement on its evolutionary place—especially after the failure of a well-equipped German expedition to find further hominid fossils at Trinil in 1907–1908. It was thus not until the mid-1920s that paleoan-

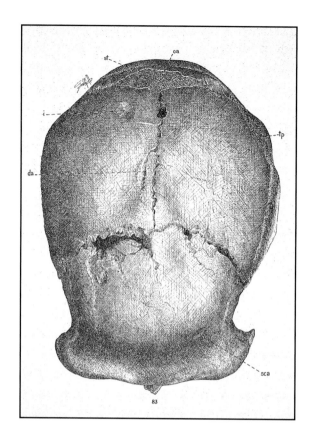

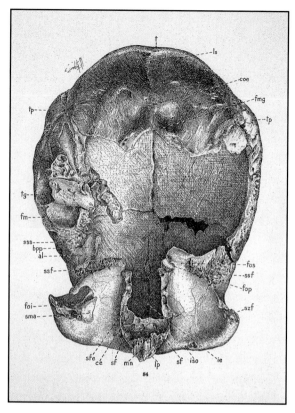

thropological attention was drawn back to the Orient, this time to China, where "dragon bones"—actually fossil mammal teeth—occurred abundantly in limestone caves, and had been ground up and used as medicine since time immemorial. Conveniently close to Beijing was one such cave, Zhoukoudian (for-merly Chou K'ou Tien), where scientists repre-senting the University of Uppsala in Sweden had by 1921 recovered a couple of hominid teeth as well as crude stone tools. The teeth, however, were not recognized as human until 1926, whereupon Davidson Black, Professor of Anatomy at the Peiping Union Medical College, took the site under his wing. By the end of the next year another hominid tooth had been recovered. Black baptized it *Sinanthropus pekinensis* ("Chinese man of Peking"), and redoubled his efforts at the cave. Those efforts began to pay off handsomely in 1929, when a hominid skullcap was discovered. [Figures 59a and b] By 1937, when work at Zhoukoudian had

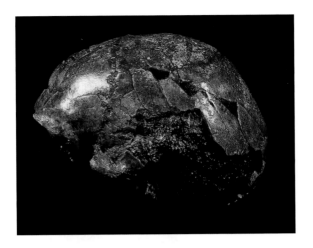 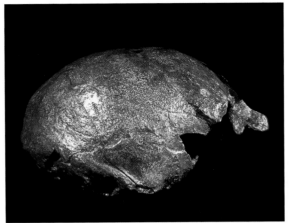

to be abandoned because of guerrilla activity, a whole series of them had been found, plus assorted facial and lower jaw fragments, and some fragmentary leg bones. The Zhoukoudian braincases looked quite similar to the Trinil skullcap, with a long, low vault that was sharply angled at the back, and that was adorned above the eyes with jutting brow ridges. What's more, in estimated brain volume the Zhoukoudian specimens spanned from 850 to 1,200 ml in volume, a range within which the Trinil skullcap fitted very comfortably. Nonetheless, Black continued to use the name *Sinanthropus* for his fossils, implying that they belonged not only to a different species but to a different genus from *Pithecanthropus*. After Black's premature death

in 1934, this usage was perpetuated by his successor Franz Weidenreich.

As the Zhoukoudian hominids accumulated, further discoveries were finally being made in Java. In 1931 and 1932 some eleven hominid braincases were found at a place called Ngandong, in the Solo Valley of central Java, not too far from Trinil. These were believed to be of late Pleistocene age, hence much younger than the Trinil *Pithecanthropus*. And although they looked generally similar to the latter, albeit with bigger braincases that ranged in volume from 1,035–1,255 ml, early descriptions emphasized alleged Neanderthal resemblances of these specimens—which thus became widely if implausibly viewed as "tropical Neanderthals." More attention was drawn, however, by finds made in central Java by the German paleoanthropologist Ralph von Koenigswald between 1936 and the outbreak of World War II. [Figure 60] The first of these was the braincase of an infant, found near the village of Mojokerto. von Koenigswald considered this to represent the same species as *P. erectus*. In deference, however, to the aged Dubois, who felt it was more like the Ngandong specimens, he named it *Homo modjokertensis.*

More finds followed, mostly from sites around the village of Sangiran, that von Koenigswald had less hesitation in naming *Pithecanthropus.* These included a braincase with a volume of 815 ml (von Koenigswald thought it was a little smaller) that was closely similar to the original Trinil skullcap, plus the base of another cranium with an apparently associated maxilla, and part of a lower jaw. [Figure 61] A small but particularly massive fragment of a lower jaw was found by von Koenigswald's collectors, but because of wartime upheavals it was not published until 1945, when Franz Weidenreich described it as *Meganthropus palaeojavanicus.* For good measure, Weidenreich at that time also created two new species of *Pithecanthropus—P. dubius,* and *P. robustus—*based on various of von Koenigswald's specimens. These species names have not found favor with later researchers, although our own examination of these fossils suggests that the hominid evolutionary picture in Java may be more complex than the by-now conventional assignment of all to *H. erectus* would suggest.

In 1939, von Koenigswald traveled to Beijing to compare his new finds with those from Zhoukoudian, where Franz Weidenreich was busy developing his own scenario of human evolution. In Weidenreich's concept, each major geographic variant of the modern species *Homo sapiens* has its roots deep in time, and *Sinanthropus* was specifically ancestral to the modern Chinese (as *Pithecanthropus* was to modern Australians). Despite differences over this interpretation, von Koenigswald and Weidenreich managed to agree on one broad conclusion, as reflected in their joint report to the journal *Nature.* These "prehominids," they said, were "related to each other in the same way as two different races of present mankind, which may also display certain variations in the degree of their advancement." The combined authority of von Koenigswald and Weidenreich ensured that from this point on Java Man and Peking Man would be widely regarded as members of the same species.

Alas, the von Koenigswald-Weidenreich encounter would be the last occasion on which these two hominids could be directly compared. For in December 1941 the human fossils from Zhoukoudian vanished in the confusion that reigned as the Japanese invaded Beijing. They disappeared in the process of being evacuated from China because of fears for their safety. Exactly what happened to them remains a mystery. The fossils were apparently shipped out of Beijing, but they probably never made it as far as the port of Tianjin, where they were scheduled to be loaded on an American freighter—which was itself torpedoed on its way into the harbor.

The Cave of Zhoukoudian

One profound difference between the Java finds and those at Zhoukoudian is context. The Java fossils were found in lake- and river-lain sands and gravels in which there is no definite association between the fossils and the very occasional crude stone artifacts that occur in the sediments. Zhoukoudian, in contrast, consists of rubble, including mammal fossils and stone tools, that accumulated in a large fissure in the surrounding limestone rocks. In 1931, Black noted that some of the animal bones recovered from the cave had been blackened by what he thought was burning. What's more, although no constructed hearths had been found, the use of fire by Peking Man also appeared to be indicated by the presence of considerable quantities of what he thought was carbon in certain areas of the deposits. Black thus concluded that Zhoukoudian was a place where Ice Age hominids had actually lived, leaving evidence behind them of their daily activities. As he saw it, the evidence hardly suggested a cozy domestic scene. Rather, some of the suggested activities at Zhoukoudian are substantially less than appealing to turn-of-the-millennium sensibilities. Thus, in 1939 Weidenreich noted that although the remains of close to 40 individual hominids were represented in the cave, there was not one even quasi-complete skeleton. Indeed, most of the remains were cranial, and all were extensively broken, as were the rest of the mammal fossils of Zhoukoudian. To Weidenreich the conclusion was clear: all the bones, human and otherwise, represented the remains of meals cooked and eaten in the cave by resident hominids. In the case of the human remains, Weidenreich was particularly graphic: "the *Sinanthropus* population [of Zhoukoudian] had been slain and...subsequently their heads were severed from the trunk, the brains removed and the limbs dissected."

Interpretations such as this garnered a lot of attention at the time they were uttered, and lent weight to the notion of early humans as brutish "cavemen" that had flourished as a result of the earlier Neanderthal discoveries in Europe. But as knowledge increased about how cave deposits are actually formed, it became evident that there are explanations other than culinary for the typical breakage of the bones found at such localities. To begin with, the simple presence of human fossils at cave sites does not necessarily mean that the humans in question actually lived in these places. What's more, we need to bear in mind that, as far as we know, early people rarely or never inhabited the dark, dank recesses of cave interiors. Rather, it was the light, airy entrances to caves that were attractive places to live. The dubious epithet "cavemen" is thus totally inaccurate. And one major reason for the failure of hominids to exploit cave entrances and rocks overhangs as much as they might have is that there is plenty of competition for such shelter. Caves are often inconveniently inhabited by carnivores (cave lions, hyenas, bears): dangerous neighbors to evict! Probably it was only the efficient domestication of fire that made humans effective competitors for space in caves. Indeed, there is currently debate over when exactly this innovation was introduced. In any event, typically the broken-up nature of bone assemblages in caves is caused by the activities of carnivores and scavengers who bring pieces of dead animals into the cave from outside. Sometimes, too, bones are simply washed into caves from the outside by water action. And this process, like the attentions of carnivores, is hardly conducive to good preservation of the bones.

At Zhoukoudian, then, it appears in retrospect that the breakage of the hominid bones, now dated to about 550–300 kyr ago, was almost certainly caused by natural factors rather than to gory cannibalistic activities—and evidence for hyena activity at the site has long been acknowledged. It is a pity that it is no longer possible to examine the original fossils for the distinctive cut-marks that would certainly have been left on them if the unfortunate individuals had been dismembered by other hominids using stone tools. It would be highly surprising, however, if any were there. Nonetheless, the notion of human habitation and cannibalism at Zhoukoudian has proven highly durable, largely because of the claimed evidence for the use of fire in the cave's interior. After Davidson Black's initial claim of 1931, various other authorities have seen evidence for enormous quantities of ash in the deposits, in some cases in layers up to several meters thick. Huge numbers of fires would have needed to burn in the cave over the millennia to accumulate ash on this scale, and the lack of evidence for individual fires was ascribed to reworking of the sediments by water action. Yet as long as it remained unquestioned that the blackened sediments of Zhoukoudian were ash deposits, a powerful reason seemed to exist for claiming that the cave was the site of human activities.

Research reported in 1998 discounted this reasoning, however. A Israeli-Chinese team carefully examined preserved deposits from which major ash deposits had been reported, and showed that many of them had been laid down under water! Some evidence of burning was discovered in the form of bones discolored by heating, but there was no indication that these bones had burned where they were found. Most probably they were washed into the cave along with other detritus, after being burned outside in a natural fire—a fairly unremarkable happening. This research has robbed Zhoukoudian not only of its status as a home for *Sinanthropus*, but also of its claim to be the earliest site bearing firm evidence of fire control by extinct hominids. This is significant, because, although we cannot necessarily conclude that hominids of this period did not use fire at living sites elsewhere, we lack good evidence for this alternative. And as long as the question of early fire control thus remains open, it is impossible to dismiss the possibility that the initial exodus of humanity from Africa, and more specifically the penetration by hominids of harsh northern climes (such as Beijing), was accomplished without the aid of fire.

New Discoveries

During the postwar period, as the linear dictates of the Evolutionary Synthesis were establishing themselves as paleoanthropological gospel, fresh discoveries of *Homo erectus* fossils continued to come in from Java and China. Particularly from the region around Sangiran there has been a steady trickle of finds, notably of the fairly complete, if distorted, cranium known as Sangiran 17, reported in 1969. (*see* Figure 46) From the same area came some very crushed specimens that have been informally grouped with the robust *Meganthropus*. This is in a way remarkable, because Java is a densely populated and well-watered island that is covered in vegetation. It is hardly the classic setting for finding fossils, which are more commonly found eroding out of desert badlands. Despite the best efforts of paleontologists, most Javan fossils havebeen found accidentally by farmers tilling their fields. One result of this unusual situation has been difficulties in dating the hominids, or even of knowing exactly whence many of them came. Diligent geological work has, however, shown that most of the Sangiran fossils come from just above or just below a distinctive layer of sands, gravels and silts known as the Grenzbank. This is a deposit that is generally reckoned, on the basis of several lines of indirect evidence, to have been laid down a little under 1 myr ago. It is thus believed that most of the Sangiran hominids date from slightly over to slightly under 1 myr ago. The Trinil hominid may be a bit younger than this, but it appears to be at least 700 kyr old. But as we'll see in a moment, there have recently been some dating surprises in Java and elsewhere in Asia.

In China, too, new *Homo erectus* finds accumulated in the postwar period, including a partial skullcap from Zhoukoudian that fits perfectly on to a cast of a prewar temporal bone, now lost. This is, alas, the only postwar hominid from Zhoukoudian, the deposit having been largely exhausted by the time excavations ceased in 1937. Earlier than the Zhoukoudian *H. erectus* fossils are a rather poorly preserved skullcap and a mandible from Lantian County that may be about 1 myr and 700 kyr old, respectively. These do not add much to our knowledge of Chinese *H. erectus*, but they do provide the earliest firm evidence for the species on the east Asian mainland. A cranium from Nanjing, dated to about 350 kyr, may eventually be more informative, but so far it has not been fully described. Several rather later finds have also been reported from Chinese sites such as Dali, in Shaanxi Province, Hexian, in Anhui Province, and Jinniushan in Liaoning Province. [Figures 62, 63, 64 and 65] However, none of these appears to represent *H. erectus*, and none has yet been adequately described, which is why this book does not include as much about the Chinese hominid record as the area warrants.

One southern Chinese site that has recently attracted attention for a remarkably early claimed age is Longgupo Cave, in Sichuan province, where an incisor tooth and a tiny fragment of lower jaw, plus some crude stone artifacts, are possibly as much as 1.9 myr old. Perhaps because of their potentially great age, the Longgupo hominids were described as being more like African *Homo ergaster* than like Chinese *H. erectus*. As we pointed out at the time, the teeth in the jaw fragment bear a close resemblance to the teeth of an orangutan relative known from a much later site in Vietnam. Moreover, the incisor, although convincingly hominid, is rather generic and difficult to assign to any particular species. Both more precise dating and more hominid fossils are needed before we will be able to assess the Longgupo evidence

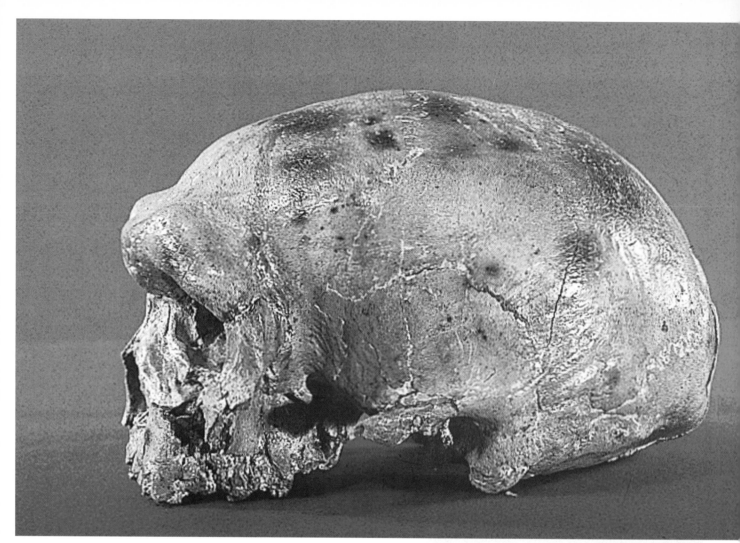

[Figures 62, 63, 64, and 65]

Four hominid crania from China, of varying affinities and some only described so far in preliminary fashion. The Dali cranium above, which may represent an East Asian version of *Homo heidelbergensis*; the Lantian skullcap facing page, left, one of the older examples of Chinese *Homo erectus*; the Hexian braincase right, whose relationships are still uncertain; and the partial cranium of *Homo erectus* discovered at Zhoukoudian in 1966 facing page, right. Compare the last of these specimens with the Weidenreich drawing in Figures 59a and b. Photographs courtesy of Wu Xinzhi.

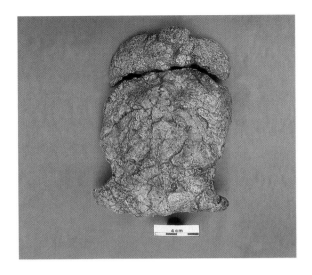

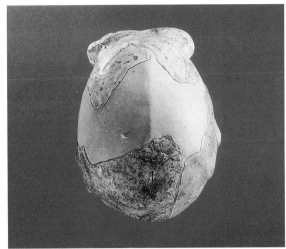

properly. It may of course be significant that, Longgupo apart, the oldest Chinese evidence for stone tools comes from sites in the Nihewan region that are only around 1 myr old: about the same age as the previous earliest fossil hominid sites in China. All of which, of course, makes the proposed date of Longgupo look a bit anomalous. It is interesting that, although Acheulean tools had been made in faraway Africa for half a million years by Nihewan times, the Nihewan tools are Oldowan-like, as stone artifacts in eastern Asia continued uniquely to be for hundreds of thousands of years. New dates suggest the reasons why.

Surprise Dates

The early date for Longgupo was unexpected, and is still highly provisional. Yet it fits with some other remarkable dating results that have been obtained from Asian hominid sites in the past few years. As we mentioned at the beginning of this chapter, it was generally believed until quite recently that hominids only left Africa for the first time at around 1 myr ago. Certainly, there were no good hominid fossils from non-African sites that were dated significantly earlier. Indeed, before the 1990s there was only one site outside Africa that contained any evidence whatever of human activity before that time. This was the site of 'Ubeidiya, in Israel, where a tiny fragment of probably hominid cranium and an abundant Acheulean stone tool industry had been dated to about 1.4 mya. And even here there was a problem of definition, because the Levant is within hailing distance of Africa and is regarded by many as part of the African faunal province. Because of all this, it came as a great surprise when, in 1994, Carl C. Swisher and colleagues at the Berkeley Geochronology Center announced that they had obtained two amazingly ancient dates for hominid sites in Java. This group used the fairly newly developed argon/argon technique to date volcanic rock samples from von Koenigswald's Modjokerto locality and a site near Sangiran that had yielded a couple of hugely crushed and distorted braincases that had been assigned to *Meganthropus* (but which most paleontologists regarded as *Homo erectus*). The results, at 1.81 myr and 1.66 myr, respectively, caused quite a stir. Although there was some-doubt about the exact locality from which the Modjokerto specimen had been recovered, it was clear that a lot of assumptions about hominid history on the Asian continent would have to be re-examined.

This necessity had, indeed, already been raised by a discovery in 1991 at the site of Dmanisi in the former Soviet Republic of Georgia. Archaeologists excavating in a ruined medieval town there discovered a partial hominid lower jaw that they attributed (more for convenience than for anything else) to *Homo erectus*. Three different dating methods suggested that this jaw might be as old as 1.8 myr. And although this great antiquity is still disputed, it fits with the growing body of evidence pointing toward an initial hominid exodus from Africa much closer to 2 than 1 myr ago. So also does the discovery by the archaeologist Robin Dennell of a few crude but clearly identifiable stone "chopping" (roughly, Oldowan-equivalent) tools at a site in Pakistan that is definitely older than 1.6 myr. At first Dennell's finding was widely ignored or attacked. But it is now looking much more plausible in light of the new Asian dates. All in all, then, even if individually virtually every report of very early Asian hominids is questionable in one way or another, together they quite powerfully support the notion of an early exodus from Africa.

They also make it easier to understand a longstanding archaeological conundrum. As we've seen, the earliest eastern Asian stone tools were remarkably primitive—Oldowan-like—although the more sophisticated Acheulean tradition had already been established in Africa for half a million years by the time those tools were made. On the fairly reasonable assumption that the use of Acheulean technology presented functional advantages compared with the Oldowan, it was difficult to understand why handaxe technology never became established in eastern Asia. Various ingenious explanations were devised for this, ranging from a lack of suitable raw materials to the exploitation of bamboo as a substitute for stone. None, however, was totally convincing. But the new dates supplied an altogether new perspective on the matter.

The Acheulean appeared in Africa only about 1.5 myr ago. If the exodus from Africa had in fact occurred before that time, as the new dates suggested, then the émigrés would necessarily have taken Oldowan, not Acheulean, technology with them. [Figure 66] Under the scenario implied by the revised chronology of events, the Acheulean was missing from eastern Asia simply because it had not yet been invented when the first immigrants left their homelands in Africa or its environs. And there was a further implication: there had been one episode of emigration from Africa to the Far East, rather than many. After an initial wave of

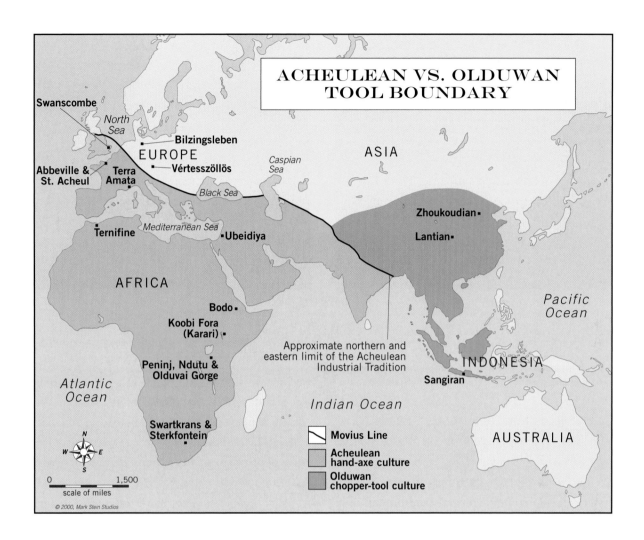

ACHEULEAN VS. OLDUWAN TOOL BOUNDARY

Swanscombe

North Sea

Bilzingsleben

EUROPE

Vértesszöllös

Abbeville & St. Acheul

Terra Amata

Black Sea

Caspian Sea

ASIA

Zhoukoudian

Lantian

Ternifine

Mediterranean Sea

Ubeidiya

AFRICA

Bodo

Koobi Fora (Karari)

Pacific Ocean

Peninj, Ndutu & Olduvai Gorge

Approximate northern and eastern limit of the Acheulean Industrial Tradition

INDONESIA

Sangiran

Atlantic Ocean

Indian Ocean

Swartkrans & Sterkfontein

AUSTRALIA

N
W · E
S

0 — 1,500
scale of miles

© 2000, Mark Stein Studios

Movius Line

Acheulean hand-axe culture

Olduwan chopper-tool culture

Oldowans had left Africa, and had managed to penetrate as far as eastern Asia, the process stopped, and there was no cultural diffusion from Africa to the Far East for a very long period of time. *Why* the Acheulean should eventually have spread from Africa as far east as India, but no farther, is of course a question that begs to be answered. But the simple fact is that there is no good evidence right now that it ever did. Which in turn supports the notion that, for

[Figure 66]

Map showing the location of some major Middle Pleistocene Afro-Eurasian paleoanthropological sites. The heavy line (the "Movius line") indicates the northern and eastern boundary of the Acheulean stone tool-making industry. More archaic tool forms are found throughout.
Map by Mark Stein.

whatever reason, the eastern part of Asia has been, for hominids at least, a kind of dead end: a cul-de-sac within which, for long periods, evolution could run its own independent course.

Homo ergaster **and** *Homo erectus:* **The Great Diaspora**

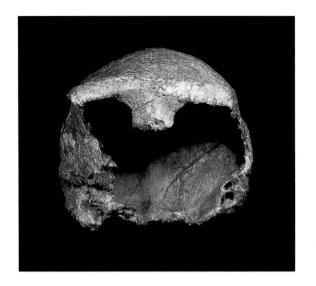 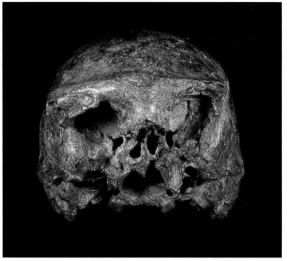

Once hominid occupation of eastern Asia had been established, cultural (and presumably also genetic) continuity between the new and ancestral areas was evidently not permanently created. Rather, the occupation of eastern Asia produced an isolate, an evolutionary outpost, within which local biological innovation became possible. The species that left Africa presumably belonged to what we can reluctantly call the *ergaster*-group, as we've already seen. And the one early species from eastern Asia that we can characterize with any confidence is the distinctively different *Homo erectus*. If it is true that *H. erectus* is an indigenous eastern Asian

development out of an at least somewhat *ergaster*-like ancestor, of course, it means that we have to rethink the position of *H. erectus* as the standard-issue hominid of its period. We can no longer follow Dobzhansky and Mayr in viewing Java and Peking Men as occupying the stage of human evolution intermediate between *Australopithecus* (or even *H. habilis* or *H. ergaster*) and *H. sapiens*, simply because its age appears to fit it for that role. We need to reconsider totally the place of *H. erectus* in human evolution: a need that has been emphasized by some further redating of Javanese hominids, this time at the young end of the age spectrum.

Ngandong Revisited

As we've already mentioned, the series of braincases from Ngandong has always been considered younger than the original *Homo erectus* material from Trinil and the fossils from Sangiran. Somehow, this has made Ngandong seem of peripheral importance to paleoanthropologists, who have never paid these specimens the attention that has been lavished on the older material. Guesses as to the age of Ngandong varied wildly, up to about 400 kyr; but all were based on the associated fauna and considerations of local geomorphology, and it was only very recently that Carl Swisher and colleagues came up with the first chronometric date for Ngandong. The Ngandong hominids were found, among many thousands of other fossils, in a very specific layer in a gravel terrace of the Solo River, and it is highly probable that all the remains, hominid and otherwise, form part of the same fauna. [Figures 67 and 68] The Swisher team collected new fossils from the same level as the original finds, and subjected them to electron spin resonance and uranium-series dating. The results were astounding. Although there was some variance between methods and samples, the average date obtained was only about 40 kyr, with a range from 27 to 53 kyr. Even at the older end, these dates are extraordinarily young, and they imply an unexpectedly long persistence of *H. erectus* in Java. What's more, if the Swisher dates for Modjokerto and the Sangiran *Meganthropus* site are correct, and the fossils involved are truly *H. erectus*, they also imply an impressive longevity for this endemic eastern Asian species: not far short of 2 myr, virtually the entire span of the Ice Ages!

The new dates also have wider implications for the pattern of events in later human evolution, for they coincide quite closely with the lat-

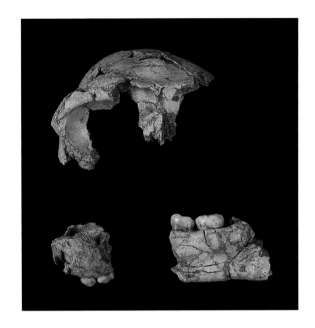

[Figure 69]
Fragmentary 780 kyr-old fossils of *Homo antecessor* from the Gran Dolina site in Spain's Atapuerca Hills. In some respects these fragments are remarkably modern-looking, especially in the lower face. Photograph by Javier Trueba.

est times of persistence of Neanderthals in the western end of the Eurasian continent. As we'll see, the species *Homo neanderthalensis* was the terminal representative of an indigenous European and western Asian hominid radiation that had been evolving in isolation for several hundred thousand years. This species became extinct shortly after the arrival in Europe of modern *H. sapiens*, presumably as a result either of competition for resources or of direct conflict, or maybe of a combination of the two. In Europe and the Levant we have substantial fossil and archaeological records to assist us in understanding the course of events in those regions.

These records are far superior to anything we have in eastern Asia, and have enabled us to pin down the chronology of Neanderthal disappearance quite closely. Nonetheless, by itself the lateness of the Ngandong dates suggests strongly that something similar to what happened in Europe also occurred in eastern Asia.

In its isolated evolutionary outpost *Homo erectus* evolved and survived relatively unchanged until a late date, maybe until some time after 40 kyr ago. At around this time modern humans finally arrived in the Far East, just as their counterparts in the west were penetrating Europe. And at both ends of the Eurasian continent the result was the same: the resident hominids lost out to the invaders, and made no further contribution to hominid history. If this was the case, we clearly have to abandon the view that *H. erectus* represented the main line of human evolution in the run-up to the appearance of *H. sapiens*. In other words, we have to step aside from the linear paradigm that has governed recent investigations in paleoanthropology. Instead, we need to accept that *H. erectus* was actually an indigenous and terminal eastern Asian development: simply—just like the Neanderthals thousands of miles away— another twig on the hominid evolutionary bush that was eventually pruned.

The Invasion of Europe

Compared with the quite abundantly documented later history of hominids in Europe, the earliest occupation of the subcontinent is poorly understood. Several putative archaeological sites in the 1-myr-old range are all disputed in one way or another, as is a claim for 2.4-myr-old tools at a site in central France. Until recently, it was necessary to wait for indisputable human fossil remains in Europe until about the half-million year mark. Dramatic new finds in Spain have, however, changed all that. [Figure 69] Level TD-6 of the Gran Dolina Cave in the Atapuerca Hills of northern Spain has recently produced a series of fragmentary human remains associated with a rather crude artifact assemblage that lacks handaxes (which, once again, only seem to have arrived in this extremity of the Eurasian continent much later). The sediments in which the fossils were found were dated to over 780 kyr, and in 1997 the discoverers of these remains assigned them to a new hominid species, *Homo antecessor*. This new species, they argued, was descended from African *Homo ergaster*, and represents the common ancestor of lineages that led on the one hand to the Neanderthals (via *Homo heidelbergensis*, which we'll read about below), and on the other to *Homo sapiens*. These interpretations have been contested on a number of grounds, including the fragmentary nature of the fossils and the fact that the best available specimen is immature. The material, however, is certainly distinctive and in our view clearly deserves to be recognized with its own species name. In a variety of respects, and particularly in the area of the face around the nose, *H. antecessor* also resembles *H. sapiens* more closely than anything else of comparable age does. Less well established is any lineal connection to later populations in Europe, especially the Neanderthals. Indeed, it seems at least as likely to us that these Spanish fossils represent an initial attempt to colonize Europe that ultimately failed, as that they gave rise to any later group of hominids. More complete finds of adults will, with luck, ultimately tell.

Meanwhile, the Gran Dolina fossils and an isolated 700-kyr-old braincase from the Italian site of Ceprano aside, the human fossil record in Europe begins at about 500 kyr, with a lower jaw from the site of Mauer, in Germany, and part of a leg bone from Boxgrove, England. These fossils are usually assigned to the species *Homo heidelbergensis*, which is more completely represented in Europe by 400-kyr-old specimens from the cave of Arago in southern France, and by a poorly dated but possibly 200-kyr-old cranium from Petralona in northern Greece. Most paleoanthropologists nowadays also include in *H. heidelbergensis* a beautifully preserved African cranium from Kabwe (Broken Hill), in Zambia, and a less complete cranium from the Ethiopian site of Bodo that is pretty firmly dated to around 600 kyr. [Figures 70, 71, 72 and 73] Closer scrutiny will probably show that the material allocated to *H. heidelbergensis* actually embraces more than just one species. For the moment, however, *H. heidelbergensis* serves as a useful umbrella for specimens whose characteristics include a sizeable brain of around 1200 ml or so. This brain resided in a braincase which was hafted behind a large face that was puffed out by the development of considerable sinuses (air spaces). Below the neck, the few bones known show that these hominids were robustly built. Still, they were unquestion-

ably perfectly efficient bipeds, with essentially modern body proportions.

Archaeologically, after a long period of tedium in the record, we begin to pick up signs of behavioral innovation in sites associated with *Homo heidelbergensis*—although not of innovation in lithic technology. The stone tools associated with this species in Europe are generally crude. But at the 400-kyr-old site of Terra Amata in southern France the foundations have been reported of large oval huts, made of saplings planted in the ground and presumably drawn together at the top. Within one such hut was found a shallow hearth where a fire had burned. Although the interpretation of Terra Amata has been disputed, a site at Bilzingsleben in eastern Germany that is not much younger has also yielded evidence of shelter building and domestic fire control. And in terms of artifacts, the open-air site of Schöningen, also in Germany, has recently yielded an extraordinary collection of carefully shaped six-foot-long wooden throwing spears (with their center of balance up front) that date to about 400 kyr ago. [Figure 74] The existence of such artifacts at that remote point in time contradicts received wisdom, which has in recent years held that until the arrival of modern *H. sapiens* more dangerous thrusting spears were the rule, exemplifying a less sophisticated approach to hunting by earlier hominids.

Why the Acheulean is vanishingly rare in Europe before about 300 kyr ago (plus or minus quite a bit: dating is a little hazy) is a major puzzle. After all, bifacial technology had by then been widely used in Africa for well over 1 myr. What's more, given the apparent late arrival of

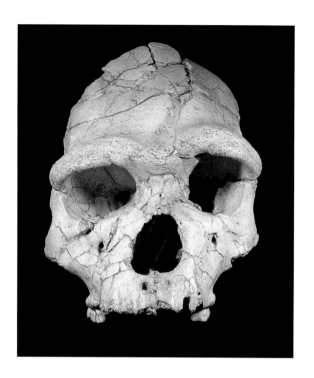 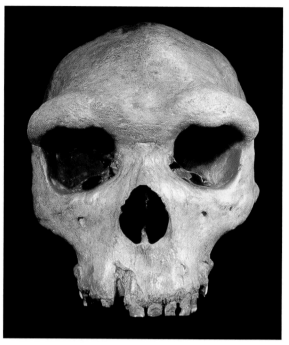

[Figures 70, 71, 72, and 73]

Front views of four crania often assigned to *Homo heidelbergensis* (although there is some variability among them, especially in the development of the cranial sinuses and in the front part of the braincase). From left to right: the 400 kyr-old Arago 21 face from France; the poorly dated "Rhodesian Man" crania from Kabwe, Zambia; another poorly dated skull from Petralona, Greece; and the 600 kyr-old Bodo cranium, from Ethiopia. Photographs by Jeffrey H. Schwartz, except Bodo, courtesy of Institute of Human Origins.

hominids in Europe we cannot claim, as in Asia, that this technology had not yet been developed when the first immigrants arrived. One suggestion is that early Ice Age Europe presented too difficult an environment to support more than a very low density of hominids who were rather unsophisticated technologically, and that in the resulting marginal economic circumstances,

earlier skills may even have been lost—something that has been documented in small isolates of recent *Homo sapiens*. [Figure 75] Well, perhaps. But at the present state of our knowledge no suggestion can rank as anything more than a guess. Equally puzzling is the apparent lateness of arrival of hominids of any technology whatever in Europe—even with the backward extension represented by the Gran Dolina discoveries. Once more—and more plausibly this time—the answer may lie in the environment. For whereas the emigrants from tropical Africa who turned eastward were able to attain the farthest reaches of Asia through a tropical or semitropical corridor to the south of the Himalayas, entrants into Europe would immediately have encountered temperate conditions or worse. But, as before, we can only speculate.

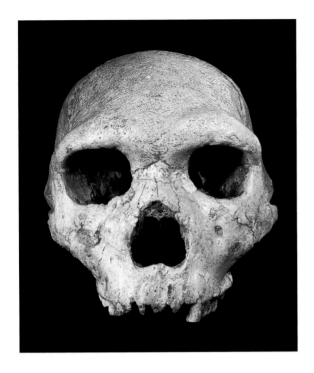

Multiple Departures?

If the hominid family originated around 5 or 6 myr ago, then for at least two-thirds of their family's history, hominids were confined to Africa, the continent of their birth. Even if one accepts the extraordinary new dates from eastern Asia, there is no suggestion that any hominid left Africa before a little less than 2 myr. This date more or less coincides with the first appearance, in eastern Africa, of the earliest known hominids that possessed essentially modern body proportions. The hominids were possibly part of the faunal turnover that marked the climatic deterioration of the beginning of the Ice Ages. It is only with the arrival of the Nariokotome youth that we have a firm indication of a hominid that was finally emancipated

from the forest edges. For, as we've seen, although the australopiths and "early *Homo*" were clearly bipedal when on the ground, they retained many features that were useful in the trees, where we can assume they spent a good deal of time both foraging and sheltering. In contrast, the Nariokotome youth showed a strong anatomical commitment to striding locomotion out on the hot, open savanna. Here, at last, was a hominid whose presence and movements on the landscape were no longer determined by the distributions of forest edges and woodlands. And once hominids were unconstrained in this way, it seems that they virtually instantaneously developed the wanderlust that has characterized their kind ever since.

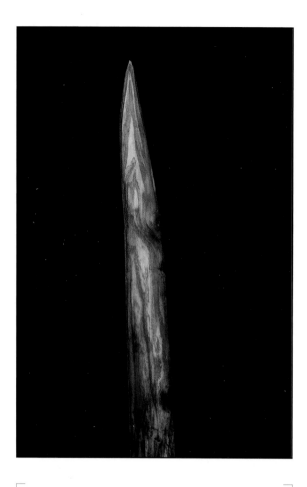

[Figure 74]

The finely-shaped point of one of the of the miraculously-preserved wooden spears, some 400 kyr old, recently excavated at Schöningen, Germany. These spears, mostly well over six feet long, were carefully crafted as throwing missiles. Photograph by C. S. Fuchs; © H. Thieme.

expand beyond Africa. The environments to the north of the African continent were at least regionally and seasonally cold and relatively harsh, with huge variations in resource availability from one time of year to another. Technology, surely, needed to develop to cope. Yet, as we have seen, it is clear that the first emigrants from Africa left that continent with only the crudest of stoneworking technologies. It is highly probable that they did not take with them the control of fire. Apparently, then, it was their physical adaptation that was paramount in enabling hominids to become a group with an Old World-wide distribution. Much has been made of the notion that humans are tropical animals, as in origin (African) they appear by definition to be. Although in his body proportions the Nariokotome youth does show a distinctive tropical adaptation—for losing heat, not conserving it—it is clear that the *fundamental* adaptation of hominids like him was not specifically tropical at all. Rather, the new lifestyle and mode of locomotion that the youth exemplified add up to a marvelously robust mechanism that is suited to the whole wide range of environments that hominids have come to occupy. Technological improvements of one kind or another were certainly necessary to make some particularly marginal environments accessible to hominids. It is hard, for instance, to imagine that hominids could ever have colonized Siberia had they not invented clothing, or controlled fire. However, the fundamental biological adaptation involved in the acquisition of modern body form has proved superbly versatile over a huge range of habitats.

Having once left Africa, they were established as far afield as eastern Asia in an incredibly short span of time.

Recognizing this involves abandoning a host of long-established preconceptions, for it has long been widely believed that technological innovation enabled human populations to

We don't know the precise identity of the first human emigrants from Africa, although given the collective weight of the new Asian dates it is reasonable to assume that they were *Homo ergaster* or a reasonably close relative. So much for the initial exodus, which at least for the moment is looking tolerably straightforward. But this was not the end of it. It appears that, ever since, Africa has been an engine of innovation in human evolution, periodically pumping out new species and sometimes new technologies into the rest of the Old World. The Acheulean, for example, had as noted reached the Levant by 1.4 myr ago (probably the first of several introductions to the northern continents), soon after its first appearance in eastern

Africa. Moving up in time, there can be little doubt that *H. antecessor* had African antecedents, whether or not this species itself was an indigenous European development, or had lost the skill of manufacturing bifacial implements. The earliest known *H. heidelbergensis* appeared in Africa, with the 600-kyr-old Bodo cranium; and within the next hundred thousand years this species was present in Europe. [Figure 76]

We cannot pass up the opportunity to say here that *Homo heidelbergensis* is an excellent example of the importance of getting basic systematics right before you proceed to more complex analyses. We have noted that some paleoanthropologists suspect that *H. heidelbergensis* as now generally recognized is not really a single biological species, but rather a name that conveniently covers a diversity of fossils. And until that diversity is clarified, it will be impossible for us to understand what exactly was going on in the 600–300 kyr period. Once more, attention has been distracted from the "bushiness" of the human family tree by an excessive adherence to a linear evolutionary model, today's reverberation of the Great Chain of Being. Provisionally, the indications are that *H. heidelbergensis*, or the group to which it belongs, arose in Africa and emigrated to Europe. It also made it as far afield as China, if, for example, the Dali cranium already mentioned actually belongs to this species.

It is by now fairly firmly established by a variety of lines of evidence that our own species *Homo sapiens* arose in Africa perhaps 150 kyr ago, and that it then spread out to take over the world. Not everybody agrees, however. This scenario contrasts with the opposing notion of "multiregional evolution," which claims intellectual descent from the ideas of Franz Weidenreich. Under this scheme, all human evolution over the past 2 myr has taken place entirely within a braided stream of evolving populations of one species all over the Old World. Over this long period these local populations each constantly adapted to local conditions. Yet all retained membership in the same species by virtue of the gene exchange that took place among them. This is a nice story, but not a very convincing one. Besides not conforming to what we know of how the evolutionary process works (remember the "genetic inertia" of large interbreeding populations), the multiregional notion is contradicted by the fossil evidence—which joins, what's more, a growing body of molecular information (notably DNA diversity data) that points toward a single and quite recent origin of *H. sapiens*, most probably in Africa. It was this continent that was the birthplace of the human family and that has been the most consistent source of innovation in human evolution.

This is not, of course, to say that Africa has been the only fount of such innovation, as the independent evolution of *Homo erectus* in Asia and *H. neanderthalensis* in Europe proves. But for some reason Africa has, it seems, consistently produced new hominid species that have successfully spread into neighboring regions, displacing indigenous relatives. As the human fossil record grows, and we learn more about hominid history, we will doubtless find that this general-

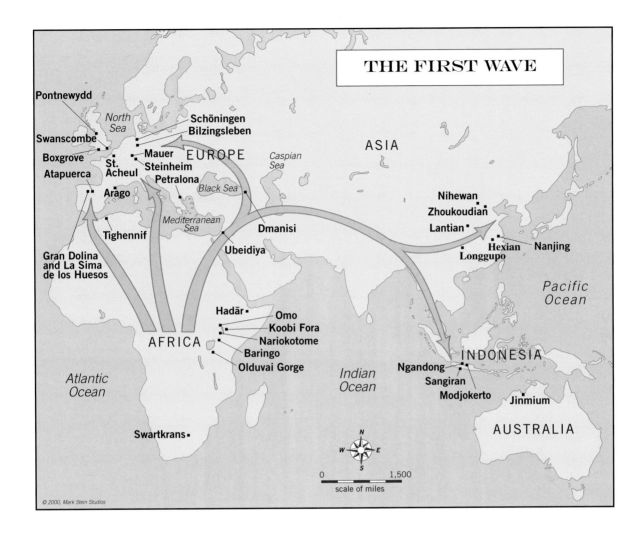

THE FIRST WAVE

Pontnewydd
North
Sea
Schöningen
Bilzingsleben
Swanscombe
Boxgrove
Mauer
EUROPE
ASIA
Caspian
Sea
St.
Steinheim
Atapuerca
Acheul
Petralona
Arago
Black Sea
Mediterranean
Sea
Dmanisi
Tighennif
Ubeidiya
Nihewan
Zhoukoudian
Lantian
Hexian
Nanjing
Longgupo
Gran Dolina
and La Sima
de los Huesos
Pacific
Ocean
Hadār
Omo
Koobi Fora
Nariokotome
AFRICA
Baringo
Olduvai Gorge
Indian
Ocean
INDONESIA
Ngandong
Atlantic
Ocean
Sangiran
Modjokerto
Jinmium
Swartkrans
AUSTRALIA
N
W   E
S
0   1,500
scale of miles
© 2000, Mark Stein Studios

ization is a little or even greatly oversimplified. It has, for example, recently been suggested that the world's human population history has been complicated by several back-migrations into Africa. However, for the moment it seems not just permissible but obligatory to conclude that the northern continents played a fairly peripheral role in "mainstream" human evolution: those events that gave rise to the direct ancestors of our own species *Homo sapiens*.

[Figure 76]

Map showing some of the major archaeological sites from the Paleolithic of the Old World, and possible routes taken by the first African émigrés into Eastern Asia and Europe.
Map by Mark Stein.

CHAPTER 7

Neanderthals and
Human Extinctions

Neanderthals and Human Extinctions

With our cocooned Western sensibilities, we tend to forget—at least when thinking of our vanished hominid precursors—that extinction without issue is a perfectly normal biological process. Extinction of old species is, indeed, both as normal and as necessary as the origination of new ones. Clearly, life could never have diversified as it has, had not millions of species given way to others over the course of biological history, freeing up space for new players on the ecological stage. Equally important is the dramatic shaping of the world's evolutionary history by an ongoing process of competition among species, both closely and less closely related to each other. This process is analogous, although not identical with the winnowing of individuals by natural selection, and the penalty for those species that lose in this game is necessarily extinction. On a planet that isn't growing any larger, how could things be otherwise?

Yet when it comes to our own family, the hominids, we seem to have a strong tendency to resist the notion of extinction without issue. With the theories of Evolutionary Synthesis and the Great Chain of Being lurking in the background, many paleoanthropologists seem to be comfortable enough with the notion of extinction via transformation, in which one species gradually gives rise to another through the gradual accumulation of physical changes over hundreds or thousands of generations. This is despite the fact that it's been abundantly evident for years that within-species processes of morphological change and diversification are functionally independent of the mechanisms that result in new species, and that gradual trans-species transformation is rare, if it ever happens at all. Implausible as it is, however, the transformational notion has historically been powerfully seductive because it avoids the conclusion that one group of ancient hominids could ever have been responsible for the extinction of another.

The unwillingness to face reality that all this implies presumably results from an understandable aversion to the idea of hominid genocide, whether through economic competition or by direct annihilation. Genocide in whatever form is, after all, among the least attractive of all of the many dubious behaviors of which modern humans are capable. And if we cling to the notion of extinction via transformation, we can pretend that our forebears (by definition the victors in the struggle) played a diminished role, or even no role at all, in the extirpation of their—and our—extinct relatives. Perhaps we can then feel better about our essential nature, however much the briefest glance around the world today, whether it be in the direction of Kosovo or the eastern Congo, would seem to indicate otherwise. But warm-hearted and wish-fulfilling though the prevailing attitude may be, it flies in the face of the evidence itself. The fossil record testifies eloquently that the history of the hominids has from the beginning been one of species diversity, with everything, including potential interspecies competition, that this implies. The survival on Earth today of only one hominid species is not only quite clearly the exception rather than the rule (and will have to be recognized as such if we are ever to understand the historical background out of which we emerged), but it also bluntly implies a high probability that some hominid species were at least indirectly responsible for the disappearance of others.

In clarifying this situation, it's unfortunate that even after well over a century of active paleoanthropological research we are still entirely ignorant of how many species made up the cast of characters in the hominid evolutionary play (although the number is almost certainly much larger than usually admitted). Even less are we able to understand precisely how these species interacted with one another. Indeed, in the entire long history of the hominids there is only one interspecies interaction into which we have any insight whatever. This is the one between the Neanderthals, *Homo neanderthalensis*, and the first modern humans, *Homo sapiens*, who invaded the Neanderthals' European and western Asian domain at around 40 kyr ago. In this chapter we will examine what is known about the interaction between *H. neanderthalensis* and *H. sapiens*, while bearing in mind that, for reasons of archaeological preservation, this is sim-

ply the best exemplar we have of a process—interspecies competition—that was going on all over the Old World in the same approximate time frame.

Still, if we had had to choose one single pair of hominids to know about in this regard, it would quite plausibly be this one. For one thing, the Neanderthals and the European early moderns are uncontestably the best documented of all hominids in the fossil record, both physically and in terms of their behaviorally. For another, during their tenure on Earth these two species overlapped in space as well as in time, so we can eliminate environment as a potential determinant of any differences between them in the ways they coped with the world. And finally, it appears that there were, indeed, many, such differences. Neanderthals and European early moderns may both have had large brains, but they did business in distinctively different ways. The moderns arrived in Europe fully equipped with unprecedented modern abilities and sensibilities, while for all their remarkable achievements the Neanderthals largely echoed the capacities of their forebears.

Especially given the excellence of the record of their activities and physiques that these hominids left behind them, the upshot is that, among all extinct hominids, the Neanderthals are incomparably the best mirror we have to hold up to ourselves, and to show us the exact nature of our own uniqueness. This is important not simply because it helps us understand our own place in nature. It is also important because in light of those very uniquenesses it may not be that the elimination of the

Neanderthals and their like was a totally routine extinction event, of the kind that had witnessed the disappearance of many other hominid species during the long history of the human family. For *Homo sapiens* interacts with the world around it in an unusual, and unusually destructive, way. Maybe this is at least in part why—as we'll see when we discuss specific theories of Neanderthal extinction—many modern paleoanthropologists seem to have such an oddly equivocal—even guilt-ridden—relationship with these extinct relatives. Before proceeding further, however, we need to pose the basic question: just who, exactly, *were* the Neanderthals?

The Neanderthals

Put most succinctly, the Neanderthals were a distinctive group of hominids who occupied Europe and Western Asia in the period between about 200 and 30 kyr ago. But how distinct were they? When the original (Feldhofer Cave; see figure 3) Neanderthal specimen was discovered in 1856, some thought it simply a pathological modern human, an idea rapidly disproved by further finds. More durable was Thomas Henry Huxley's notion, articulated in his 1863 essay "On Some Fossil Remains." As we've seen, Huxley felt that these hominids, then known as adults only from Feldhofer, were little more than an extension back in time of the morphology of the Australian aborigines, who were regarded in Victorian times as the most "brutish" of living humans. Here was yet another unfortunate lega-

cy of the Great Chain of Being notion. Yet even those paleoanthropologists who maintain today that Neanderthals represent nothing more than a variant of *Homo sapiens* can, like Huxley, articulate a remarkable series of differences that exist between these two hominids.

So, what were the Neanderthals like? In considering this it is convenient to start with what our colleague Al Santa Luca termed the "core" (i.e., uncontested) group of Neanderthals. The earliest probable such specimen is a partial lower jaw with some teeth from the French site of Montmaurin. This may be older than 150 kyr, even 200 kyr. Otherwise, the oldest core Neanderthal is represented by the back of a skull from the French site of Biache, dated to 150–160 kyr ago. The youngest specimens—a mandible and part of a leg bone—are from the from the Spanish site of Zafarraya (dated to approximately 30 kyr), and the next youngest—the right side of the face and forehead and lower jaw, as well as a few other bones—are from the French site of Saint-Césaire (at approximately 36 kyr). What should be noted about these upper and lower dates for the supposedly "cold-adapted" Neanderthals is that they do not bracket a consistently cold time period. Indeed, the famous Neanderthals of Krapina, in Croatia, actually enjoyed a much more pleasant climatic and seasonal regime than present-day residents of the northeastern United States. In general, only the European sites toward the younger end of the core group's chronological distribution fall into the picture of deep freeze that is typically associated with these hominids.

Most hominid sites that fall within the Neanderthal time range are in Europe, one of the oldest being Krapina (at about 130 kyr), and the majority falling between 40–60 kyr. Among the later sites are many in France (such as La Chapelle-aux-Saints, La Quina, La Ferrassie, Regourdou, Le Moustier, and Peche de l'Azé), Italy (such as Grotta Guattari, Archi, and Saccopastore), Belgium (Spy and Engis), the Iberian peninsula (Gibraltar), Croatia (Vindija), Hungary (Subalyuk), and, of course, the original Feldhofer site in Germany (for which, miraculously, a date of about 40 kyr has recently been obtained from bones found in the detritus dumps left by the original miners). In the Near East, the sites of Kebara and Amud (Israel) and Shanidar (Iraq) are more or less contemporaneous with these European sites, but the site of Tabūn, in the Mount Carmel range in northern coastal Israel is still being worked out, estimates ranging from 178 to 38 kyr (!). [Figures 77-91]

THE NEANDERTHALS

Neanderthals—*Homo neanderthalensis*—have traditionally been perceived as displaying an array of variation that flows into the stream of variation that is believed to characterize *H. sapiens*. Truly, as the adult specimens in the following series of plates illustrate, *H. neanderthalensis* was indeed a variable species. But the variability lies both within the domain of the morphologies that are specific to being a Neanderthal and that of those that are characteristic of other species. Variability in Neanderthals is expressed just as it is in ourselves, or any other species for that matter. An individual may be larger or smaller than others, and have a shorter or longer or narrower or wider skull, more massive or less well-developed brows, deeper or thinner cheek bones, more upturned or downwardly sloping nasal bones, more or less protrusive occipital bones, or taller or shallower lower jaws. These are the kinds of differences one expects to find between individuals of the same species. And the more closely related species are to one another—and *H. neanderthalensis* and *H. sapiens* are closely related—the more features, including similar variants, they will have in common. But just because features of closely related species may vary in similar ways, this does not mean that there is a continuum of variability or evidence of evolutionary change from one species to another.

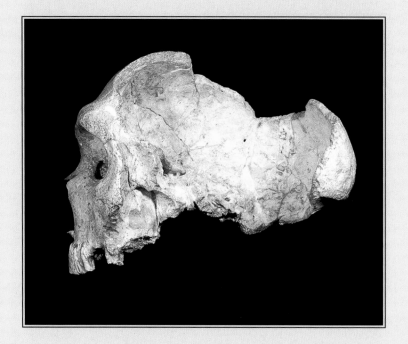

[Figures 77a and b]

As typified by the Gibraltar 1 adult skull when viewed from the front, specifically Neanderthal morphology is seen in the enormous size of the nasal opening, the protruding, "wedge-shaped" snout, the swollen or "puffy" face and medial region of the eye socket, and the "swept back" cheek bones. In this specimen, a pair of large swellings protruding medially within the nasal cavity is particularly well preserved. The configuration of the brow—smoothly rolled from top to bottom, arced over each orbit, and continuous across the midline—has also been thought of as a uniquely Neanderthal feature. But its presence in hominid specimens that do not share other Neanderthal features suggests that the "Neanderthal" brow is characteristic of a larger group of related species, of which *H. neanderthalensis* is but one. Although Neanderthals, such as the Gibraltar 1 specimen when viewed from the side, can also be described as having the face at the front of their relatively long and low brain case, so, too, can other hominids— but not *Homo sapiens*.

PHOTOGRAPHS BY JEFFREY H. SCHWARTZ; COURTESY NATURAL HISTORY MUSEUM (LONDON).

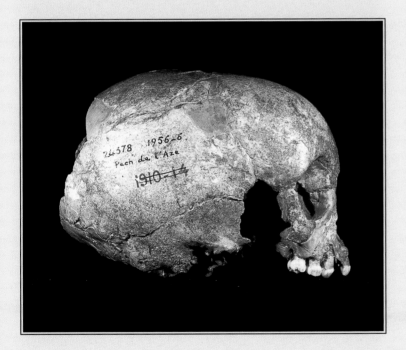

JUVENILE NEANDERTHALS

One can learn a lot about a species' morphologies by studying growth and development. With some morphologies, such as the medial projections within the Neanderthal nasal cavity and the large nasal region and protruding snout, unique structures are already present in children, as seen in the three-year olds from Pech de l'Azé [Figures 78a and b], Roc de Marsal and Subalyuk, and the slightly older juvenile from Teshik-Tash [Figures 79a and b], in whom these regions are preserved relatively intact. Other features, such as the puffy face, develop over time, since this externally expressed configuration results from growth and expansion of the maxillary sinus in this region. In the Peche de l'Azé child, and the somewhat older juvenile from Teshik-Tash, the face is not yet puffy. The details of the so-called Neanderthal brow also emerge during growth. In the Peche de l'Azé child, the brow region is essentially smooth. In the Teshik-Tash juvenile, low swellings are visible arcing over the orbits. And in the teenager from Le Moustier [Figures 80a and b], the brow is more recognizable as a structure. In *Homo sapiens*, the two-part brow that is otherwise unique to this hominid species also takes shape during growth.

[Figures 78a and b]
Child from the site of Pech de l'Azé, France.

PHOTOGRAPHS BY JEFFREY H. SCHWARTZ.

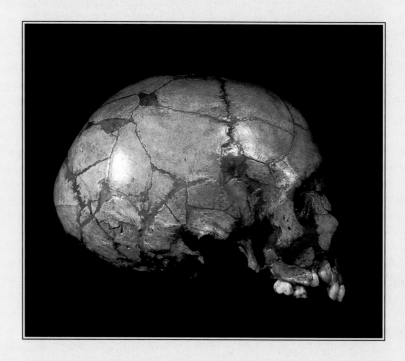

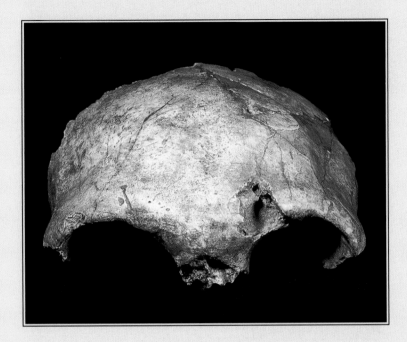

[Figures 80a and b]

Frontal bone of teenager from the site of Le Moustier, France.

PHOTOGRAPHS BY JEFFREY H. SCHWARTZ.

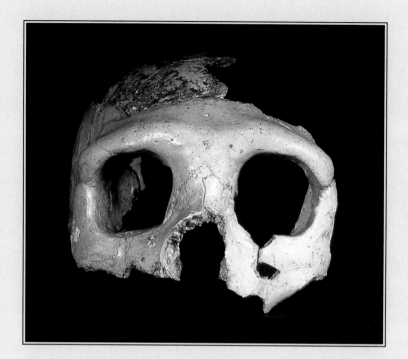

[Figures 81a and b]

Adult Neanderthal (Skull C)
from the site of Krapina,
Croatia.

PHOTOGRAPHS BY JEFFREY H. SCHWARTZ.

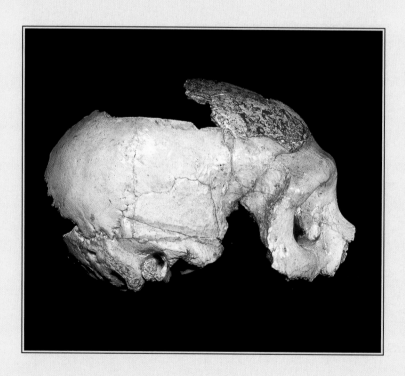

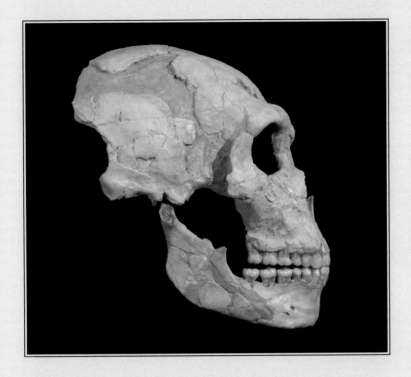

NEANDERTHAL PECULIARITIES

Although the sites of Krapina and St. Césaire differ in age by 100 ka—and as one of the youngest Neanderthal sites at approximately 36 ka, St. Césaire is also younger than some "Cro-Magnon" sites—the hominids from each are clearly Neanderthal. They have large nasal openings, distinct medial projections within the nasal cavity, protruding, "wedge-shaped" snouts, "puffy" faces, and "swept back" cheek bones. They are also like some other hominids, but different from *Homo sapiens*, in having the facial skeleton positioned at the front of the brain case and brows that are smoothly rolled and "double-arched."

[Figures 82a and b]

Adult Neanderthal (cast) from the site of St. Césaire, France.

DIGITAL SCANS BY ANTHONY LOCKWOOD AND KENNETH MOWBRAY; COURTESY OF AMERICAN MUSEUM OF NATURAL HISTORY.

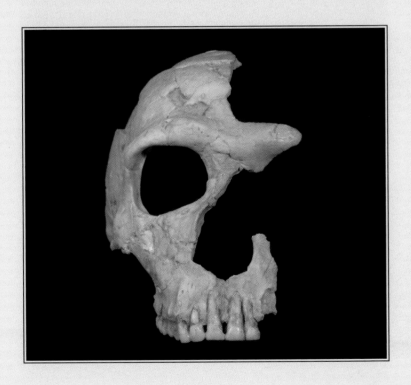

NEANDERTHAL GEOGRAPHIC VARIATIONS

Although one can define "Neanderthal" on the basis of various unique morphologies, there is some geographic variation among the specimens of *Homo neanderthalensis*, just as there is in other species, including *H. sapiens*. Compare, for instance, nuances in the expression of the brow, size of the nasal opening, curvature of the nasal bones, puffiness of the face, or protrusion of the snout, as well as length of the brain case, rise of the forehead, or swelling of the back of the skull in Gibraltar 1 [Figures 77a and b], Krapina C [Figures 81a and b], and St. Césaire [Figures 82a and b], and the following adult Neanderthal specimens.

[Figures 83a and b]

The Neanderthal from La Chapelle-aux-Saints, France, lost most of its teeth due to infection. This Neanderthal had very upturned nasal bones, an extremely wedge-shaped snout and puffy face, quite a low frontal rise, a long brain case, and a bulge at the rear of the skull. The medial projections in the nasal cavity are also less protrusive than in Gibraltar 1 (see Figures 77a and b).

PHOTOGRAPHS BY JEFFREY H. SCHWARTZ.

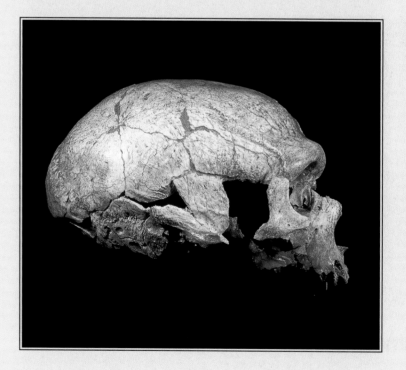

Extinct Humans

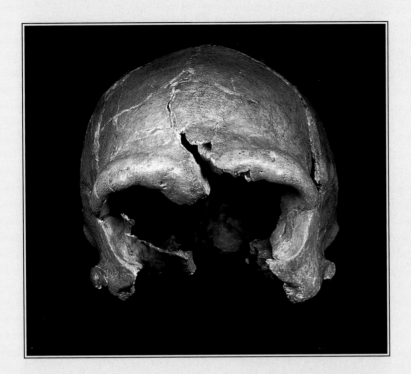

[Figures 84a and b]

The partial skull from the site of La Quina, France, is slightly smaller and narrower than the La Chapelle-aux-Saints specimen, but the degree of development of the brow is similar. In side view, the general profile is similar to that of La Chapelle-aux-Saints (see figures 85a and b).

PHOTOGRAPHS BY JEFFREY H. SCHWARTZ.

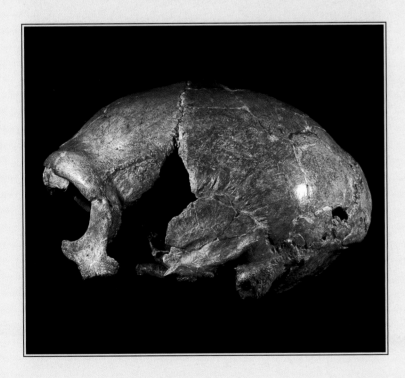

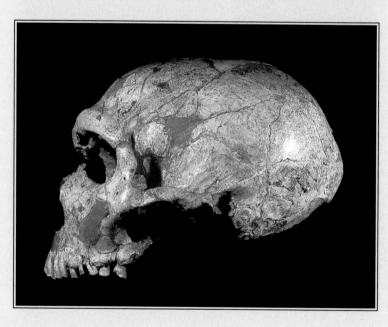

[Figures 86a and b]

The Monte Circeo skull from Italy, also known as Grotta Guattari 1, is reminiscent of the La Chapelle-aux-Saints cranium in having a very, long, low, and wide brain case, but its brow and nasal region are less protrusive.

PHOTOGRAPHS BY JEFFREY H. SCHWARTZ.

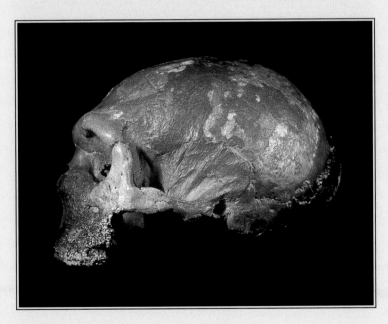

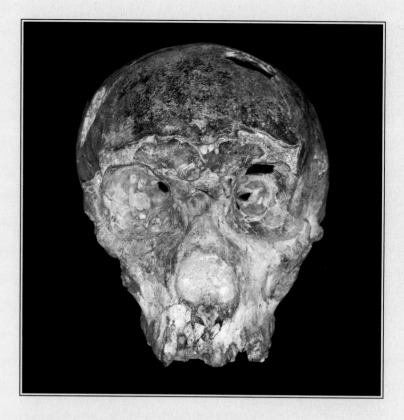

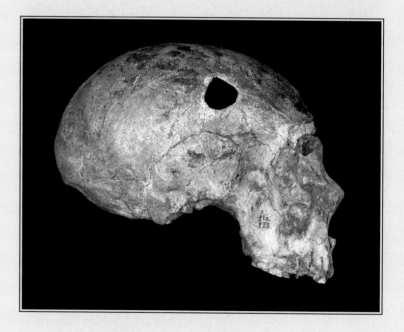

[Figures 87a and b]

The skull from the site of Saccopastore, Italy, is smaller than most Neanderthal crania, but is recognizably similar in its puffy though narrower face, protruding, wedge-shaped snout, and retreating cheek bone regions, as well as in its low and wide brain case. Although the brow ridges are not preserved, the configuration of the exposed, large but not excessively expansive frontal sinuses suggests that these structures would have been continuous above the nasal region and have followed the contour of the eye sockets. In side view, as in other Neanderthals, the long nasal bones of Saccopastore project markedly forward and the brain case is long, with some swelling at the rear.

PHOTOGRAPHS BY GIORGIO MANZI, MUSEO DI ANTROPOLOGIA OF THE UNIVERSITY OF ROME "LA SAPIENZA."

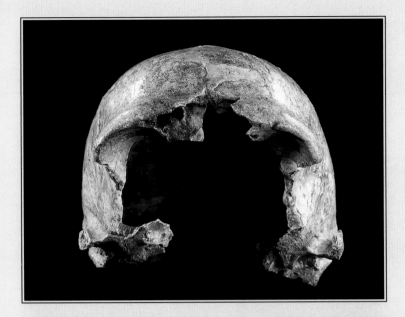

[Figures 88a and b]

The brain case of the Spy 1 partial skull from Belgium is not as low rising or wide as in some Neanderthals, and the preserved brows, although of similar configuration, are on the thinner side of the range of variation. In profile, the Spy 1 partial skull is not quite as low or projecting at the rear as are some other Neanderthals.

PHOTOGRAPHS BY JEFFREY H. SCHWARTZ.

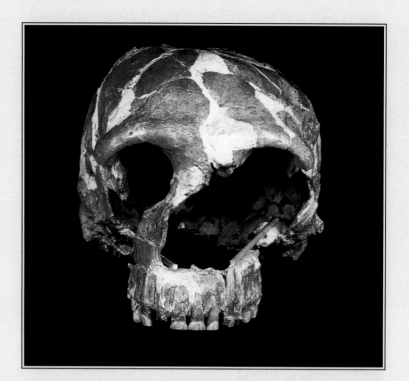

[Figures 89a and b]

The skull from the site of Tabun, Israel, is quite small, but very reminiscent of the markedly larger skulls from La Chapelle-aux-Saints and Monte Circeo in the relative width of the face and brain case, low rise of the forehead, and prominence of the brows. In side view the Tabun partial skull is also similar to various larger Neanderthals in the protrusion of the brow from the forehead and the long profile of the brain case.

PHOTOGRAPHS BY JEFFREY H. SCHWARTZ.

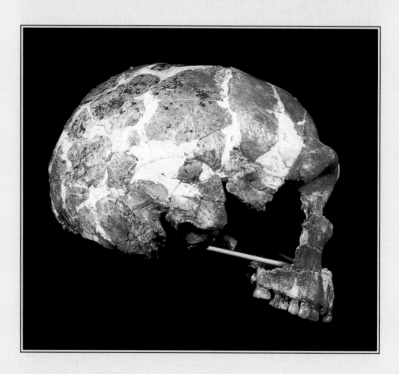

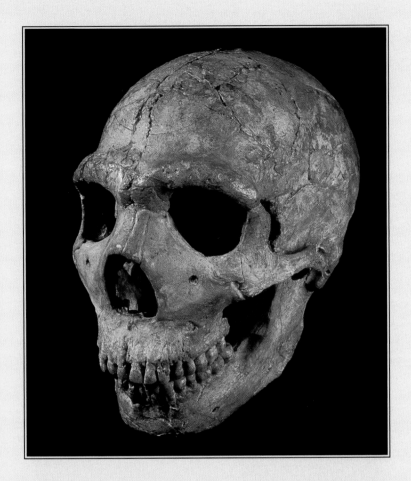

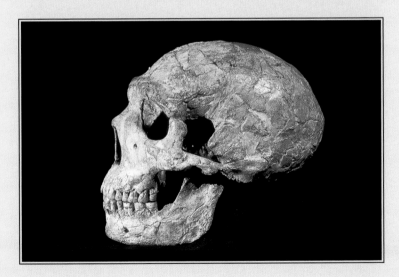

[Figures 90a and b]

Although the central face and nasal region of the Amud skull from Israel were reconstructed, perhaps, to look less Neanderthal-like in aspects of the snout, the preserved brows, partial face, and brain case are distinctly Neanderthal in their features.

PHOTOGRAPHS COURTESY OF ISRAEL ANTIQUITIES AUTHORITY.

Neanderthals and Human Extinctions

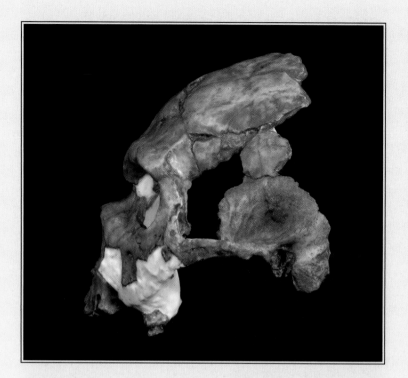

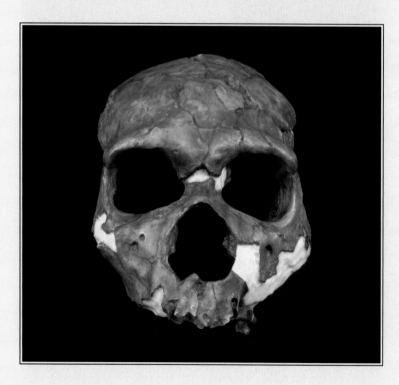

[Figures 91a and b]

The skull (cast) from the site of Shanidar, Iraq, known as Shanidar 5, has a somewhat narrower face and brain case than some of the other large-skulled Neanderthals, but the protruding, wedge-shaped snout, retreating cheek bones, and well-developed medial projections in the nasal cavity are recognizably "Neanderthal," as is the configuration of the brow region. The long profile of the brain case and forwardly positioned face of Shanidar 5 are characteristically Neanderthal.

DIGITAL SCANS BY ANTHONY LOCKWOOD AND KENNETH MOWBRAY; COURTESY OF THE AMERICAN MUSEUM OF NATURAL HOSTORY.

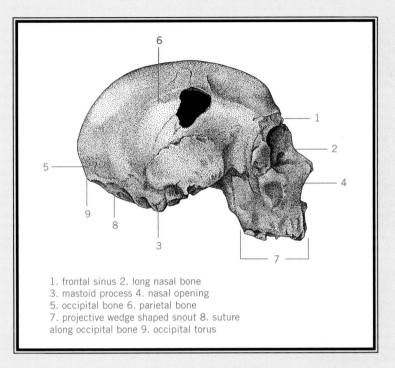

1. frontal sinus 2. long nasal bone
3. mastoid process 4. nasal opening
5. occipital bone 6. parietal bone
7. projective wedge shaped snout 8. suture
along occipital bone 9. occipital torus

[Figures 92 and 93]

Regional and temporal variation in Neanderthals is noted,
for instance, in a comparison
between the smaller and more
ancient Saccopastore skull from
Italy (top) and the larger and
more recent cranium from La
Chapelle-aux-Saints, France
(bottom). Of more immediate
note are the ways these individuals differed in upward flexure
of the long nasal bones, vacuity
of the nasal opening, rise of the
forehead, and distension of the
back of the brain case.

DRAWINGS BY DON MCGRANAGHAN.

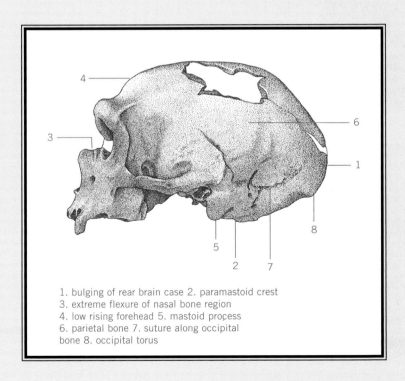

1. bulging of rear brain case 2. paramastoid crest
3. extreme flexure of nasal bone region
4. low rising forehead 5. mastoid process
6. parietal bone 7. suture along occipital
bone 8. occipital torus

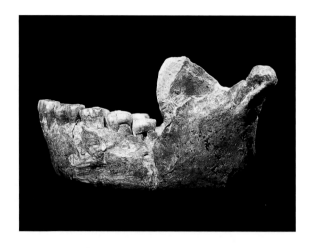

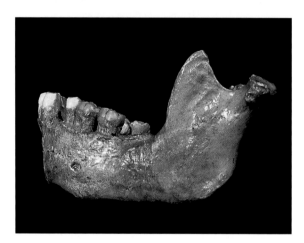

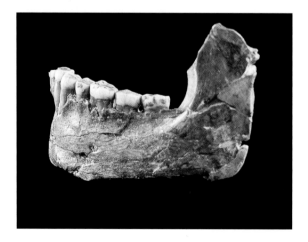

Neanderthal Anatomy

Since the discovery of the Feldhofer skull cap and its associated limb skeleton, Neanderthals have been characterized as having thick-walled bones. This is pretty much the case, but it is not constant across all specimens, particularly with regard to the skull. Neanderthals were also described as having long and low skulls, but this, too, is not entirely accurate. There is individual variation in skull length and slope of the forehead, just like there is in modern humans. In fact, one of the most satisfying things about studying Neanderthals is that, with so many specimens, it is possible to discuss individual variation. Thus, for instance, there appears to be a "French" kind of Neanderthal nose, with the nasal bones flexed quite severely upward (but not quite horizontal). In the Croatian, Italian, and southern Iberian Neanderthals, the slope of the nasal bones is a bit more downward. [Figures 92 and 93] There is also variation

[Figures 94, 95 and 96]
The Neanderthal Mandible

The Neanderthal mandible, or lower jaw, can be characterized by various features, such as being very broad across the front and having the last molar exposed in front of the vertical part, whose upper notch is asymmetrical in profile and whose inner surface bears well-developed muscle attachment sites. These characteristics are evident in the three mandibles pictured here: from of Tabūn, Mount Carmel range, Israel (top); One of the Croatian Krapina Neanderthal mandibles (middle), and from the site of Spy, Belgium (bottom). These individuals vary from one another such as in the degree to which the mandible is thin (Tabūn) or robust (Spy), its front is flat (Tabūn and Krapina) or slightly bulging (Spy) and/or rather vertical (Krapina) or tilted forward (Tabūn), the lower margin of the front of the mandible is raised and cornered at its sides (Krapina and Spy) or level with smooth bone (Tabūn), and the roots of the front teeth curve out and overhand the front of the jaw (Spy).

Photographs by Jeffrey H. Schwartz.

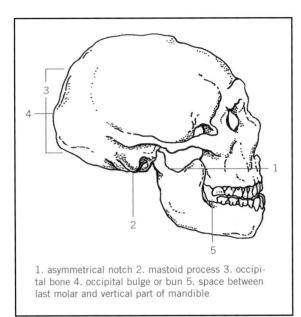

1. asymmetrical notch 2. mastoid process 3. occipital bone 4. occipital bulge or bun 5. space between last molar and vertical part of mandible

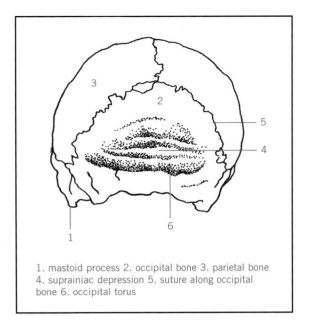

1. mastoid process 2. occipital bone 3. parietal bone 4. suprainiac depression 5. suture along occipital bone 6. occipital torus

[Figures 97a and b]
Various features of the skull that are typical of Neanderthals and discussed in the text. Drawings by Bridget D. Thomas.

in the slope of the front of the mandible when viewed from the side. [Figures 94, 95 and 96] In one mandible from Israel's Tabūn, for instance, the front of the lower jaw slopes down and back very strongly. But in some of the Krapina mandibles, this surface is almost vertical. And in the Spy mandible, the profile of the mandible is fairly vertical but the front surface is slightly swollen.

This list can go on and on: is there or is there not a prominent bulge or "bun," or an extensive or restricted indented and pitted area at the back of the skull? [Figures 97a and b] Is there a large or small space between the back of the third lower molar and the edge of the vertical part of the mandible; a shallow gutter or a smooth transition between the brow ridges and the forehead; a marked or a slight tapering of the lateral portions of the brow ridge? Are there large- or medium-sized bony projections into the nasal cavity; large or small pulp cavities in the molars; totally unseparated or partially separate molar and premolar tooth roots; extensive or slight wrinkling of the enamel on the molar teeth? Are the thumbs extraordinarily or only markedly long? There is plenty of variation here; but if you focus only on this level of morphological expression, you'll miss the evolutionary boat in terms of answering the most important question: do the Neanderthals represent a distinct species? Indeed, if you only paid attention to this kind of individual variation in

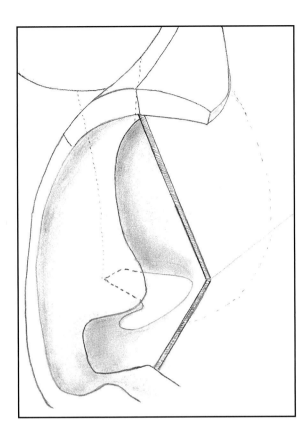

[Figures 98a and b]

One of our discoveries about Neanderthals is that they had
structures in the nasal cavity that are not found in other
mammals, much less hominids. The most obvious is the
development of a pair of swellings or medial projections
from the sidewalls of the nasal cavity. Behind the medial
projections, the wall of the nasal cavity balloons out.
Image by Jeffrey H. Schwartz.

Homo sapiens, you'd never be able to tell if we
constituted our own species or not.

As for derived features that do characterize
our core group of Neanderthals—that is, distinguish them from other hominids regardless of
whether any particular specimen has a large
"this" or a small "that"—they are present in
bountiful number. For instance, one of the
most amazing things that we have run across in
our multi-year study of these hominids is a feature that no one had described before. [Figures
98a and b] On the very first day of our study, we
were in London at the Natural History
Museum, looking at the Gibraltar adult
Neanderthal. Just inside the rim of
Neanderthal's huge nasal opening, on each
side, was a huge bony projection, behind which
was an even larger swelling of the inside wall of
the nasal cavity. And this specimen is not
unique. Every Neanderthal specimen that has
the nasal region preserved as completely as the
Gibraltar adult specimen not only has the typical large nasal opening, but also has these features within the nasal cavity. Size may vary
from individual to individual, but the swelling
is always there. You can even see the first projection already beginning to develop in the
skulls of various 3- or 4-year-old Neanderthal
children. The more posterior swelling is not yet
visible in these children because the maxillary
sinus has not yet expanded into the huge air-
space it becomes in the adult; but there's no
doubt that given time it would have developed.

A detailed comparison with other
hominids, and mammals in general, indicated
that, without a doubt, here was a truly unique
Neanderthal derived character. Although some
of our colleagues have argued that there are
hints of such structures, especially the projections toward the front of the nasal cavity, in
modern humans with broad noses—such as the
San—this is simply not the case. No other
mammal, much less hominid, that we've studied has these features. And what this means, as

our colleague Jeff Laitman has pointed out, is that some very important aspects of breathing in Neanderthals had to have been completely different than in other mammals. Even in the absence of any other features, if that kind of uniqueness doesn't demand recognition at the species level, what could?

But there's more, a lot more, that's derived about being a Neanderthal. For one thing, these hominids had huge maxillary sinuses that not only distended the inner walls of their nasal cavities, but puffed out the face just below the orbital region and even extended a bit up into the side walls of the nasal region and into the floor of the orbit itself. Clearly, Neanderthals certainly haven't been traditionally described as having a puffy face for no reason. When viewed from the top, the face of a Neanderthal looks like the prow of a ship: the forwardly placed snout juts right out there and the puffed-out cheekbones give more or less straight sides to the receding outline.

As the Harvard paleoanthropologist W. W. Howells pointed out years ago, if you made a triangle by connecting lines from the first lower molar to the suture at the front of the cheek bone that comes to the bottom of the orbit, and then on to the suture in the middle of the cheekbone, it would be large in Neanderthals and very thin in present-day humans. This is because the Neanderthal face is so forwardly positioned, and it correlates in turn with the fact that the upper teeth are very forwardly placed, well in front of the cranial vault. And, because upper and lower teeth develop so as to be in occlusion with each other, the lower teeth of Neanderthals lie very far

forward along the mandible, which is why the famous gap exists between the back of the third molar and the vertical part of the mandible behind it. It is also why the horizontal body of the mandible is relatively long.

The last major facial feature that is accepted as typically Neanderthal is the configuration of the brow ridge. Viewed from the front, it has the general shape of McDonald's famous double arches because it curves over the top of each orbit. However, it is not uniformly thick, as it has sometimes been portrayed. The brow is actually thinner to some extent at its lateral extremities than in its midsection. When viewed from the side, the brow rolls smoothly out and up from the upper margin of the orbit and then over and back into the forehead. The brow has no sharp or otherwise delineated margins, top or bottom.

The rest of the Neanderthal skull is less riddled with derived features than is the front of the skull. Howells and Santa Luca, for instance, thought that Neanderthals might have an oddly configured and arranged set of crests on the base of the skull, not too far in from the ear. Our own experience, however, suggests that, once you have sorted out the crests, there's too much individual variation to make this a reliable suite of anatomical traits. But there is one region of particular interest—an area on the occipital bone, at the very back of the skull.

In the "old" days of the 1960s and 1970s, Neanderthals were described as having an occipital torus (a bar of bone of relatively uniform thickness) that coursed horizontally across the occipital bone. Above this bone lay a

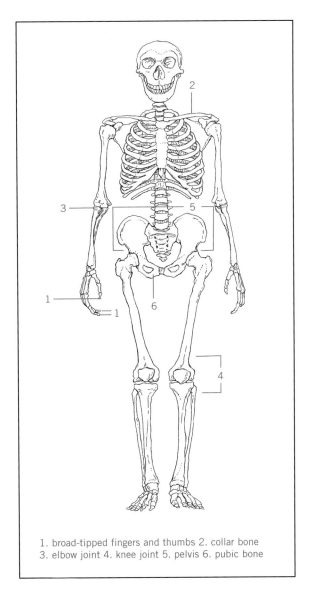

"suprainiac depression" with crisply defined margins and a pitted surface. Well, as it turns out, that's sort of correct. We found in the course of our studies that the torus is indeed defined below by an inward displacement of the bone below it. In contrast, a true upper border to the occipital torus can only be observed immediately below the suprainiac depression (whose edge is usually only crisply defined down near the torus). The depression, which is always there, can be larger or smaller, and the upper edge of the torus is thereby better or more poorly defined.

While we were studying the occipital region, we also noticed that the outline of the occipital bone, which is delineated by its sutural edge, was different from other hominids. When viewed from the side, the lateral part of the bone's edge (suture) does not veer up and back in Neanderthals from its contact with the adjoining parietal bone and the mastoid region of the temporal. Instead, for some distance this portion of the suture runs back fairly horizontally, before turning upward. When viewed from behind, the rest of the suture follows a low arc up and across the midpoint of the bone. It doesn't come to a peak in the midline as it does in us, for example.

Neanderthals also show uniquenesses in various other aspects of the skeleton. [Figure 99] For instance, their collar bones are extraor-

1. broad-tipped fingers and thumbs 2. collar bone 3. elbow joint 4. knee joint 5. pelvis 6. pubic bone

dinarily long. Their finger tips are very broad. Their elbow and knee joints are broadly delineated from the shafts of the bones on either side of the joint—somewhat as in camels! The Neanderthal pelvis is also unusual in that the pubic bone—which runs on each side from the

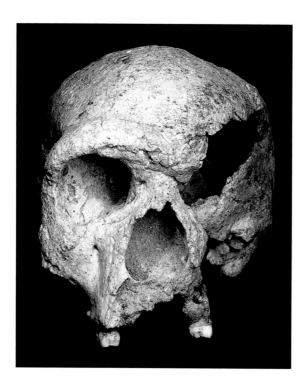

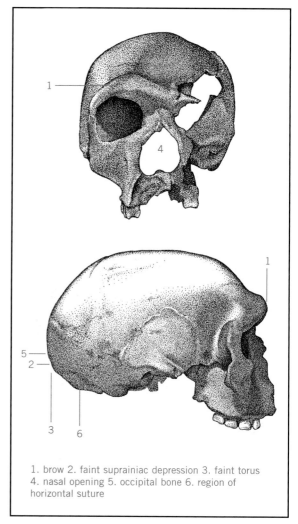

[Figures 100 and 101a and b]

The Steinheim skull (above), from Germany, is similar to Neanderthals in the configuration (right) of its brow, the large size of the nasal opening, the horizontal suture near the occipital bone, and the forward position of the face on the long, low brain case. Because the Steinheim skull has only a faint suprainiac depression and weak occipital torus (which are more marked in Neanderthals) and does not have a puffy face and protruding, wedge-shaped snout (unlike Neanderthals altogether), we think it represents a different species, but one that is related to Neanderthals.

Photograph by Jeffrey H. Schwartz;
drawings by Don McGranaghan.

1. brow 2. faint suprainiac depression 3. faint torus 4. nasal opening 5. occipital bone 6. region of horizontal suture

hip joint to the midline—is remarkably long. In addition, the end of the pubic bone that contributed to the midline joint (the symphysis) is tall from top to bottom and relatively thin from front to back.

We could go on and on, into the finer details of Neanderthal morphology. We think,

however, the point is already made: there is a plethora of features that emerge as distinctive of Neanderthals among hominids, especially when compared with modern humans. Clearly, these features point to a species distinction. But what does the picture look like when we add other European specimens to the comparison?

Well, for one thing, there are associated occipital, right and left parietal bones from the

English site of Swanscombe, which is anywhere from 250–350 kyr old. The hominid it represents has been touted as being on the way to becoming modern human. But the occipital has the sutural outline, the inferiorly defined torus, and the pitted depression of Neanderthals. As old or perhaps even older are specimens from the German site of Weimar-Ehringsdorf. These are Neanderthal-like in the various preserved cranial bones and (unfortunately worn) teeth. On the basis of these specimens, it appears that we can extend the temporal range of Neanderthals back at least another 100 kyr beyond the limits defined by the core group alone (to well over 200 kyr).

Penecontemporaneous with the Swanscombe specimen (and perhaps also with another, rather different-looking hominid from the German site of Reilingen) is a small, partially damaged skull from Steinheim, also in Germany. [Figures 100, 101a and b] Because of its Neanderthal-like brow and large nasal opening, this specimen has been linked to Neanderthals. However, because it lacks a puffy face, and its occipital torus and suprainiac depression are weakly developed, the Steinheim skull has generally been taken as an early, not-yet-fully-developed Neanderthal. From our perspective, however, this specimen seems not to be simply a poor man's Neanderthal, but a member of a distinct species that is closely related to Neanderthals. This species declares its relationship to Neanderthals by the shared configuration of the shared brow ridge and the large nasal opening, as well as by features of the occipital bone and

the long horizontal suture on its side. And what this means is that we cannot view the form of the brow ridge, the large nasal opening, and the horizontal occipital suture as derived Neanderthal features. It seems instead that these characteristics were present in the common ancestor of a group of related species that includes *H. neanderthalensis*. However, because the features of the occipital are not as pronounced in the Steinheim specimen as in Neanderthals, we conclude that the degree to which these features are expressed in Steinheim more closely reflects the common ancestral condition. Neanderthals became more specialized and, subsequently, developed a more strongly delineated occipital torus and suprainiac depression.

The same kind of argument applies to features within the nasal region. To our surprise, when we looked inside the nasal cavity of the Steinheim specimen, we found preserved on the right side (the left side was damaged) a small projection—a miniature version of the larger projection seen in Neanderthals. Again, it seems most likely that the last common ancestor of the Steinheim species and the Neanderthals had a small projection of this kind, which became much more pronounced in Neanderthals after the two species separated. There are, however, some features in which the Steinheim specimen is distinctly more primitive (like the common ancestor) than the Neanderthals. The most obvious of these is in the facial region, just below the orbits. Whereas in Neanderthals this area is puffed out, in the Steinheim specimen it isn't. It is nicely sunken, just as in *Homo sapiens* and a lot

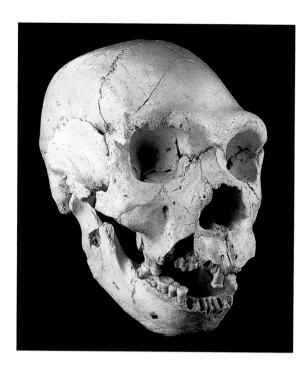

the Atapuerca region north of Madrid, just outside the city of Burgos. [Figure 102] This site,
which is still being excavated by Juan Luis
Arsuaga and a team of gifted experts, has been
dated to approximately 300 kyr ago, and will
probably end up holding the all-time record for
the largest number of hominid specimens to
come from one place. Because of this, Arsuaga
and his colleagues have been engaged in the
study of individual variation within this assemblage, which to us, at least, appears to represent
yet another, as yet unnamed, species of *Homo*.
A striking feature of the Sima skulls is their
Neanderthal-like (and Steinheim-like) large
nasal openings and brow ridges. They also
share the horizontal lateral part of the occipital
suture with Neanderthals and Steinheim,
adding yet another hominid to the Neanderthal
clade. Because the Sima skull can be readily distinguished from the skulls of all other
hominids, we think it will eventually be accepted by paleoanthropologists as representing a
distinct species. By linking the Sima material
with the Neanderthal-Steinheim group we conclude that the brow configuration, the large
nasal opening, and the horizontal lateral part of
the occipital suture would have characterized
their last common ancestor—which is why, of
course, all these hominids have these features.

But, in the meantime, what about *Homo
sapiens*? Clearly, Neanderthals are easily distinguished as a species, even among the diverse
group of European hominids within which they
fit. As for ourselves, however, the problem has
been that history has always had us at the top of
the heap, being more everything than any other

of other primates. What this means is that the
puffy face of Neanderthals—of which the hugely
expanded maxillary sinus is the underlying cul-
prit—is definitely a derived feature of *H. neanderthalensis*, a feature in which the Steinheim
specimen and *H. sapiens* remain primitive.

Is that it for the larger Neanderthal-related
group to which we referred earlier? We think
not. There's a least one other group of relevant
specimens, from the Sima de los Huesos site of

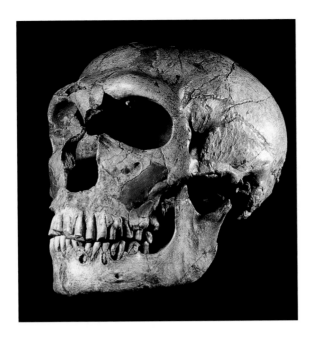 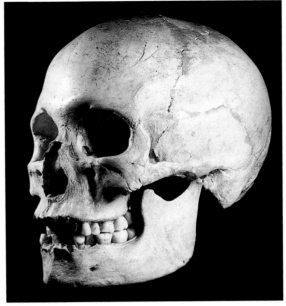

[Figures 103 and 104]

As seen in the La Ferrassie adult Neanderthal (left), the "chin" region is essentially smoothly rounded from side to side and featureless. In contrast, the "chin" region of *Homo sapiens*, as seen in the specimen from Abri Pataud (right) is unique and distinctive among hominids in having a raised vertical keel along the midline that fans out, thickens, and becomes more protrusive toward the lower margin of the jaw; there is also a shallow depression on each side of midline keel. Photographs by Jeffrey H. Schwartz.

animal, extinct hominids included. And because of this, there hasn't been much attention paid to sorting out exactly what features do distinguish us as a species. *Nosce te ipsum*, again! But we have to undertake this task before we can even begin to figure out who our closest fossil relatives may have been.

One of the features that Blumenbach pointed to as diagnostic of our species is our protruding chin. But the character "protruding" isn't specific enough to use to distinguish one specimen from another. On this basis you would lump together—as indeed some of our colleagues have done—such disparate specimens as the Spy mandible—with its low-mounded profile—and modern human mandibles—in which the chin takes the distinctive form of an inverted letter T. But the T configuration is actually something very special, and it develops very early in life. No Neanderthal specimen (including the children, in whom you would expect to find such clues if they existed) has such a configuration at the front of the lower jaw. [Figure 103] This feature is something truly distinctive of *Homo sapiens*, and we can use it as the starting point to morphologically define our own species. [Figure 104]

Another feature that has been suggested as being distinctive of *Homo sapiens* is the development of what's been called a bipartite brow. This means that our brow region has two com-

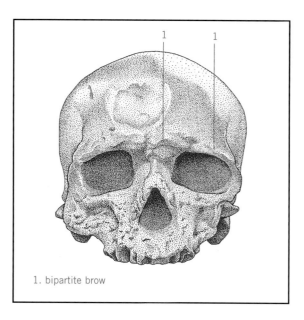

[Figure 105]
Homo sapiens is also unique and distinctive among hominids in having a two-part or bipartite brow. Even mineral deposits and severe weathering on the Cro-Magnon 1 skull from France cannot mask this derived feature of our own species. Drawing by Don McGranaghan.

1. bipartite brow

ponents to it: a variably bulbous area in the center that extends some way on each side over the eye, and a "plate-like" lateral portion. If you try to feel this on your own brow, about midway over each eye you will detect a "break," often in the form of a very perceptible notch or thin depression. [Figure 105] Many fossil crania and lower jaws—such as those from the well-known French sites of Cro-Magnon and Abri Pataud, and at least some of those from the much earlier Levantine locality of Jebel Qafzeh (approximately 100 kyr)—show these features of living *H. sapiens*. On the other hand, some other specimens that have been traditionally designated "anatomically modern *H. sapiens*," (some other

specimens from Qafzeh, for instance) don't have them, and in our view cannot be regarded as members of our species.

Other features that have been considered to be typical of *H. sapiens*, are basically generalities. For instance, we are supposed to have a more lightly built skeleton, a more vaulted or rounded cranium, and smaller teeth. Of course, these are comparative statements, and have usually been made under the assumption that "archaic *H. sapiens*" (i.e., usually Neanderthals) were our own anatomical precursors. In which case, our own evolution was simply a matter of becoming more gracile, and all boundaries are arbitrary. But such speculations basically do little more than reflect the notion that we are at the top of the evolutionary pile. And meanwhile, in the broader realm of looking at our own species, there's still a lot of work to be done. Delineating that unique "chin" and the bipartite brow is only the beginning.

The Ice Age Environment in Europe and Western Asia

The Neanderthals, then, were highly distinctive in their anatomy. They were their own species, and need to be dignified as such if we are ever to understand them. There is no evidence whatever that Neanderthals evolved directly into *Homo sapiens* as the lingering devotees of the Great Chain of Being would like to claim. As far as we can tell, then, for two hundred millennia or so the Neanderthals inhabited Europe and western Asia untroubled by competition from other hominids. Such tranquillity apart, what kind of world did they inhabit?

Well, these were times of extraordinary climatic extremes. As we've seen, during the Ice Ages the more northerly parts of Europe were covered periodically by ice sheets up to a mile thick. In the inhabitable areas to the south of the ice sheets summers were short, if not hugely cooler than those of today, and the winters were long and cold. In contrast, today's world climates are fairly typical of a major warmer interglacial period. The transition between peaks of warmth and troughs of cold was not a smooth progression, for within each major cold/warm cycle there were many short-term oscillations in temperature and humidity. These variations profoundly affected environments in the Neanderthals' world. The broadleaf forests that form the climax vegetation of mid-latitude Europe in interglacial conditions yielded in glacial times to open steppe and tundra. During the Ice Ages a huge variety of large-bodied mammals roamed over the steppes and tundra. With this in mind, it's important to remember that, for hunting/gathering hominids, cold times were not necessarily hard times, uncomfortable though they may have been by our modern standards. For killing herding mammals in an open landscape would certainly have been a lot easier and more energy-efficient than pursuing red deer or wild boar through dense oak forests.

But perhaps the most important thing of all to bear in mind is that the Ice Ages were not a monolithic period of harsh, cold environments. Just as today, Ice Age environments varied at any one time from locality to locality, depending on such geographically variable factors as latitude, elevation, local topography, and the proximity of the ocean, as well as on prevailing temperatures and humidities. And just as the vegetation would have varied locally, so also would have the fauna available to be exploited by the Neanderthals. In flatlands, for instance, a typical plains fauna would have embraced horses, wild cattle, and bison, whereas in areas of more jagged topography mountain sheep and ibex would have dominated, posing a totally different—and much more difficult—set of problems. There is thus no "typical" Neanderthal habitat, to which these hominids were specifically "adapted." Indeed, what the Neanderthals are most remarkable for is their success in occupying and exploiting a vast range of different habitats over a very long period of time. Yet it is still common for paleoanthropologists to argue that the Neanderthals were cold-adapted, and several of their physical specializations, for example their limb proportions and their large nasal cavities, have been "explained" as adaptations of this kind. On the face of it some of this is quite plausible, at least as regards body shape. For the Neanderthals were rather stocky, something also characteristic of Arctic *Homo sapiens* today. Adaptation of the nasal tract to cold environments is, on the other hand, little more than pure speculation. More important is that we do not know where or at what point in the glacial/interglacial cycle the Neanderthals actually originated and acquired their distinctive morphologies. The dating and characterization of the earliest putative Neanderthals is so poor

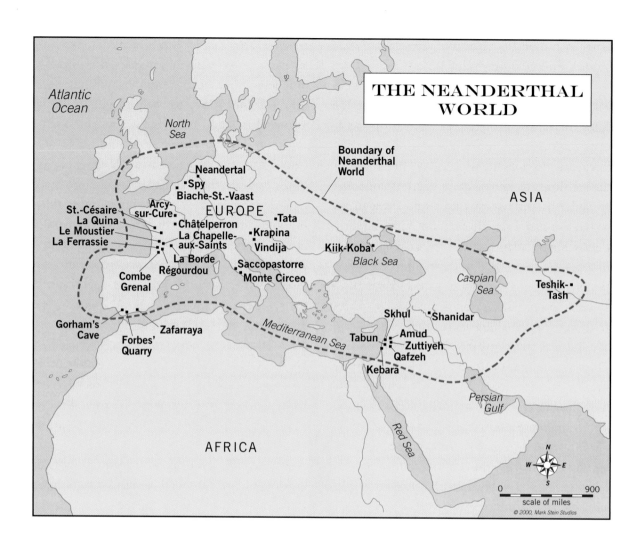

THE NEANDERTHAL WORLD

Atlantic Ocean

North Sea

Boundary of Neanderthal World

ASIA

EUROPE

Neandertal
Spy
Biache-St.-Vaast
St.-Césaire
Arcy-sur-Cure
La Quina
Le Moustier
Châtelperron
La Chapelle-aux-Saints
La Ferrassie
Tata
Krapina
Vindija
Kiik-Koba
La Borde
Régourdou
Saccopastorre
Monte Circeo
Combe Grenal
Black Sea
Caspian Sea
Teshik-Tash
Gorham's Cave
Zafarraya
Forbes' Quarry
Mediterranean Sea
Skhul
Shanidar
Tabun
Amud
Zuttiyeh
Qafzeh
Kebara
Persian Gulf
Red Sea

AFRICA

N W E S

0   900
scale of miles
© 2000, Mark Stein Studios

that there is no way in which we can associate the origin of these distinctive hominids with a particular set of climatic conditions.

The notion of cold-adaptedness among Neanderthals is thus largely an historical artifact, stemming principally from the incontrovertible fact that the largest concentration of Neanderthal sites and fossils is known from the last glacial period, subsequent to about 100 kyr ago. Even so, however, concrete evidence for

> **[Figure 106]**
>
> During the period between 200 kyr and 27 kyr ago, the Neanderthals inhabited a vast swath of Europe and western Asia, from the Atlantic east to Uzbekistan and from Wales south to Gibraltar and the Levant. The dotted line encloses all regions from which Neanderthal fossils are known.
> Map by Mark Stein.

Neanderthal occupation of areas close to the glacial fronts, or of regions of tundra, is actually quite poor. [Figure 106] What's more, we have to remember that the long Neanderthal record stretches back, albeit in a fairly spotty fashion, well beyond the last glacial period. Indeed, the record embraces all of the warm last interglacial period, and extends well into the colder period before it—and maybe further yet. Given all this, then, perhaps the most important thing to know at present about the Neanderthals is not how they were biologically adapt*ed*, but the simple fact that they were evidently highly adapt*able*. It was, after all, surely this flexibility—partly, at least, based on technology—that above everything else ensured the Neanderthals' ability to flourish for a long period in a huge variety of ever-changing habitats. These ranged from the relatively benign and sheltered conditions of littoral western France to the harsh plains of central Europe and beyond: a sweep of environments that, as far as we know, no earlier hominid had ever matched.

Neanderthal Technology

The Neanderthals faced this suite of circumstances armed with a fairly sophisticated and modestly homogeneous stone tool kit that is known as the Mousterian industry. The Mousterian represents the finest expression of a new technology of stoneworking that first shows up in Europe something over 250 kyr ago (though it didn't become ubiquitous until much later). We don't know who the first makers of "prepared-core" tools of this kind were, but it's clear that this innovation marked a major waypoint in stone toolmaking technology: one that

was in its way just as radical as the advance from the simple Oldowan cutting flake to the carefully shaped Acheulean biface. In this new technique, a stone core was carefully shaped, to a point at which a single blow would detach a quasi-finished tool (or series of tools) of predefined form. Such flake implements were co-opted to a variety of different uses: large ovoid flakes, for instance, were often employed as hand-held cutters and scrapers, and small triangular "Levallois points" may have been hafted to spear-ends. Whatever their exact uses, however, all such tools had the advantage of possessing long, continuous cutting edges right around their peripheries. During the middle of the twentieth century an elaborate typology of Mousterian stone tool-types was devised, with more than 60 separate sorts of flake tool recognized, plus a large number of handaxe types. [Figure 107] However, it has been found subsequently that many of these apparent tool-types resulted from repeated resharpenings of individual tools that actually belonged to a much smaller group of beginning categories. Each individual tool, moreover, may well have served a series of different functions as it became smaller and differently shaped as a result of the resharpening process. What's more, it is also becoming clear that differences between toolkits in different localities may be because of the intensity with which tools were reused—something that, in turn, depended on influences that were independent of the technological tradition itself. Raw materials, for instance, are obviously a key factor in stone toolmaking. And more resharpening may have been done in

[Figure 107]

Mousterian tools from various sites in western France.
From left: scraper on flake; two small handaxes; scraper
and point on flakes. Photograph by Ian Tattersall.

localities where good raw materials were harder to come by, purely because they were more difficult to obtain.

Making—and even resharpening—stone tools of this sort is by no means a simple activity. And although prepared-core techniques improved over time, it's clear that even the earliest makers of such tools were cognitively quite sophisticated. It seems, however, that Neanderthals made only limited efforts to import better types of raw material to areas where high-grade stone was scarce (which is, apparently, why Mousterian tools made from the best materials tend to have been intensively resharpened). What's more, they rarely employed other preservable materials in their toolmaking activities. Occasionally we find at Mousterian sites a piece of bone or antler that appears to have been used as a hammer in knapping stone tools. Rarely, however, were bone or antler themselves used as raw materials for implement manufacture. At one seashore site in Italy, some simple tools made from flaked sea shells were found, but such implements are remarkable for being the exception rather than the rule. On the other hand, studies of the marks left by wear on the cutting surfaces of Mousterian stone tools have shown that many of them had been used in working wood, which itself rarely preserves but which leaves a characteristic polish on tools used to cut or shape it. We can never know for sure about the range and accomplishment of Neanderthal woodworking. However, one obvious way in which stone tools could have acquired such a polish is by being used in the sharpening of spears. Weapons of this kind were at least occasionally tipped with stone, as the damage patterns exhibited by some Levallois points studied at Levantine sites testify. However, as the Schöeningen spears we encountered in the last chapter eloquently demonstrate, sharpened wood by itself makes a formidable weapon—especially, as it turns out, when it has been hardened by charring.

It is interesting that stone tools that have been found to bear woodworking polish are not typologically consistent. Implements that archaeologists had described from their form as diversely as "knives," "scrapers," and "points" have all been found to exhibit this same polish—suggesting that the traditional method of describing and classifying the function of Mousterian tools from their form may not be a reliable procedure. What's more, it may also give us pause by suggesting that the Neanderthals themselves saw their stone implements with eyes very different from our own.

One final point about the Mousterian industry: it is generally associated with the Neanderthals, but it is not synonymous with them. There are plenty of Mousterian sites in northern Africa, for example, but not one Neanderthal fossil is known from there. Similarly, Mousterian industries in the Levant are positively associated both with Neanderthals and with early anatomically modern humans. And in Europe, very late-occurring Neanderthals are associated with various non-Mousterian industries, the best-known of which is the French Châtelperronian. These industries, although apparently derived from the Mousterian, show features that suggest cultural contact with the *Homo sapiens* who began arriving in Europe at around that time. We'll look at these in more detail shortly.

Neanderthal Lifestyles

Like their predecessors since time immemorial, the Neanderthals were hunters and gatherers, living off the bounty afforded by nature. Like all hunter-gatherers the Neanderthals must have lived a shifting existence, moving from one campsite to the next as local resources became depleted. Given the Neanderthals' early reputation as "cavemen," it's important to emphasize that although light and airy yet sheltered spots such as cave entrances and rock overhangs were certainly desirable places to live—especially if they faced south—they were not the only places in which Neanderthals camped. Intensive

"landscape archaeology" is beginning to reveal that Neanderthals frequently stayed at open-air sites. Nonetheless, it is with the Neanderthals that we begin for the first time to find abundant evidence of the repeated revisiting of favored sites, and these happen generally to be in places such as rock shelters and cave entrances simply because these are where preservation is most likely. Typically, however, such occupations appear to have been rather short—weeks, perhaps, rather than months—and in many cave sites, especially, there is evidence that carnivores moved in during the times when no hominid occupants were in residence.

Most Neanderthal sites show little evidence of any structuring of the living space, or of attempts to improve it, although in a few places local concentrations of stones and bones have been interpreted as showing the outlines of tent- or windbreak-like structures. At the French site of Combe-Grenal was found a natural cast of something that looks unambiguously like a tent-peg. At a couple of other spots quite extensive "floors" have been identified that consist of closely laid cobbles. At Combe-Grenal and one or two other sites in France, Neanderthals appear to have dug shallow pits into their living areas. Nobody knows for certain what these were for, but it's been suggested that they may have been places where food was stored. In the Levant, the important Neanderthal site of Kebara shows evidence of some rudimentary organization of space, with hearths concentrated in one area and food refuse in another. But as far as the organized use of space is concerned, that's about it. For of the hundreds of Mousterian sites known, almost all are relatively haphazard, lacking any clear evidence that their ancient occupants had consciously partitioned off the living space according to different functions.

One telling feature of Mousterian sites is that they tend to be comparatively small, which suggests in turn that social group sizes were rather limited: perhaps to a couple of dozen individuals at most. We know nothing for certain about how Neanderthal groups were organized, although based on his preliminary interpretation of the single site of Combe-Grenal, the archaeologist Louis Binford has come up with the startling conclusion that males and females there had led largely—though not totally—separate lives: something never recorded among modern hunter-gatherers. And whether or not this idea turns out to be widely accepted, it is valuable in reminding us powerfully of the folly of trying to interpret the behavior of extinct humans in terms of what we know of *Homo sapiens* today or in the historic past. It is certainly convenient, and at some level even satisfying, to interpret the facts of a vanished world in terms of a "living model" that we can actually observe in action. But we are assuredly deluding ourselves if we try to draw such parallels too closely when the living model is the highly unusual *H. sapiens.* Of course, whatever the reasons, our extinct relatives are just that—extinct. Hence, there is a strong temptation to see them as "losers" in the evolutionary game—just as we, for the moment at least, are "winners." But if we succumb to this temptation it's almost inevitable that we will come to see those vanished relatives as no more than inferior versions of ourselves; and if we do this, we will never succeed in doing them justice as entities that in most cases flourished on the world scene for much longer than *H. sapiens* has yet contrived to do. There are many ways of doing business successfully in this world, and ours is only one of them.

A major ingredient in Binford's reconstruction of life at Combe-Grenal is the evidence for differing uses of fire there. As we have already hinted, there are considerable uncertainties over when fire was effectively domesticated. Very early intimations of fire use well over 1 myr ago in Africa remain controversial, and some classical examples in the 400-kyr range, such as Zhoukoudian and Terra Amata, have also been challenged of late. Even if further research should bear out some early occurrences of fire use such as these, it will still remain true that they are exceptions rather than the rule. It is only within—well within—the time-span of the Neanderthals that domesticated fire became a regular—and even then, far from inevitable—feature of hominid living-sites. Of course, preservation is always an issue here: evidence is much less likely to survive of fires that did not burn in hearths scooped out in the ground, and/or lined with stones, and absence of evidence of fire-use often cannot be taken as reliable evidence of absence. Nonetheless, the regular construction of hearths was certainly a highly significant element in the incorporation of fire-use into hominid domestic lifestyles, and this innovation seems to have come fairly late. Apart from a few questionable occurrences at European and Asian sites, the earliest well-defined collections of hearths (not all stone-lined) have been found at Mousterian sites about 60 kyr old (the age of Combe-Grenal), and as widely separated as Portugal, Israel and Ukraine. Further, after this date hearths become much more common, although they are still far from an inevitable feature of Neanderthal occupations.

Fires provide warmth, light, and protection from carnivores. They permit the cooking of food, which kills parasites, as well as rendering many animal and plant products more digestible, and thus available. They are useful in the hardening of wood and flint. And perhaps most importantly of all, with wide ramifications, they provide a spatial focus for group activities. In the longer term, fire control opened the door to technologies such as ceramics and metalworking. Clearly, the control of fire was one of the most significant innovations in the entire long history of hominid technology, and the most basic of its advantages would have been available from the very beginning. Yet it's at least possible, perhaps even likely, that the regular use of fire lagged significantly (hundreds of thousands of years, perhaps more than a million) behind its first use. This is a major mystery; and it's particularly frustrating that the early record of fire use is so cryptic.

Equally frustrating is our lack of knowledge of Neanderthal clothing. Few would contest the notion that the Neanderthals' (and their predecessors') successful penetration of some areas of pretty harsh climate strongly implies that at least seasonally they wore clothing as protection against the cold. But the only even semi-direct information we have on this matter comes from studies of the wear-surfaces of some Mousterian stone tools. These tools bear a characteristic type of polish that indicates their use in scraping animal hides. Of course, what those hides were used for once scraped we don't know, because no Mousterian hides have been preserved. Yet although hides may have been used for all sorts of purposes, including the improvement of living spaces and making containers, it is practically inconceivable that they were not also used—even regularly used—for clothing. Exactly what that clothing was like is now entirely conjectural; for even in late Mousterian times the bone needle, hence tailoring as we understand it, was still a thing of the future. It's possible to imagine that a typical suit of Neanderthal clothing consisted of hides with slits or holes cut in them for heads, arms, and so forth, the whole tied together with thongs or leather strips. But unfortunately, barring some altogether unexpected discovery, we will never know for sure.

Neanderthal Economies

There has been considerable debate over how efficient the Neanderthals were as hunters. At one time hunting was considered to be a central aspect of hominid behavior, going back to the very beginning of the human lineage. However, once it had been recognized that extrapolating from modern human behaviors carries the risk of making us see extinct humans simply as inferior versions of ourselves, the role of hunting in the economic lives of those extinct species had to be rethought. Of course, the pendulum effect being what it is, there was a resulting tendency to minimize the role of hunting in any hominid species other than *Homo sapiens*, including *H. neanderthalensis*. Nowadays, however, some archaeologists are coming around to the view that, at least in certain times and places, Neanderthals were at least reasonably proficient hunters of medium-bodied mammals, such as reindeer. For example, caves in western Italy preserve evidence of Neanderthal occupation at two periods, one during the last interglacial around 120 kyr ago, and the other at about 50 kyr ago, in the run-up to the peak of the last glacial. In the earlier period occupations appear to have been rather brief, and the preponderance of animal remains were cranial parts of older individuals. This is in contrast with the later period, which had longer occupations. Most mammal remains from the later period were those of individuals in the prime of life, and a wider variety of body parts was represented. The archaeologists who investigated these sites concluded that most of the bones from the earlier period represented the scavenged remains of individuals that had died of natural causes, although at the later time the occupants had employed ambush-hunting techniques to kill animals whose carcasses they transported entire to their camp sites. This interpretation certainly reflects some flexibility in Neanderthal behavior patterns, although to what extent the differences in behavior represented direct responses to climate changes is not clear. Whatever the case, at least in the later period there does appear at these sites to be some evidence for quite efficient predation by Neanderthals upon deer-sized mammals.

Nonetheless, the notion of ambush-hunting by Neanderthals sits rather uneasily with the concept, put forward by Lewis Binford, that the Neanderthals were foragers, in contrast to modern humans, who are, or rather were, collectors. The distinction here is that while foragers roam relatively randomly around the landscape, opportunistically exploiting any resources they may encounter, collectors actively monitor their environments and plan the exploitation of the resources they offer. There is, of course, no sure way to know exactly how the Neanderthals obtained the animal remains that litter their living spaces. Although it seems very likely that these early humans were quite adaptable in the ways in which they made their living, there is very little evidence available to refute Binford's notion that the Neanderthals lacked modern human levels of forward planning and anticipation. Certainly, the sites they left behind tend to lack the structure and complexity of those of early modern humans, and it is reasonable to suppose that this reflects a fundamental difference in lifestyle.

Hunting is, of course, a relatively complicated behavior that tends to attract the attention of archaeologists because of the durable bone refuse it generates. It is also the kind of dramatic activity that captures our imaginations in a way that the more prosaic gathering of plant resources fails to do. We must never forget, however, that, even in highly carnivorous modern societies, meat rarely forms the bulk of the diet. Instead, plant-derived proteins and carbohydrates provide most of the nourishment in the daily menu, just as it seems reasonable to conclude they also did in Neanderthal times and earlier. The problem is one of evidence: soft plant remains rarely preserve over the millennia, so that no matter how important vegetable resources may have been to the Neanderthals (and other early hominids), we have no access to quantifiable proof of their nutritive role. Thus, although pollen preserves well, we cannot be sure that it represents plants used as dietary resources. Moreover, it is quite plausible that plant foods (and possibly also fish and small mammals, whose bones are rare at Neanderthal sites) may normally have been consumed where they were found, rather than being transported back to camp sites for consumption—a habit that would have exaggerated any bias toward medium-bodied mammals at central living sites. Diet can leave a signature in the chemistry of bones; and a recent preliminary study of collagen (an organic bone component) extracted from Neanderthal fossils from sites in France and Belgium, about 40 kyr old, suggests that the individuals concerned were quite highly carnivorous (unless they had died after a prolonged periods of starvation, which might have mimicked the effect observed). A couple of specimens is not of course, a great statistical sample upon which to base statements about the diet of an entire species. But findings such as this point to an important potential future source of information on the diets of extinct hominids.

Neanderthal Burial and Symbolic Behaviors

One of the main reasons for the relative abundance of Neanderthal fossils is that these hominids, as far as we know, were among the first to practice the burial of the dead. After all, it is not easy to become a fossil, because fresh remains are of the greatest interest to a variety of scavengers, including such legendary bone-crunchers as hyenas. Escaping such attentions is the essential first step toward becoming decently fossilized, and there's no better way of achieving this result than via successful burial. Indeed, it's quite possible that the motivation for Neanderthal burial was no more than this: to discourage the interest of scavengers in the places where they lived, which are also the places where the burials have typically been found. Certainly, it would seem on the face of it unwise to assume that burial held the same symbolic significance for Neanderthals as it does for modern humans today. Still, the matter of burial is invariably invoked whenever the question of Neanderthal symbolic behavior is raised. And at the other end of the spectrum, the notion has been challenged that the Neanderthals ever buried their dead at all. What can we reasonably conclude from the evidence advanced for Neanderthal burial?

First, we have to concede that burial was indeed practiced, at least from time to time, and simply. Enough Neanderthal skeletons have been found in what were clearly pits excavated into pre-existing cave sediments to make this claim pretty robust. Where there is room for argument is over the elaborateness of such burials. Among early modern humans the dead were typically inhumed along with grave goods: articles intended to ease the existence of the departed in an afterlife. And it is generally agreed that true grave goods of this kind are effective proofs of spiritual belief, with all that implies for symbolic awareness. Yet it can be hard to distinguish between intentional grave goods and items that may have randomly found their way into a grave. Thus, although once in a while we may find animal bones or stone tools in a Neanderthal grave, these are invariably objects of a kind that lay around living sites in some abundance, and that were quite likely kicked or shoveled into the grave simply as part of the filling process. Indeed, as we'll see in the next chapter, there are only a couple of cases where animal bones found in Mousterian graves might plausibly be interpreted as grave goods in the strict sense. And in these cases the association, although Mousterian, is not with Neanderthals.

Such prosaic interpretations are a far cry from the dramatic stories of Neanderthal "bear cults" that were rife earlier in this century. Between 1917 and 1921, for instance, when modern archaeology was still in its infancy, excavations at the Drachenloch cave in the Swiss Alps revealed Mousterian tools in association with large numbers of fossils of the giant cave bear. In itself this was hardly surprising: during the Ice Ages these fearsomely enormous bears regularly frequented caves, where the nests they dug for hibernation are standard features still easily visible today. But Emil Bächler,

the excavator of the Drachenloch, thought there was something unusual about the way in which the cave bear remains were arranged. He reported the presence of dry stone walls in the interior of the Drachenloch, defining "cists" that were filled with bear skulls and capped with stone slabs. Bächler's preferred explanation for this remarkable phenomenon lay with the Neanderthals, whose former presence at the Drachenloch was attested by the Mousterian implements they had left behind. The cave bear bones and stone blocks, he declared, were distributed as they were because the cave had been the scene of rituals that might even have included deliberate sacrifice of these formidable animals. Whatever the exact details, however, Bächler's perception fed precisely into the equivocal public image of the Neanderthals as rather frightening quasi-human creatures, with glimmerings of spiritual awareness combined with dark and powerful "primitive" instincts. Other reports of "bear cults" began to flood in, and soon became mingled with the notion that the Neanderthals had practiced cannibalism: an idea that had been innocently introduced at the turn of the century by the paleontologist Dragutin Gorjanovic-Kramberger, in an attempt to explain why the Neanderthal fossils he was finding at the Croatian site of Krapina were so fragmentary.

Familiar, yet bizarre; human, yet repulsive: this was the image of the Neanderthals as mid-century neared. And nothing did more to reinforce this rather unflattering and ambiguous portrait than a report that emanated from the Italian site of Guattari Cave on the eve of World

War II. Here workmen discovered a well-preserved Neanderthal skull, its base broken, and surrounded by stones. According to A. C. Blanc, the paleontologist called in to investigate this remarkable find, the unfortunate individual had been killed by a blow to the right side of the head. Subsequently he (or she) was decapitated, the skull base being broken off to remove the brain. The skull was then placed upside down in the middle of a ring of stones, where it formed the centerpiece of some obscure Neanderthal ritual—or perhaps even many of them—that involved drinking from the braincase. What story could possibly exert a more repellent fascination, and better feed into the popular perception of what the Neanderthals had been like?

The public devoured it eagerly. Fortunately, though, an ugly theory can occasionally be slain by a (relatively) beautiful fact; and the fact in this case is that the Guattari site was an ancient hyena den, its floor littered with stones and broken animal bones, the Neanderthal skull simply one more among them. And not only had the skull been moved before Blanc first saw it, but there is no way that any object lying on the cave floor could avoid being in the center of a circle of stones, which were all over the place. Far from being a ritual object, the skull was simply another victim of hyena activity in that dark and messy den.

This revised explanation for the circumstances of discovery of the Guattari Neanderthal may lack drama, but it frees us to make a more dispassionate assessment of Neanderthal behavior. What's more, it prompts us to re-examine other accounts of Neanderthal ritual behavior, such as Bächler's. And it turns out that Bächler had not reported the actual evidence discovered by his workmen, but rather his subjective post-hoc interpretation of that evidence. Further, the stone cists apparently did not consist of piles of stones, but rather of single blocks that fell from the cave roof and were later shattered *in situ* by frost action. Similarly, the dense clumps of cave bear bones seem to have resulted from the activities of generations of the bears themselves, as they excavated out new nests in which to hibernate (and occasionally to die).

Once we have eliminated interpretations of Neanderthal behavior that, like Bächler's and Blanc's, are a bit irrationally exuberant, we are left with evidence that is hard to decipher. As we've seen, burial by itself, without clearly identifiable grave goods, is at best an ambiguous indicator of spiritual awareness. Nevertheless, there are some burials that we need to look at particularly carefully. Foremost among these are the burials excavated during the 1950s at the site of Shanidar, in northern Iraq. [Figure 108] Some nine Neanderthal individuals were disinterred at this site, one group of them probably dating from about 60 kyr ago, and another from perhaps 70–80 kyr. What really caught public attention at Shanidar was the claim that one of the graves was particularly rich in pollen: pollen that, moreover, implied that its occupant had been laid to rest in the springtime, on a bed of flowers. Hence the subtitle of the excavator's popular account of his findings: *The First Flower People*. It has been pointed out, however, that a simple concentration of pollen does not neces-

[Figure 108]

A recreation in Japan's Gunma Museum of Natural History of the 50 kyr-old Neanderthal "flower burial" from Shanidar, Iraq. Courtesy of Shuichiro Narasaki, Gunma Museum of Natural History.

sarily indicate flower burial, because various post-depositional processes, such as the burrowing of rodents, can produce a similar result. And although flower burial, if it happened, almost certainly implies some degree of empathy with the deceased, its implications for symbolic reasoning among those who practiced it are not entirely clear. More telling, perhaps, is the biological evidence itself.

One of the Neanderthals interred at Shanidar (possibly as the result of a rockfall) bears healed injuries to his head and shows a withering of the right arm that might have been with him since birth. Yet he survived to the age of forty or even more—a highly advanced age for a member of his species. This is something that, in the harsh world of the Neanderthals, he could hardly have achieved without the active support of his social group, possibly over decades. Here, then, we have powerful presumptive evidence for empathy and caring within the social group, and possibly for complex social roles as well, for it may well be unlikely that support for this individual would have been forthcoming over this long period had he not made some countervailing contribution to the life of the group. Perhaps we should set against this the evidence—a rib bearing a deep cut—that yet another Shanidar Neanderthal had been stabbed in the chest with a sharp instrument. The individual survived this trauma for at least a few weeks, but it's hard to say exactly what historical scenario the few known facts in this case imply. All in all, the evidence from Shanidar is more tantalizing than conclusive, at least as far as the cognitive abilities of its inhabitants are concerned.

The same conclusion is true of the other more spectacular reported cases of Neanderthal burial. For example, the famous finding at the cave of Teshik-Tash, in Uzbekistan—an adolescent buried within a ring of ibex horns—was probably overenthusiastically interpreted by its discoverers. However, plausible reported instances of defleshing of the dead—as in some forms of modern secondary burial, and documented in the human fossil record as far back as 600 kyr ago—are extremely rare at Neanderthal sites. Thus, although burial of the departed was at least occasionally part of the Neanderthal behavior pattern, the motivations behind this practice remain pretty obscure.

Burial in the simple Neanderthal style thus falls short of furnishing us with convincing proof of symbolic activity among these extinct hominids. Is there anything else in the record bequeathed us by the Neanderthals that might suggest such a thing? Well, actually, rather little. That the Neanderthals had curiosity and some form of aesthetic sense is suggested by the finding at one site of an occasional fossil imported from another. There are, however, few convincing instances of actual symbolic productions. The German site of Bilzingsleben, about 350 kyr old and thus pre-Neanderthal, has yielded a bone plaque bearing a series of incisions that may have been deliberately made; the site of Berekat Ram in Israel, about 230 kyr old, has produced a rather unimpressive pebble allegedly shaped to the outline of a human female.

Within Neanderthal times, the 50-kyr-old site of Quneitra on the Golan Heights has yielded a plaque engraved with sinuous lines that were certainly deliberately made. This Mousterian site, however, might just as well have been the work of early modern humans as of Neanderthals. At the Mousterian site of Tata, in Hungary, which we can more confidently associate with Neanderthals, a plaque made from a mammoth molar tooth was apparently deliberately polished. At other Mousterian sites we find the occasional pierced tooth, or piece of bone. And at La Ferrassie in France was found a block of very hard stone that bears a deliberately made series of scooped-out hollows. But such rather obscure expressions are about it; and even if some or all of these items are evidence of deliberate symbolic production, they only serve to emphasize the rarity of such behaviors among the Neanderthals: something that contrasts dramatically with the torrential outpourings of symbolic artifacts by the early moderns who succeeded the Neanderthals in Europe. The evidence is poor that the shared cultural expressions of the Neanderthals were routinely or even ever symbolically mediated.

There is one possible exception. Toward the end of the Neanderthals' tenure, about 35 kyr ago, a set of short-lived new industries, apparently developments out of the Mousterian, emerged in various parts of Europe, notably France, Italy, and Hungary. The best-known of these industries is the Châtelperronian, which was concentrated in western France and adjacent regions. This industry combined aspects of the Mousterian tradition of the Neanderthals with the "Upper Paleolithic" technology brought with them by the first modern humans to enter western Europe. About half of the Châtelperronian stone tool assemblage consisted of "flake" tools typical of the Mousterian. The balance, however, consisted of long "blade" tools, struck successively from cylindrical cores. Even more impressively, the Châtelperronians diversified into the working of materials such as bone and antler: something the Mousterians had virtually never done. What's more, from the Châtelperronian site of Arcy-sur-Cure we have evidence of some of the earliest unquestioned symbolic objects, including an impressive carved and incised bone pendant. [Figure 109] Inevitably, two questions were long debated: first, was the Châtelperronian the last phase of the Middle Paleolithic, or the first phase of the Upper Paleolithic? And second, was it the work of

[Figure 109]

The Châtelperronian bone pendant from Arcy-sur-Cure, France. Whether this elegant piece was made by a Neanderthal or otherwise acquired is still debated. Photograph by Alex Marsheck.

Neanderthals or moderns?

There is now fair unanimity on both these matters. Archaeologists see the Châtelperronian as a terminal industry that emerged from one local variety of the Mousterian, and there is also fossil evidence that it was Neanderthals who produced this industry. Yet this is clearly not the whole story. The Châtelperronian emerged after the first modern humans had entered Europe; and indeed at a couple of French sites Châtelperronian and Upper Paleolithic deposits are interlayered, demonstrating overlap in occupations between the two hominid types. It has thus been suggested that the Châtelperronian represents some kind of cultural interchange between Neanderthals and moderns: that the Neanderthals learned from the moderns how to make blade tools and to use materials other than stone and wood. It's even been suggested that the Arcy pendant might have been acquired by Neanderthals from moderns by trade or in some other way. Here we are, of course, in the realm of pure speculation. But it remains true that the only good association of symbolic objects with Neanderthals comes in a period during which contact of some kind between these native Europeans and the arriving moderns was inevitable.

Neanderthal Extinction

The Neanderthals were the last surviving representatives of a long history of hominid evolution in Europe and western Asia. They were the latest and—at least until the moderns turned up—the most successful members of a group that was entirely indigenous to this region. Analysis of the only DNA sample so far isolated from a Neanderthal suggests that this lineage may have separated from that leading to ourselves as much as 650 kyr ago. Our own species, *Homo sapiens*, thus evolved somewhere else—plausibly Africa, although there is no conclusive proof of this—and only spread into the Neanderthals' European homeland very late in time. It was thought that the story of the colonization of Europe by modern humans was a fairly straightforward one, because the earliest European dates for industries associated with *H. sapiens* came from the eastern part of the subcontinent, as much as 10 kyr before their equivalents in the west. These dates suggested that moderns had entered Europe through a portal in the east, and had gradually spread westwards, displacing the Neanderthals in the process.

Now, however, the plot has thickened, with new dates for modern human occupation of Iberia coming in at about 40 kyr, just about as old as anything in the east. Clearly we are looking at a more complicated situation than a single stream of invaders sweeping all before them in their advance to the west. Whatever the details, however, there is no doubt about the outcome of this invasion. By 27 kyr ago, the Mousterian was gone from Europe, and we find no more Neanderthal fossils. Although Iberia has furnished some of the earliest dates for modern arrival, it has also yielded the latest dates for Neanderthal survival (apart from one of 28 kyr just reported from Croatia), indicating that coexistence of the two hominids was possibly most prolonged in this area. This may have been because of the relative isolation and rugged terrain of the Iberian peninsula, but in the end the pattern there was just the same as elsewhere: *Homo neanderthalensis* and *H. sapiens* were unable to coexist in the longer term, and it was the Neanderthals that gave way. [Figure 110]

So what, exactly, happened? Several interpretations of the interactions between the two species are current, and how you choose among them depends in large part on your view of how the evolutionary process works and on just how different you consider the Neanderthals and moderns to be. The most extreme viewpoint is that Neanderthals simply evolved locally into moderns—in which case, there was no replacement at all. Given the lack both of time and of satisfactory "intermediate" fossils, and the fact that the archaeological record (much more extensive than its fossil equivalent) consistently emphasizes the abruptness of the change from the Mousterian to the Upper Paleolithic, support for this idea is fading rapidly. This is true even among those who embrace the notion of multiregional continuity. The fallback position from this scenario involves assuming that Neanderthals and moderns were no more than variants of the same species, and could thus have interbred efficiently. In which case, the disappearance of Neanderthal morphology can be ascribed to a "genetic swamping" of the Neanderthals by limitless hordes of invading moderns, all eager to miscegenate. After ten thousand enthusiastic years of this, the story would have it, there was precious little Neanderthal culture or morphology left, although it is claimed that all Europeans still carry some unspecified "Neanderthal genes" as a result of this process.

Once again, we run into the problem of intermediates. On the behavioral side, the Châtelperronian and similar short-lived (and distinctive) cultures apart, there is no evidence for cultural mixing. And even in the case of the Châtelperronian, it appears that what we have is evidence for adoption by Neanderthals of certain Upper Paleolithic technologies, rather than a wholesale cultural blending. Biologically, too, we lack any good evidence of mixing; indeed, we have no credible evidence of it at all. The latest Neanderthal fossils we know of show no sign of "dilution" by modern genes; and

[Figure 110]
The Zafarraya cave, in southern Spain. This may have been one of the last redoubts of the Neanderthals prior to their final extinction at about 27-28 kyr ago. Photograph courtesy of Cecilio Barroso Ruiz.

although enthusiasts have claimed that various "Neanderthal" features show up in certain early modern specimens from Central Europe, such claims are based on a mistaken interpretation of morphology. Thus, although a few early Upper Paleolithic skulls have prominent brow ridges and skull rears, somewhat as Neanderthals do, on closer inspection the morphologies of these areas are quite distinctive. For example, modern brow ridges may be large, small or virtually nonexistent, but in no case do they at all closely resemble their Neanderthal equivalents. A recent claim that a 24.5-kyr-old child's skeleton from Portugal represents a member of a hybrid population does not stand close scrutiny.

The alternative is to admit that *Homo neanderthalensis* and *H. sapiens*, as befits two organisms whose bony structures differ so strongly, belonged to two different species. In which case, they could not or would not have interbred. This is not to say that no matings ever took place between the two (after all, even today some humans are notoriously undiscriminating in such matters!) It is simply to say that any biologically significant exchange of genes would have been minimal to nonexistent. And, if true, this has powerful consequences for what we can infer about the interaction between Neanderthals and moderns. For if Neanderthals did not evolve into moderns, or blend with them, then the two kinds of humans must have been in competition of some sort, just like any other pair of closely related species attempting to share the same environment. Such competition would have been fundamentally economic: a contest for those resources that were available on the landscape.

In theory, the competition might have rested there, the inferior exploiter of those resources gradually being edged out by the superior until the population of Neanderthals fell below the point of no return. But, modern humans being what they are, this seems unlikely—whatever the essential nature of the Neanderthals may have been. We have, of course, no idea what the Neanderthals were like temperamentally, or what they may have learned by experience that it was in their best interests to be. We don't know whether they were peaceful or aggressive, quick or slow to react, tolerant or hostile to outsiders. What we do know, however, as we'll see in the next chapter, is that the first Upper Paleolithic peoples of Europe were fully modern in their behavior, just as in their anatomy. In other words, they were *us*: humans with all of the attributes, appalling as well as admirable, that this implies. History abundantly shows the horrendous ways in which invading humans have tended to treat resident peoples, let alone members of other species, as they have moved around the world. And we only have to know one side of the equation to realize that encounters between Neanderthals and modern humans cannot always have been happy ones.

Whatever Neanderthals were like, then, it seems highly unlikely that they usually brought out the best in the strangers who invaded their territory. The details of the interaction between Neanderthals and moderns are probably best left to novelists to explore—and this is surely the ultimate story for examining the darker recesses of human nature as well as the genius that produced Lascaux. But it is staying well within the bounds of science to suggest that the extinction of the Neanderthals involved at least a certain amount of direct conflict as well as of more generalized economic competition. Clearly this was not a simple process, for after all it took thirteen thousand years to complete. Indeed, it was probably every bit as murky and complicated as human nature itself.

CHAPTER 8

And Then There Was One

[And Then There Was One]

In the last chapter we focused on the Neanderthals because these extinct humans are incomparably the best-known of the competitor species that *Homo sapiens* saw off on its way to becoming the only hominid on Earth—quite possibly, for the very first time since soon after the ancestral biped took its first hesitant steps away from the forest. It would be quite wrong, however, to imagine that the interaction between Neanderthals and moderns was the only—let alone the most significant—such interplay that went on in the millennia after the origin of our species. Even if we cannot yet perceive the details at all clearly, there can be no question that similar things were happening all over the Old World in the period after about 100 kyr ago. It is interesting that the only other such specific instance of which we can catch even a fleeting glimpse comes from another evolutionary cul-de-sac— this one at the opposite end of the Eurasian continent from Europe. For, as we saw in Chapter 6, the Ngandong hominids of Java have recently been dated to 40 kyr ago or even less: a finding that suggests that *Homo erectus*, or something like it, survived into the period during which the first modern humans penetrated eastern Asia. And if so, it is not hard to imagine an interaction between the two species that closely paralleled the unhappy experience of the Neanderthals all those thousands of miles to the west.

Where did this alarming new phenomenon come from? This is the question of questions in paleoanthropology; and it's thus particularly frustrating that the evidence of the emergence of *Homo sapiens*, such as it is, is not easy to read—and all the more so because the acquisitions of modern bony anatomy (which we find in the fossil record) and of modern behavior patterns (reflected in archaeological evidence) do not appear to have occurred in synchrony. Fortunately, however, at least as far as the broad outlines are concerned, there has in recent years been a convergence of our readings of traditional lines of evidence—fossils and archaeology—with the newer data provided by molecular studies.

Out of Africa

Remarkably, the African paleoanthropological record, so rich in information about our ancestors during this continent's monopoly of the first half to two-thirds of human evolution, begins to falter a little once the initial exodus of hominids from the continent had been achieved. After about 1.5 myr, when we lose track of *Homo ergaster*, all we have in the entire vast African continent are sporadic occurrences of isolated hominid fossils, and our understanding of these has been severely handicapped by the tendency of paleoanthropologists to place all hominids of the last 0.5–1 myr into another "wastebasket," this time "archaic *H. sapiens.*" It is, of course, a generous sentiment that drives these scientists to include all hominids with even modestly large brains within our own species *H. sapiens.* But it is not a particularly helpful one when we wind up with a miscellaneous collection of very different hominid fossils that are all synonymized under a single epithet. For while a rose may indeed be a rose by any other name, what we have here is in reality a diverse bouquet: a whole meadowful of wildflowers, not just a couple of dozen quasi-identical long-stems. Almost certainly, then, the human evolutionary story in Africa over the past million years has been an eventful one, although at present we can't at all clearly perceive what those events were. During this period new kinds of hominid continued to arise in Africa, almost certainly including the ancestors of the fossils now increasingly referred to as *Homo antecessor* and *H. heidelbergensis*—and, fatefully, the ancestor of *Homo sapiens.*

Africa declares itself paleontologically as the birthplace of our species for the most traditional of reasons: quite simply, that the earliest dates for potentially modern human fossils come from that continent. Unfortunately, beyond this point the simplicity ceases, because the fossils in question tend either to be fragmentary or poorly dated, or sometimes both. For example, during the late 1960s, a braincase and a fragmentary skull were recovered from deposits of the Kibish Formation, in the Omo

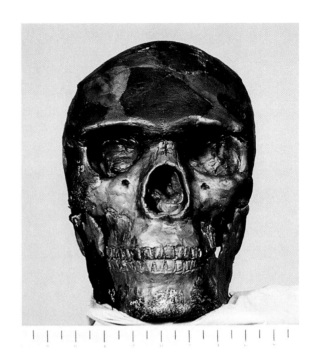

[Figure 111]

Front view of the reconstructed Omo 1 cranium from the Kibish Formation, southern Ethiopia. At possibly up to 130 kyr old, this fragmentary specimen may be the oldest anatomically modern human fossil known. Photograph courtesy of Michael Day.

Basin of southern Ethiopia. [Figure 111] The braincase is rather archaic in appearance but, once reconstructed, the other skull appeared to have all the attributes of modern *H. sapiens.* The problem was that nobody knew the age of these specimens: an uncertainty that continues to plague studies of them. One investigation suggested that the deposits in which the specimens were picked up were about 130 kyr old. However, both hominids were found lying on the surface, so it's hard to eliminate the possibility that one or both were washed down to where they were found from younger deposits above. This is a particularly frustrating situation, because if the more modern-looking specimen is indeed 130 kyr old, it is quite likely the earliest readily recognizable *H. sapiens* yet known from anywhere. Equally tantalizing is the new date of about 133 kyr recently derived for a specimen found in 1924 at Singa, in the Sudan. The daters are quite confident in their results, but the problem of interpretation lies with the fossil itself, which consists of a braincase that appears fairly modern in form but that may be distorted by pathology.

Almost rivaling Omo Kibish and Singa in age is the site of Klasies River Mouth, near the southern tip of Africa, where some human remains may date to as much as 120 kyr ago. The dating methods used there are somewhat experimental, but several lines of evidence converge on this age. Unfortunately, the remains themselves are highly fragmentary, and have given rise to a great deal of debate over their modernity. They are quite *Homo sapiens*-like; but whether any or all of them actually represent our species still awaits definitive clarification. It has been quite convincingly argued that the charred and fragmentary nature of these fossils indicates that they represent victims of cannibalistic activities: if so, this is the earliest reliable case of such behaviors that has yet been reported. The Omo specimens are without archaeological context, but the Klasies hominids are clearly associated with a Middle Stone Age lithic industry: roughly speaking, the local version of the Mousterian. The site's excavator believes that he can discern some evidence for the organization of space that is so rare at Mousterian sites.

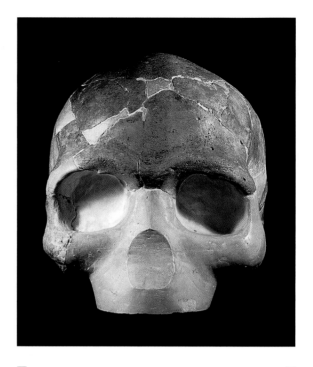

[Figure 112]
Front view of the Border Cave 1 cranium from South Africa. Lightly built and clearly modern in morphology, this specimen is of debatable antiquity but may be over 100 kyr old. Photograph by Jeffrey H. Schwartz.

Another southern African locality that may yield very early *Homo sapiens* fossils is Border Cave, high in a cliff on the frontier between South Africa and Swaziland. It is believed that some unarguably anatomically modern specimens from Border Cave may be as much as 100 kyr old, or even considerably more; but unfortunately the stratigraphy in the cave was disrupted by early mining activity, and it's also possible that some apparently ancient burials may have been dug into earlier levels at a later time. [Figure 112] Nonetheless, taken together, the Klasies and Border Cave fossils do suggest that

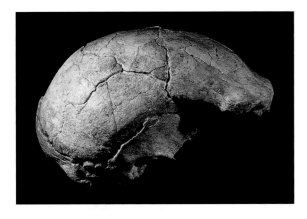

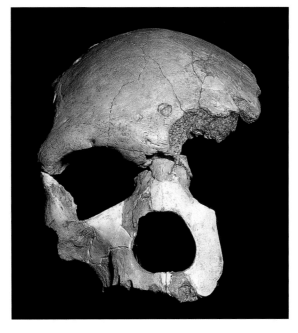

[Figures 113 and 114]
Two early near-modern African crania. Left: the LH 18 (Ngaloba) cranium from northern Tanzania; Right: the Florisbad face from South Africa. Photographs by Jeffrey H. Schwartz.

H. sapiens may well already have been present in southern Africa by 100–120 kyr ago.

The plausible early emergence of modern hominids in Africa did not, however, mean the immediate elimination of other members of the human family. The 120-kyr-old Ngaloba Beds of Laetoli, in Tanzania, have produced the braincase and partial face of a hominid with the relatively modest brain size of 1200 ml, and a suite of archaic features in the skull. [Figure 113]

Whatever species this individual may have belonged to, it was not the immediate ancestor of *Homo sapiens*. A much earlier partial skull from Guomde, in Kenya's Turkana Basin, looks more modern. This specimen has now been dated to at least 180 kyr ago, and may be older. In turn, the Guomde specimen contrasts strongly with a fossil face from Florisbad, in South Africa, that may be of around the same

age. [Figure 114] The picture we gain from tantalizing glimpses such as these into Africa's paleoanthropological past is thus not only of the rather early emergence of anatomically modern humans in that continent. It is also the image of a complex set of morphologies in the period between 250–100 kyr ago, suggesting that the process of evolutionary experimentation among African hominids continued right into *H. sapiens* times. As the record expands, we can hope to figure out how many players there were in the evolutionary theatre at this fateful juncture in the history of life that saw the emergence of our own species. For the present, however, it is already evident that the proto-*H. sapiens* was far from having had the stage to itself. Once again, we have to conclude that our species' current monopoly of hominid life on Earth is an unusual state of affairs.

African Eve

During the 1980s new techniques of molecular analysis began to have a significant impact on scenarios of modern human emergence. This was not because scientists had perfected techniques for extracting the molecule of heredity, DNA, from actual early *Homo sapiens* fossils. Indeed, the only successful example so far of this type of research is the very recent isolation of a short stretch of mitochondrial DNA (mtDNA) from the original Neanderthal fossil, which was hardly surprisingly shown thereby to lie well beyond the limits of all modern human populations combined. Rather, the new evidence on the geographic origin of modern humans came from the analysis of mtDNA variation in representative samples of living human populations from around the world. Before we follow up on this evidence, just what is mtDNA, and what makes it attractive to molecular systematists?

Human body cells contain not only the DNA that resides in their nuclei, and that furnishes the "blueprint" for the construction of each new individual. They also carry a small quantity of DNA in their mitochondria, the structures in the outer part of the cell that function as the "powerhouse" behind cell operations. This mtDNA has several qualities that make it particularly useful to those interested in what molecules can tell us about relationships. First, it lacks the elaborate self-repairing mechanisms of nuclear DNA, and thus accumulates mutations at a very high rate, giving molecular systematists lots of differences to look for even

when they are studying quite closely related populations. Second, it is largely free of the "junk" (non-coding) DNA that composes so much of the nuclear DNA complement. Third, modern human mtDNA consists of about 16,500 nucleotides (the minimal units that are strung together to make up the DNA strand). This is in contrast with more than three billion nucleotides in the human nuclear DNA genome—obviously using mtDNA simplifies comparisons. Fourth, mtDNA is always transmitted between generations as a single unit, unlike the nuclear DNA which is carried on chromosomes that sometimes exchange material. And finally, and most interesting of all, everyone's mtDNA is often inherited only from their mother. This is because the mother's egg contains mitochondria but mitochondria are present only in the tail of the father's sperm. Usually only the head of a sperm cell penetrates the egg. But sometimes a piece of the tail also gets included. Most of the time, then, mtDNA avoids the mixing-up in every generation that accompanies the transmission of nuclear DNA, thereby avoiding the complicated consequences of sexual reproduction.

In a landmark study published in 1987, a group of molecular systematists at the University of California at Berkeley sampled mtDNA from representatives of a variety of human groups of different geographical origin. They used the data thus obtained to test the two major paleontological hypotheses of modern human origins and diversity that were current then (and still, in essence, are). On the one hand was the multiregional continuity idea, whereby the major geographical groups of modern humankind have roots very deep in the past. On the other was the "single origin" notion, whereby all modern human populations share a close common ancestry, probably in Africa, and have only diversified quite recently. The researchers found that their sample of Africans contained much more mtDNA diversity than did the representatives of other populations, suggesting that the African population had been accumulating mutations for much longer than either Europeans or Asians. Further, a "family tree" of mtDNA resemblance seemed to have its roots within the African sample, and from this the researchers derived the notion of "African Eve," the female founder of all surviving mtDNA lineages. Finally, assuming an average rate of change in mtDNA sequences of about twenty percent every million years (a big assumption, of course), they concluded that Eve had lived about 200 kyr ago. [Figure 115] This rather short chronology seemed, however, to fit well with the observation of a very low mtDNA diversity in humans when compared with modern ape populations. The best explanation for this seems to be that humans went through a population "bottleneck" (dramatic shrinkage) in the fairly recent past. And, quite obviously, all of these findings conform much better to the "African Origin" paleontological model than to the multiregional idea, which predicts that mtDNA diversity should be roughly equally distributed among modern populations.

Early criticism of this research focused on the nature of the sample of modern humans that the Berkeley group had used (which includ-

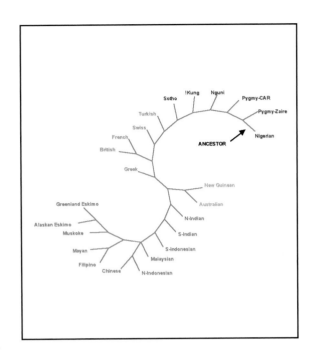

[Figure 115]
An estimate of affinities among some 24 modern human populations worldwide, based on mtDNA differences. This tree is "rooted" at the "ancestor" arrow. Courtesy of Mark Stoneking.

ed African Americans rather than individuals born in Africa). But later studies on larger samples obtained in diverse geographic regions, including Africa, came up with similar results. The work was also attacked on the grounds that the published family tree was not actually the best one that could be constructed on the basis of the available data sets. Again, however, there appears to be no getting away from the fact that the diversity data do seem to be telling us that humans have been diversifying longest in Africa, and that Asian and European populations appear to have been derived ultimately from emigrants from this older African population. The extrapolated dating of African Eve was also questioned, but studies incorporating later refinements continue to indicate a bottleneck in the period of about 150–200 kyr ago. Recent comparative studies of the human Y chromosome (uniquely passed along by men, presumably from an "African Adam") suggest a pattern similar to that suggested by the maternally derived mtDNA. Even more interesting, is that in China, one hotbed of multiregional thinking, a recent study of microsatellites (repeats of short nuclear DNA segments) has suggested a derivation of the Han Chinese from an ultimately African ancestry.

One important point to bear in mind here is that the postulated African Eve was not necessarily the first *Homo sapiens*. She was simply the individual from whom our mtDNA lineage was descended. Such are the vagaries of the speciation process (which isolates one population from another but not population members from each other) that she might actually have been a member of an earlier species. In which case *H. sapiens* itself could have originated subsequent to Eve's tenure on Earth. Such quibbles aside, and especially when taken together with the minimal existing paleontological indications, the mtDNA data do provide us with quite a strong signal that our species emerged not only in Africa, but relatively recently.

Unfortunately, there is in Africa no equivalent of the "symbolic explosion" we find in Europe (albeit fairly late on) that announces the abrupt arrival of a fully formed modern human sensibility. There are, however, certain tantalizing hints in the archaeological record of "mod-

ern" behavior patterns in Africa at an unexpectedly early date. Earliest of all are recent findings that the manufacture of blade tools (the long, thin flakes typically made by the first *Homo sapiens* to enter Europe) at one site in eastern Africa dates to well over 200 kyr ago. Evidence of the hafting of projectile points is almost as old. Equally, recent reports have come from a Central African site of bone tools that may be as much as 80 kyr old. [Figure 116] Africa also furnishes the earliest evidence of such "modern" activities as flint mining and the long-distance transport (trading?) of prized materials, as well as of efficient fishing in the form of abundant fish bones at living sites. What's more, there are also early inklings of overtly symbolic behaviors, such as the decorative or notational incising of ostrich eggshell fragments almost 50 kyr ago. And whereas even putting all this evidence together lacks the astonishing impact of the European symbolic record subsequent to about 40 kyr ago, it is hard to avoid the conclusion that important behavioral developments were afoot in Africa well before we see them so dramatically expressed in Europe.

On the other hand, even if Africa offers the earliest suggestions we have of both anatomical and behavioral modernity, it is clear that *Homo sapiens* did not make these twin acquisitions in lockstep. Indeed, the record we currently have leaves little doubt that modern anatomical form was achieved well before modern behavior found its fullest expression. Which, when you consider the matter, should come as no great surprise, for as we've already noted, there is only one place in which a new behavior can be

[Figure 116]
Bone harpoon point from the Katanda 9 site, Zaire.
Although associated with Middle Stone Age stone tools,
this sophisticated artifact may be 80-90 kyr old.
Photograph by Chip Clark; courtesy of Alison S. Brooks.

acquired, and that is *within* a species. Any new behavior, after all, whether momentous or trivial, has to originate with a single individual. And that individual has to belong to a pre-existing species and can hardly differ too much from his or her parents or offspring. To find evidence that for all its unusual attributes *H. sapiens* is no exception to this pattern, we need look no far-ther afield than the Levant (specifically, Israel)—a region that, incidentally, many consider to be a biogeographic extension of the African continent.

The Levant

Tentative dating of the earliest levels of the site of Tabūn, a huge cave in the western foothills of Israel's Mount Carmel, suggests that Mousterian tool technology was already established in the Levant by well over 200 kyr ago. A precursor industry from the site of Zuttiyeh, a few dozen miles to the east, may be a good bit older. This industry is associated with a skull fragment that has traditionally been touted for its "archaic" characteristics, but that bears several strong Neanderthal resemblances. Exactly who made the earliest Mousterian implements at Tabūn cannot at present be known for sure, but what is clear is that the two hominid finds at the cave, which come from deposits perhaps 125 kyr old or thereabouts, are fully formed Neanderthals. One of the specimens, assumed to represent a burial because much of the skeleton was present in articulation, is lightly built and thought to be female. The other specimen consists of an isolated and robust lower jaw that has numerous Neanderthal characteristics but which is often said to boast a chin, something normally associated with *Homo sapiens*. Our own examination of the fossil shows that although the area of the chin is broken, enough remains to demonstrate that no "inverted T" structure is present. Tabūn thus offers a pretty strong association of the Mousterian with Neanderthals, as also do various other, much younger, Levantine sites. Among these are the cave of Kebara, which we discussed in the last chapter, and which has yielded an extremely robust Neanderthal skeleton dated to about 60 kyr ago. Younger yet is another Israeli site, Amud, at which Neanderthal burials are also associated with Mousterian stone tools. An adult male burial is dated to about 45 kyr, and an infant skeleton is a little older, at between 50 and 60 kyr. Despite its tender age and incompleteness, this specimen shows distinctive Neanderthal morphologies.

So far so good; and it is of course no surprise to find Neanderthal bones associated with a Mousterian technology. But there are other Israeli sites at which the Mousterian is equally definitely associated with remains of anatomically modern humans. The clearest such association is found in the cave of Jebel Qafzeh, where the lithic industry is plainly Mousterian but where more than a dozen human burials, found in various parts of the cave, are rather oddly assorted. Of the two best preserved specimens, one looks just a little odd for a modern human, while the other (Qafzeh 9) is as representative a *Homo sapiens* as you could wish to find. [Figure 117] This individual was laid to rest, arms folded and knees bent, in a shallow grave. And, because an infant was buried in the same grave, at the adult's feet, it has been generally assumed that here we have the skeleton of a female, buried with her child. However, our own observations show that if you apply the criteria generally used by anthropologists to sex modern skeletons to both skull and body skeleton, it is hard to avoid the conclusion that in fact these are the remains of a male. Even more remarkably, recent dating has shown that this Mousterian modern died well over 90 kyr ago. About the same age or possibly even more ancient yet is a series of burials from the site of Skhūl, just a few minutes' stroll from Tabūn. Ever since their excavation in the early 1930s these Mousterian remains have posed a puzzle to paleoanthropologists, appearing to be almost but not quite modern humans. Ironically, the stone tools found in some abundance along with the Skhūl burials compare closely to those associated with both the Tabūn and Qafzeh hominids. At its simplest, then, the Levantine record shows clearly that more or less indistinguishable Mousterian industries were produced both by Neanderthals and by *H. sapiens*; and the known fossils hint that the situation may have been more complex yet, at least on the biological side.

Neanderthals were thus quite likely already present in the Levant close to or even well over 200 kyr ago. And Neanderthals appear to have persisted in the region until 40–45 kyr ago. Anatomically modern humans appeared later, at a little under 100 kyr ago. Further, once arrived, moderns never left, at least for long. Obviously, then, there was a protracted period of coexistence between the two species, minimally from about 100 to 40 kyr ago. Exactly what form this coexistence took is a matter for speculation.

[Figure 117]
Cranium 9 from Jebel Qafzeh, Israel. This specimen is unequivocally modern in morphology, and is dated to over 90 kyr. Photograph courtesy of Israel Antiquities Authority.

Extinct Humans

On the basis of the supposed cold-adaptedness of the Neanderthals, for example, it has been suggested that these now-extinct hominids moved south into this region when the climate cooled, and the "tropically adapted" (i.e., Africa-derived) moderns retreated toward the continent of their birth. The reverse, it is proposed, would have occurred in warmer times, as the Neanderthals sought the welcoming cool of the north. Well, perhaps, although rigid "time-sharing" of this kind seems a bit unlikely given what we know about the adaptability of both hominid species. But what does seem inescapable is that, after the arrival of the moderns, coexistence of some kind continued for almost exactly as long as both hominids shared a similar stoneworking technology (and whatever other behavioral patterns this implies). Unlike the situation in Europe, where the "Upper Paleolithic" technology of the first *Homo sapiens* was introduced by invaders from outside, in the Levantine region Upper Paleolithic stone tool making was initially an indigenous development, with Mousterian techniques being used at first to produce utensils of Upper Paleolithic form. We find the first evidence for this innovation at Israel's Boker Tachtit, a site that dates from about 47 kyr ago. We don't know what other behavioral advances might have accompanied this technological development. However, it is probably not coincidental that it was not long afterwards that Neanderthals disappeared from the Levantine record. Thus, for as long as *H. sapiens* and *Homo neanderthalensis* employed essentially similar technologies, it evidently remained possible for them to share the Near East landscape in some

way. But, once their technologies diverged, coexistence was apparently doomed.

It is thus particularly regrettable that we have so little other evidence of the lifeways of Neanderthals and moderns in the Levant at this critical juncture in the human evolutionary story, especially because the key to the problem of coexistence seems to lie in what we might call "behavioral modernity." *H. sapiens* has at least intermittently existed as a distinctive anatomical entity in the Levant for at least a hundred thousand years, and in Africa quite probably for a lot more. But until we begin to pick up—unfortunately highly indirect—intimations of modern human behavior patterns, our species appears to have been capable of sharing its environment with a spectrum of relatives. *H. sapiens*, in other words, was just another hominid. But once hints of modern human cognition appeared, everything changed. How it changed is without question incomparably best reflected in the archaeological record of Europe. Charges of Eurocentrism are often leveled at those who succumb to the fascination exerted by the astonishing archive left behind them by the first—both anatomically and behaviorally—modern Europeans. Yet even if this record is biased by the lack of comparable evidence elsewhere, it is also hugely compelling. We would be grievously wrong to ignore it, even as we recognize that Europe is and was merely a cul-de-sac tacked on to the western end of the Eurasian continent— and that, by the time the Upper Paleolithic record began there, the most momentous events of all in the history of the human species had already taken place somewhere else.

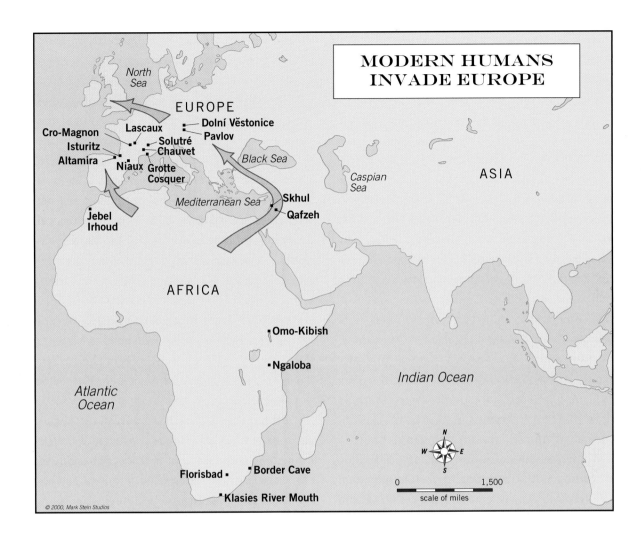

MODERN HUMANS
INVADE EUROPE

North
Sea

EUROPE
Dolní Věstonice
Lascaux   Pavlov
Cro-Magnon
Isturitz   Solutré
Altamira   Chauvet   Black Sea
Niaux Grotte   ASIA
        Cosquer
Mediterranean Sea   Skhul   Caspian
                                    Sea
Jebel   Qafzeh
Irhoud

AFRICA

Omo-Kibish

Ngaloba
                                    Indian Ocean
Atlantic
Ocean

Florisbad   Border Cave

Klasies River Mouth   0   1,500
                                 scale of miles

© 2000, Mark Stein Studios

The First Modern Europeans

As we've seen, the first modern human invaders erupted into the (relatively) serene world of the European Neanderthals around 40 kyr ago, appearing more or less simultaneously in both the eastern and western extremes of the subcontinent. [Figure 118] Whether eastern or western, these *Homo sapiens* brought with them a single distinctive Upper Paleolithic industry, known as

[Figure 118]

Map showing major Old World archaeological sites that have contributed to our knowledge of the emergence and spread of anatomically modern humans. The two southern arrows show two routes via which modern humans may have invaded Eurasia from Africa; during the period of intense cold at the height of the last glacial sea-levels were low, and Britain was connected to France via a land-bridge, represented by the northern arrow. Map by Mark Stein.

the Aurignacian after a site in southern France. This new technology is quite distinct from the indigenous early Upper Paleolithic of the Levant, and nobody is sure exactly when or where it originated. Technologically, the Aurignacian is distinguished from the Mousterian by stone tools made from long, narrow blades struck successively from carefully shaped cylindrical "prismatic" stone cores, and by the widespread adoption of bone and antler as raw materials in toolmaking. These new materials were worked with an exquisite sensitivity to their mechanical properties: something that contrasts with the rather crude as well as rare Middle Paleolithic treatment of these substances. What's more, the relative monotony of the Mousterian was completely gone from early Upper Paleolithic tool assemblages: toolmakers from different sites apparently freely followed their own creative impulses, making the classification of the many local variants of the Aurignacian an enormous headache for archaeologists. At the same time, however, individual tool types become easier for modern humans to analyze because they were evidently made by people who saw the world and the interaction of its parts in the same way that we do. The categories that made sense to them are the categories that make sense to us. So, for the first time, we can have no doubt whatever that we are dealing with beings whose cognitive processes were essentially similar to our own.

But as impressive as the new technology may have been, it certainly does not furnish us with the most dramatic evidence for major cognitive innovation. For the most remarkable change in the archaeological record from the Middle to the Upper Paleolithic consisted not of a shift in the character of functional objects, but rather of the appearance of a wealth of symbolic or ceremonial artifacts. We have to look very hard at the Neanderthal record to discern anything at all that we can describe as symbolic with even the most modest confidence. In stark contrast, however, the Upper Paleolithic was drenched in symbol. Quite simply, if the archaeological record they bequeathed us means anything at all, it indicates that the Aurignacians were beings of an entirely different order from the Neanderthals who had preceded them. The best evidence we have of the arrival of this unprecedented sensibility comes from France and Germany, where the earliest Aurignacian sites have been dated to the period of 32–35 kyr ago.

Perhaps as good a place as any to start an account of this flowering is the lovely and tranquil little valley of the Lone River, in southern Germany: a place evidently as greatly favored by the Aurignacians during the last Ice Age as it is by ramblers today. Here, within a mile of each other, are two caves in the valley walls that were used for shelter by Aurignacians some 34 kyr ago. At one of them, Vogelherd, was found a whole series of animal figurines carved in mammoth ivory, among them a two-inch-long image of a horse that is still unrivaled today for its elegance and grace. Polished by long contact with someone's skin, this figurine was probably worn originally as a pendant. What is particularly interesting about it is that it is not in the least a straightforward representation of the stocky horses that roamed the steppes of Ice Age Europe. Rather, with its long arching neck and the exquisite line of its back, it is an evocation of the graceful essence of all horses. As simple representation and craftsmanship this figurine is already remarkable. But the abstraction of form that it embodies places it in the most refined category of art. What more could we ask for as proof of a fully formed modern sensibility? Well, how about an intriguing foot-high figure, also carved in mammoth ivory, from the nearby cave of Hohlenstein-Stadel? This piece is less impressive as art than the Vogelherd figurines, but it is more aggressively symbolic, consisting as it does of a man's standing body surmounted by a lion's head. We will never know exactly what the man/lion emblem represented to the individual who made this carving, or to the society to which he or she belonged. But nobody could ever doubt that this remarkable object was fashioned by someone possessing all the mysterious complexity of a fully modern human.

Impressive as such pieces of early "portable" art are, in the public mind the Aurignacians are more closely associated with the art they left on the walls of numerous caves that dot the limestone landscape of southern France and northern Spain. Until recently this was not technically the case, for it was generally believed that in Aurignacian times cave decoration (difficult or impossible to date directly) had been largely restricted to hand stencils and a few geometrical signs. The great period of deep cave art, it was thought, had began much later, maybe less than 20 kyr ago. But the astonishing

discovery in late 1994 of the southern French cave of Chauvet has made it evident that extraordinary cave decoration, too, dates from the very beginning of the Upper Paleolithic in western Europe. [Figure 119] An early estimate of the age of the art of Chauvet, based on its style and craftsmanship, had placed these images at about 18 kyr old. Imagine, then, the astonishment of scientists and art historians alike when direct dating of some of the images using new radiocarbon techniques revealed that some of them at least were painted as much as 32 kyr ago! At Chauvet a wealth of animal and abstract images, some 300 counted so far, cascade across the cave walls. Some are painted in red or black outline. Some are finger tracings in the soft coating of the cave walls. Some are represented by dots. And some gain their interior volume from shading, although others use the natural relief of the cave walls to achieve the same effect of bulk. Each of the most spectacular elements of the mammal fauna of the Ice Age Rhone valley is there: lions, woolly rhinos, mammoths, reindeer, horses, wild cattle, bears, ibexes, a leopard, and—most unusually—an owl. And all of them are depicted with the vitality, economy, and grace that have always marked the finest of graphic productions. It is interesting that some of the animal images of Chauvet were evidently "re-used" by the addition of body parts (horns, for example, or legs) to pre-existing images: a foreshadowing of later practices that emphasizes the functional as well as the aesthetic aspects of this art.

Just as do the masterpieces of portable art from the Lone valley, the Chauvet images

[Figure 119]
Footprint left in the floor of the French cave of Chauvet by a Cro-Magnon child, perhaps up to 30 kyr ago. Photograph by Michel-Alain Garcia; courtesy of Direction Regionale des Affaires Culturelles Rhône-Alpes, France.

very little Ice Age art is overtly narrative, at least in the way that we understand this term today. Indeed, of the thousands of Ice Age images known, only a handful are assembled in such a way as to suggest to modern eyes that a specific story is being recounted. The best such example, probably around 17 kyr old, is painted on the wall of a vertical shaft at the incomparable cave of Lascaux, in France. Here a very schematically represented bird-headed man falls backwards in front of a bison that has apparently been disemboweled by a spear. A woolly rhinoceros is beating a retreat behind the man, and the ensemble is completed by some dots and a staff bearing a bird symbol. Almost certainly significantly, the same scene seems to be enacted in simplified fashion (just the man and the bison) on the wall of the cave of Villars, not very far away from Lascaux. But that, literally, is about it for narrative in Ice Age art, at least in a form that we can readily recognize (if not interpret) today. In sensibility the Aurignacians were our equals, but their cultural traditions are, of course, lost in time. Thus most Ice Age animal images are juxtaposed with others, and it is obvious that such creations as the "parade" of polychrome animal images that tumbles across the wall of the Hall of Bulls at Lascaux—as powerful an ensemble as has ever been painted— are not simply random arrangements of the symbolic elements. [Figure 121] But they are not evidently telling a sequential story, as in the case of the man and bison.

At one level this certainly seems curious, especially given how hard it is to escape the conclusion that the animal art of the Ice Age, and

announce the arrival of the modern human sensibility in an incomparably direct way. We don't have to understand what this art meant to its makers to know, viscerally, that it is not simple representation, but is rather a distillation of the artists' view of the natural world, and of their place in it. Clearly, these images have, or had to their makers, a symbolic significance that went far beyond the mere cataloguing of animal species. [Figure 120] Perhaps it's odd, then, that

the geometric and other symbols associated with it, reflect a coherent, complex, and extensive body of knowledge, myth, and belief. At another level, it is easy enough to appreciate that the original Ice Age observers, inheritors of a rich and complex cultural tradition, would have responded readily to the symbolic references that the art embodied, including the juxtaposition of images that appears so mysterious to us. After all, to them this art was part of a living tradition. And even if, many thousands of years later and in an entirely different social milieu, we are in the end obliged to admit that for us the art of the Ice Age is art to be experienced rather than art to be understood, the power of this art to move us tens of millennia after its creation is as eloquent a testimony as could ever be found to the fact that its makers were people with whom we can identify at the most profound of levels.

Perhaps no more eloquent; though, than the arrival of music, another common denominator of modern human societies. From the site of Isturitz, in the French Pyrenees, comes a whole set of bone flutes, at least 32 kyr old.

[Figure 122] We will never know exactly what sounds echoed off the walls of the Isturitz cave during those long-ago Ice Age evenings; but in the hands of modern musicians, replicas of such wind instruments show remarkably complex sound capabilities. Music—even sophisticated music—is, it seems, inseparable from being human. And as if this were not enough, right from the beginning of the Aurignacian, at least 32 kyr old and possibly a good bit more, is a polished bone plaque from the site of the Abri Blanchard, in southwestern France. This plaque bears a long, curving series of deliberate

[Figure 121]
Cave painting from Lascaux, France. Seventeen thousand years ago a team of artists created an unparalleled cascade of animal images on the walls of this cave. Many of the animals are depicted with an associated symbol. A small horse appears between the horns of the two aurochs (wild cattle); and three stags can be seen below. Courtesy of Norbert Aujoulat, Centre National de Préhistoire, Ministère de la Culture, France.

notations, and has been interpreted as a lunar calendar. Whether or not this interpretation is historically accurate, it is incontestable that this piece, and others like it of similar age, are testimony to recordkeeping of some kind.

Aurignacians not only lived in a symbolically mediated world, but they kept accurate track of their experience. This fits in well with what we know, from the sites they left behind, of their social existence. On the basis of the relative complexity and size variations in their sites, we can conclude that Aurignacians lived in social groups that were much more complex and variable in size than any earlier groups. There is, indeed, good reason to believe that such "modern" socioeconomic features as division of labor and social stratification had already appeared in Aurignacian times.

Sculpture, engraving, painting, music, notation, elaborate burial, specialized social roles, recordkeeping, ever-evolving technology —it may seem remarkable that all of these quintessentially human activities are documented in Europe immediately upon the arrival of anatomically modern humans in this part of the world. But what the record appears to be suggesting very strongly is that the modern human sensibility—what has been called "the human capacity"—was acquired as a package, rather than bit by bit over the millennia. And this, as it happens, fits well with what we know about the evolutionary process itself. Of course, given the innate human urge to refine and improve, we should not be surprised to discover, as we do, that technological advances continued to be made throughout the Upper Paleolithic, even after the basic modern human behavior patterns had been established. Thus the "Gravettian" culture that replaced the Aurignacian introduced the eyed bone needle and, presumably, tailored clothing, by about 26

[Figure 122]
Ice Age bone flutes. The one in the center is about 27 kyr old, from the cave of Pair-non-Pair in France. Photograph by Alain Roussot.

kyr ago. At around the same time we find the first ceramics, in the form of figurines baked at high temperatures in simple but remarkably effective kilns. Not too long after this, spear-throwers were introduced, devices that would have considerably improved hunting efficiency; and barbed harpoons announce advances in fishing techniques. Bows and arrows had become current by the end of the Ice Age, about 10 kyr ago, when the high cultures of the Upper

Paleolithic were already on the wane. Throughout the Upper Paleolithic, in other words, technology continued to be refined and elaborated—as is, indeed, still happening today. But what is equally inescapable is that even at the very beginning of this period—right from the very earliest modern human occupation of Europe—all of the essential modern human characteristics were already established. What happened—or rather, what had happened—to create this new phenomenon? How did our ancestors come to buy this package? This is, of course, the mystery of mysteries, and there is probably no simple answer to it. But it's possible to make a few suggestions.

Becoming Human

Significant behavioral innovation has, as we've seen, been sporadic and quite rare in human evolution. Even as new species came and went, the general pattern over the eons was one of adding the occasional refinement to ancestral lifestyles, rather than of radical changes in ways of doing business. But with the advent on Earth of *Homo sapiens*—or at least, of *H. sapiens* with modern behavior patterns—this was emphatically no longer the case. Indeed, there has never been a more fateful arrival on the biological scene than that of our extraordinary species. On the other hand, however, there is absolutely no reason to believe that the rules of the evolutionary game had been even slightly bent in paving the way for our arrival. We can look nowhere else than at conventional processes of evolution

in explaining the advent of our very unconventional selves. [Figures 123 and 124] Let's briefly look again at some of those processes.

It is often believed, if only implicitly, that natural selection is in itself a "creative" process that somehow "drives" evolution. But a moment's thought is enough to show that this cannot be the case. Any new structure must arise *before* it can assume a function, and thereby qualify as a target of natural selection. What's more, natural selection itself is a pretty blunt instrument. It can, after all, only vote up or down on the reproductive success of entire organisms, each one a complex bundle of characteristics. However convenient we may find it for analytical purposes to think in terms of the evolution of the brain, say, or of bipedalism, there is in fact no way in which natural selection can single out one particular trait to favor to or condemn. It's the whole individual whose reproductive success is at issue, just as at another level it is whole species that must succeed or fail. The story of evolution is thus much more than the simple sum of the direct results of natural selection alone. It is, instead, completed by the histories of entire organisms, populations, and species, all competing at their respective levels to make it in the ecological arena. And once (but not until) we understand that evolution cannot simply be a matter of fine-tuning of individual traits by natural selection, the way is open to comprehending in broad terms what might have happened to give rise to the extraordinary phenomenon of modern human cognition. Unfortunately, we are handicapped here by our ignorance of how human consciousness is gen-

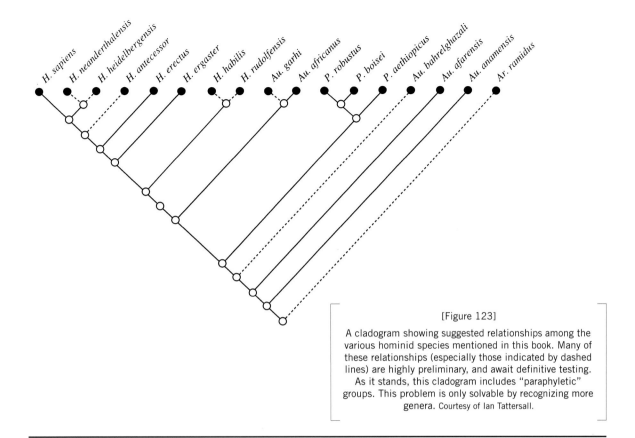

[Figure 123]
A cladogram showing suggested relationships among the various hominid species mentioned in this book. Many of these relationships (especially those indicated by dashed lines) are highly preliminary, and await definitive testing. As it stands, this cladogram includes "paraphyletic" groups. This problem is only solvable by recognizing more genera. Courtesy of Ian Tattersall.

erated in the brain. We know a lot about how the human brain is put together, and about how various parts of it are recruited in performing various specific functions. But, quite simply, we have as yet no idea whatever about how a mass of electrical and chemical discharges within the brain is converted into what we individually and subjectively experience as consciousness. To explain ourselves to ourselves completely, we shall ultimately have to achieve this knowledge. Fortunately, however, we do not need to command this level of detail to understand in principle what might have happened to bring our extraordinary consciousness about.

A routine phenomenon in the histories of organisms is what has been called "exaptation," whereby new characteristics arise in one functional context well before being recruited in another. Thus, for example, birds appear to have acquired feathers in the context of body temperature regulation long before these structures were recruited in the service of flight. Flight would ultimately not have been possible if feathers had not already been there, but feathers are not inherently flight-associated. For millions of years (as we can know only in retrospect), feathers were exaptations for flight, available to be co-opted in this new function

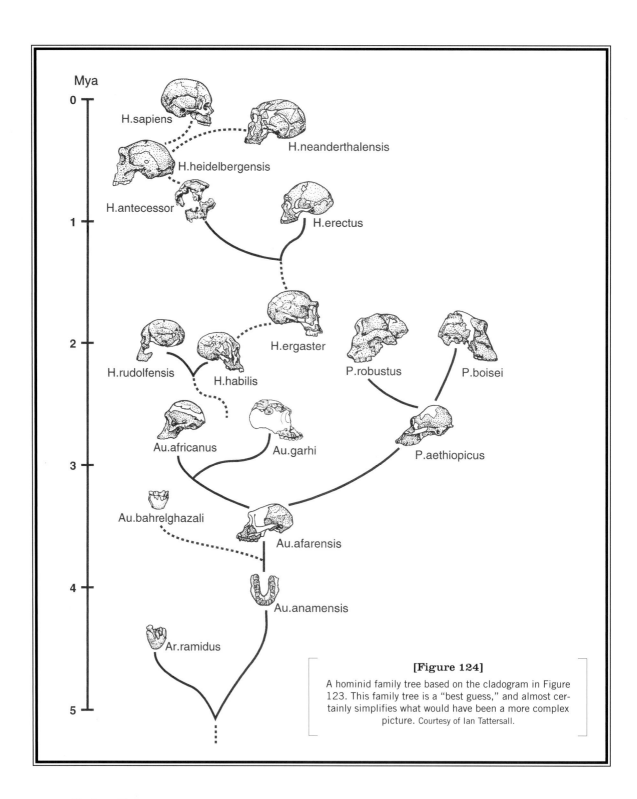

[Figure 124]

A hominid family tree based on the cladogram in Figure 123. This family tree is a "best guess," and almost certainly simplifies what would have been a more complex picture. Courtesy of Ian Tattersall.

when circumstances permitted, but already performing another essential role. In the case of human evolution, as good an example as any of exaptation is provided by the structures of the vocal tract that permit speech. The vocal tract itself is, of course, made of soft tissues that do not fossilize. But the roof of the tract is also the base of the skull, which sometimes does. And it turns out that a distinct downward flexion of the skull base is associated with the possession of a humanlike vocal tract capable of producing the sounds associated with language. What's more, this downward flexion can be traced all the way back to some members, at least, of *Homo heidelbergensis*—perhaps as much as 0.5 myr ago. Yet the archaeological record before about 50 kyr ago contains no evidence of the ability to manipulate symbols that almost certainly accompanied the advent of language. The modern vocal tract (which has a distinct downside—it makes it possible for its possessors to choke to death) must thus have been acquired in another context, possibly but not inevitably a respiratory one. In any event, the record is saying pretty clearly that our ancestors possessed an essentially modern vocal tract a very long time before we have any solid grounds for believing that they used it for linguistic purposes—something we'll return to in a moment.

The other concept that is useful to bear in mind as we seek the origins of the human capacity is that of the "emergent quality." Frequently, complex systems can add up to much more than the simple sum of their parts, and combining two or more unrelated elements can give rise to unexpected (emergent) results.

The classic case of this is water, whose properties, so essential to life, are entirely unpredicted by those of its constituent atoms, hydrogen and oxygen. Perhaps the extraordinary phenomenon of modern consciousness is a quality of this kind, a chance combination of exaptations that were locked into place as an unexpected functioning whole by a final "keystone" acquisition that appeared, like all novelties, independently of any functional role. What that acquisition was in physical terms will have to await a more profound knowledge of the functioning of the human brain than anything we can lay claim to at present. But it does seem likely that, whatever it was, it lay fallow for a considerable period before being co-opted into its new role. For, as we've seen, modern anatomical structure considerably predated modern cognitive functioning. This is most clearly evident from the Levantine record, which shows Neanderthals and moderns behaving, as far as we can tell, in more or less indistinguishable ways for perhaps as much as 60 kyr.

What can we infer from this? Well, one possibility is that Neanderthals and early moderns initially possessed brains that were functionally identical, but that some radical biological reorganization eventually arose among the moderns that permitted them to express modern behavior patterns. This seems on the face of it a bit unlikely. For this scenario depends on the acquisition by anatomically modern *Homo sapiens* of a key heritable biological innovation at perhaps 50 kyr ago. Spreading such an innovation around the Old World would have involved the wholesale replacement throughout this vast region not only of osteologically and behaviorally archaic hominids (Neanderthal, Ngandong, and so forth), but of osteologically modern (but neurologically archaic) populations. Not only is the time available for such an extraordinary replacement episode rather short, but (in an admittedly sketchy record) there is no evidence for it (such as might be furnished, for instance, by abrupt replacement, at individual sites, of behaviorally archaic moderns by behaviorally advanced moderns). The alternative is to conclude that the human capacity was born in potential by some "keystone" acquisition at or close to the birth of our species as an anatomical entity. This innovation then lay fallow, as an exaptation, until it was activated by some kind of behavioral invention in a particular local population. And, if that invention was highly advantageous, it's reasonable to expect that it would have spread rapidly by cultural contact among anatomically modern human populations, all over the Old World, that would already have possessed the biological potential to acquire it.

What could this innovation have been? There is no way at present of knowing for sure, but the obvious candidate is the invention of language. Language is not simply a refinement of earlier ways of communication, but is almost certainly integral to our reasoning abilities. Language and thought as we know them both involve forming and recombining mental symbols; and it is, indeed, virtually impossible for us to conceive of one in the absence of the other. Language is thus not simply the medium by which we communicate our thoughts to each other, but is rather basic to the thought process

itself. And once we have symbolic thought we can live, not simply in the world as presented to us by Nature, but rather in the world as we reconstruct it in our minds: an ability that has had profound and fateful consequences. None of this means, of course, that many kinds of sophisticated understanding were not already possible before the advent of symbolic reasoning. Indeed, in their day the Neanderthals, whose record shows what remarkable achievements can be made on the basis of intuitive processes, clearly knew and understood their environment with unprecedented precision. Although they evidently had an advanced intuitive intelligence, there is no compelling evidence that the Neanderthals possessed symbolic reasoning. There is, indeed, some dispute over whether Neanderthals had the vocal equipment to produce speech.

Thus, it seems rational to conclude that the prosaic phenomenon of exaptation was what set the stage for the emergence of the astonishing and totally unprecedented human capacity. For whatever historical reasons, a set of neural and peripheral structures were in place early in the evolution of anatomically modern *Homo* that both permitted and capitalized on the invention of language by individuals of one local population, somewhere in the world. The resulting language need not have sprung forth full-blown, with all of the many subtleties and complexities that characterize languages worldwide today. Even a relatively simple language would have made the most profound of differences in the way in which our ancestors were able to view and interact with the world around them, simply by making it possible to create symbols in the mind, and to recombine them and ask questions such as "what if?"

Whatever the case, it is a related change in ways of interacting with the world around us that accounts for the fact that *H. sapiens* is the lone hominid on Earth today. The switch by our ancestors from intuitive to symbolic intelligence (or, more accurately, the grafting of symbolic onto intuitive intelligence) clearly made it impossible for our fossil relatives to coexist with us. Earlier in human evolutionary history, small differences in relative advantage doubtless led to the overall replacement of one hominid species by another over the long term. But typically such differences would have been sufficiently small that replacement was probably a fairly long-drawn-out process. What's more, the relative advantage would presumably have changed depending on local environments (that themselves oscillated), leading to a situation whereby various hominid species competed on different footings in different places. With the advent of symbolic reasoning, however, the behavioral advantage of *H. sapiens* became so overwhelming that other hominids could no longer compete under any ecological circumstances. And, once these closest relatives were gone, we turned our attention to a remoter group of relatives, the apes—and beyond.

In closing, it is worthwhile to point out that, as a model to explain the emergence of human beings and their remarkable attributes, the Great Chain of Being has once again let us down. There was nothing inevitable about how we got to where we are today, and in the truly unique and important aspects of our being we are not simply the result of steady improvement in a linear progression. The emergence of behaviorally modern *H. sapiens* was emphatically not just an extrapolation of earlier trends; and cognitively we are not merely a refinement of what went before. For reasons, and through mechanisms, that we still don't fully understand, something truly unprecedented happened in one of the terminal branches of our bushy family tree, and we are still learning how to live with the consequences.

FURTHER READING

INDEX

Further Reading

The literature relating to human evolution is vast. Below are some recent popular titles that further explore some of the themes followed in this book. Most contain pointers to the primary literature.

Bahn, P. and J. Vertut. 1998. *Journey Through the Ice Age.* Berkeley, CA: University of California Press. A beautifully illustrated account of French and Spanish Paleolithic art, and its interpretation.

Byrne, R. 1995. *The Thinking Ape: Evolutionary Origins of Intelligence.* Oxford: Oxford University Press. A thoughtful and wide-ranging consideration of primate cognition and its evolution.

Darwin, C. 1981. *The Descent of Man, and Selection in Relation to Sex.* John Tyler Bonner (ed). Princeton, New Jersey: Princeton University Press. A classic and engaging account, if somewhat flawed by the assumptions of its times.

Deacon, T. 1997. *The Symbolic Species: The Co-evolution of Language and the Brain.* New York: W. W. Norton. Highly informative review of the function of the human brain and the potential pathways of its evolution, from a gradualist perspective.

Eldredge, N. 1998. *The Pattern of Evolution.* San Francisco: W. H. Freeman. A leading expert in evolutionary theory considers evolutionary mechanisms and the expected biotic patterns arising from them.

Huxley, T. 1894. *Man's Place in Nature and Other Anthropological Essays.* London: Macmillan. Currently out-of-print, but well worth a trip to the library for this provocative and opinionated series of essays on the "question of questions."

Johanson, D., L. Johanson and B. Edgar. 1994. *Ancestors: In Search of Human Origins.* New York: Villard Books, 1994. Companion volume to a TV series, in which the discoverer of "Lucy" conducts an engaging and very personal tour of the human fossil record.

Johanson, D. and B. Edgar. 1996. *From Lucy to Language.* New York: A Peter N. Nevraumont Book, Simon and Schuster. A superbly illustrated and produced volume of human fossil images, structured around informative considerations of many of the most-frequently asked questions about human evolution.

Lieberman, P. 1998. *Eve Spoke: Human Language and Human Evolution.* New York: W. W. Norton. A distinguished linguistician provides his views on the evolution of language in an easily accessible form.

Pinker, S. 1994. *The Language Instinct: How the Mind Creates Language.* New York: William Morrow & Co. A leading cognitive psychologist and linguistician, and fluent writer, explains the intimate relationship between language and the functioning of the modern human brain.

Rudwick, M. 1985. *The Meaning of Fossils* (2nd ed.) Chicago: University of Chicago Press. An accessible and comprehensive account of paleontology from Renaissance times to Darwin.

Schwartz, J.H. 1993. *What the Bones Tell Us*. New York: Henry Holt. An osteologist and paleontologist provides a variety of perspectives on what we can learn from the study of bones—both fossil and modern.

Schwartz, J.H. 1995. *Skeleton Keys: an introduction to human skeletal morphology, development, and analysis*. New York: Oxford University Press. A detailed overview of the human skeletal with an eye toward distinguishing between features of the species and individual variation within the species.

Schwartz, J.H. 1999. *Sudden Origins: Fossils, Genes, and the Emergence of Species*. New York: John Wiley & Sons. A readable and informative account of a new theory of the evolutionary process, based on the latest advances in our understanding of genes and developmental processes.

Stanley, S. 1996. *Children of the Ice Age: How a Global Catastrophe Allowed Humans to Evolve*. New York: Harmony Books. A lively and readable account by a distinguished paleontologist of how the vagaries of climate have affected human evolutionary history.

Stringer, C. and R. McKie. 1996. *African Exodus: The Origins of Modern Humanity*. New York: Henry Holt. A prominent exponent of the "Out of Africa" model of modern human emergence provides a personal perspective on the later phases of human evolution.

Tattersall, I. 1995. *The Fossil Trail: How We Know What We Think We Know About Human Evolution*. New York: Oxford University Press. A history of human evolutionary thought and the human fossil record through the eyes of a practicing paleoanthropologist.

Tattersall, I. 1998. *Becoming Human: Evolution and Human Uniqueness*. New York: Harcourt Brace. A personal investigation of what makes us different from the rest of the living world, and of how those differences came about.

Tattersall, I. 1999. *The Last Neanderthal: The Rise, Success, and Mysterious Extinction of Our Closest Human Relative* (Revised ed.). Boulder, CO: A Peter N. Nevraumont Book, Westview Press. A beautifully illustrated account of our closest well-documented extinct relatives, of their background, and of what may have befallen them.

[Index]